Contested issues in training ministers in South Africa

Editor
Marilyn Naidoo

Contested issues in training ministers in South Africa

Published by SUN MeDIA MeTRO under the SUN PReSS imprint.

All rights reserved.

Copyright © 2015 SUN MeDIA MeTRO and Marilyn Naidoo.

The author(s) and publisher have made every effort to obtain permission for and acknowledge the use of copyrighted material. Please refer enquiries to the publisher.

No part of this book may be reproduced or transmitted in any form or by any electronic, photographic or mechanical means, including photocopying and recording on record, tape or laser disk, on microfilm, via the Internet, by e-mail,
or by any other information storage and retrieval system, without prior written permission by the publisher.

Views expressed in this publication do not necessarily reflect those of the publisher.

First edition 2015

ISBN 978-0-992236-00-7
ISBN 978-0-992236-01-4 (e-book)
https://doi.org/10.18820/9780992236014

Set in Bembo 11pt
Cover design and typesetting by African Sun Media.

SUN PReSS is an imprint of African Sun Media. Academic, professional and reference works are published under this imprint in print and electronic format. This publication may be ordered directly from www.sun-e-shop.co.za.
Produced by African Sun Media.

This publication can be ordered from:
orders@africansunmedia.co.za
Takealot: bit.ly/2monsfl
Google Books: bit.ly/2k1Uilm
africansunmedia.store.it.si (e-books)
Amazon Kindle: amzn.to/2ktL.pkL

Visit africansunmedia.co.za for more information.

TABLE OF CONTENTS

Foreword vii
Rev. Prof. Emeritus John S. Pobee

Acknowledgements xi

Contributors xiii

Introduction 1
Marilyn Naidoo

PART 1   STRUCTURAL REALTIES OF THEOLOGICAL EDUCATION

Is the re-integration of theological education viable? 13
Ernst Conradie

Accreditation and ministerial formation: Serving two masters? 27
Craig Dunsmuir and Michael McCoy

The African Renaissance and the decolonisation of theological education 43
Phillip Higgs

Choosing the better part: Engendering theological education 57
Janet Trisk

Dealing with the Other: Managing diversity in theological education 69
Marilyn Naidoo

PART 2   MINISTERIAL FORMATION CHALLENGES

Contesting spiritual formation in theological education 85
Lyzette Hoffman

Challenges in moral formation for ministerial training 99
John Klaasen

Relations between Church and training institution: A symbiotic association? 113
H. Mvume Dandala

PART 3   NEW DEVELOPMENTS

Entrepreneurial leadership training and theological education 127
Chris L. de Wet

Educational technologies: Exploring the ambiguous effect on the training of ministers 141
Anita Cloete

Diversification in training models: A key to overcome challenges in ministry training 155
Johannes P. van der Walt

Foreword

REV. PROF. EMERITUS JOHN S. POBEE

My Akan background and wisdom encourages me to undertake this contribution in two proverbs. Firstly, *se nnkɔr obi efua mu a, wodwen dɛ wo nko ara na eyɛ okuafo,* i.e. without venturing out into another person's farm, one may be tempted to conclude he/she is the only farmer, or even the champion of famers. We need outsiders and their contributions to assess the rightness and fullness of our perspectives. Secondly, *adwen wotoa-toa,* i.e. wisdom is pieced together from different, diverse and even divergent perspectives and inputs. Against the background of the foregoing Akan wisdom, I have been uneasy about 'contestation' which is often held in terms of competition and struggle for victory. However, going back to the etymology, it helps holding together the mission and ecumenical vocations of theology. Both Akan proverbs, in their own way, pull us towards the ecumenical perspective which is a biblical imperative (Ps. 24:1; John 17:20-26; Eph. 1:10; Rev. 7:9ff; Rev. 21:1-7) and a catalyst of renewal (Pobee 1997). Ecumenical imperative is about making connections and building communities.

The submission of this contribution is that the twin words, namely contextuality and viability, are the ultimate test of the authenticity, integrity and relevance of any theological construct and endeavour. To put it another way, each contribution in this symposium may be assessed on how it corresponds to the heartbeat, the hopes and fears of Christians in South Africa, and their renewal. Contextuality and viability may be planks of 'contestation', but are fundamentally still about owning the products of theological and ministerial programmes by various constituencies.

Viability

Viability etymologically derives from the French word *'la vie'* (life) and the English 'able'. Hence, viability signals the ability to give life, renewal, change and transformation. Scripture itself is insistent that God's wisdom is spirit(ual) and, therefore, is revealed by the spirit (I Cor. 2:6-16). John 20:30-31 corroborates the Pauline statement to suggest that the dynamo of theology (education) is spirituality. And so, the Church Father, Evagrius Ponticus (345-397), monk from Egypt who influenced such giants of Christian history as Palladius, Bishop of the Ireland, John Cassian (c. 360-435), abbot of the monastery of St Victor near Marseilles, Dionysius the Areopagite, and Maximus the Confessor, asserted that "a theologian is one who truly prays and one who prays is a theologian" (Greensclade 1964:3). Prayer life is one aspect of tuning in to God, but spirituality is prayer and more. John Chrysostom (347-407), a celebrated expositor of scripture who was initially the Elder of the Church of Antioch and later Bishop/Metropolitan of Constantinople, spoke the length and breadth of spirituality when he introduced the idea of two altars – one in the sanctuary, the other in the marketplace (Bria 1996). In other words, theology's concern with spirituality is not only liturgical acts of worship but also to pass social, economic and political issues through the prism and microscope of the God-word, with the ultimate good of redeeming everything to and for God. It is this that brings viability to the discipline of theology. Theology is not only to know the truth; it is to do the truth, too. My humble challenge is for us to critique our theological work by whether it equips us to know and do the truth, God's truth, which like Joseph's coat (Genesis 37) is as a coat of many colours.

The presentation thus far has attempted to suggest the crucial place of viability for what we do in theological education. It is that which makes Janet Trisk's use of 'engendering' as the subtitle of her contribution most appealing. Marilyn Naidoo's use of 'managing diversity' in her title, or Craig Dunsmuir and Michael McCoy's tying of ministerial formation into the Church's vocation and mission are useful resources for ventilating the viability of theological education. The chapter on Pentecostal-Charismatic traditions is very much on target as we pursue viability which facilitates change. Indeed, Part Two on ministerial formation focusing on spirituality and morality is perhaps the most rewarding part of this publication.

Contextuality: Blessing our memories

The theme of viability, as traced through spirituality as the dynamo of vibrant theology like the rest of theological education and ministerial formation in Africa, came with models minted in the North, especially the Latin West. As such, spirituality as a discipline has been mediated and shaped by scripture and some classics from the North/West: The Greek epic poet, Homer (c. 800 BCE-c. 701 BCE), the Greek philosopher Plato (427-347 BC), the Greek philosopher Aristotle (284-322 BC), the Roman poet Virgil (70-19 BC), the Church Father Augustine of Hippo Regius, Roman North Africa (AD 354-430), the Italian philosopher-theologian, Thomas Aquinas (1225-1274), the Italian poet Dante Alighieri (1265-1321), the English poets John Milton (1608-1674) and William Shakespeare (1564-1616), and the Spanish author Miguel de Cervantes Saavedra (1567-1618). With the exposure of students to these landmarks of formational and spiritual development, the student's life "becomes a practice of ecumenism of time – and their journey through life is enriched by having (them) as partners along the way" (Weigel 2013:14).

This classical input, however, may not be completely precise because of Christian faith's core message of the Incarnation (John 1:14, Gal. 4:3). It is that incarnational thrust that we highlight with the word contextuality. The contribution by Phillip Higgs on "The African Renaissance and the decolonisation of theological education" is a refreshing exploration of this theme. In the South African context, however, for precisely the reason of the painful experience of the ideology of apartheid, theology and education must be most attentive of issues of the social, economic and political life which will necessitate the reorientation of theology to look beyond dogma towards the fundamental meaning of religion as concerned with the human (Bonhoeffer 1967:118). However, in engaging issues of human dignity and rights, we must be careful not to turn theology into a programme or crusade; rather it may never lose its *raison d'etre* as good news and gospel (cf. Higgs' chapter in this publication). Theology may not start from the problem of the community and a predetermined framework to articulate the Christian message – that leads to legalism rather than gospel.

There is a context of multiple plurality and pluralism in South Africa – ethnic, race, gender, religion and denominations. Those identities involved in the pluralism should lead us to engage, firstly, the different people, and then to explore the philosophy of truth that will not short-change the being of other humans. The vision of contextualisation has for some time now, especially since the nationalist era, been bubbling on the African theological scene. The desire for contextuality passes under such descriptions as accommodation (Rahner and Vorgrimler 1965:12), adaptation (Hermandes 1958), inculturation (Waliggo et al. 1988) and African theology (Ela 1988, Pobee 1979). The endeavour to culture the word of God in the South African context has gone under the designation of black theology (Mosala 1989, Mofokeng 1983), liberation (Frostin 1988) and reconstruction (Villa-Vicencio 1992).

All the foregoing attempts are rooted in the realisation and conviction regarding the crucial importance of environment, physical, external and interior for viable theology. By the former is meant modern surroundings and features. By interior environment is meant mental and spiritual climate (Niblett 1955:234), which is perhaps more influential than exterior environment. The contribution by Conradie lays out how the University of the Western Cape is grappling with the environment/context in the South African context so as to sustain the missiological orientation of theological education.

Language, the vehicle of culture and people's identity, has long been recognised to be critical for engaging people. It, therefore, comes as no surprise that missionaries take the credit for reducing African vernacular to writing (Pobee 2011:20-29). On the other hand, much of theological work in South Africa is done in English or Afrikaans to which the biblical languages are added. Ela (1988:44) is right in his critique that "in Africa, the confrontation between the message and the African universe must bring forth meaning with the power to transform the lives of African Christians." Today the faith of the Church in Africa is in danger of death because the Church tends to forget the cultural dimensions as marked by the Greco heritage. If the faith of Africa is not to die (cf viability), it must become a vision of the world that they can feel is theirs; European cultural dimensions must be stripped away. There is an urgent need to reject present models of expression if we are to breathe new life into the spoken word. Our Church must express a Passover of language, or the meaning of the Christian message will not be understood. In place of the cultural presuppositions of Western Christianity, namely *logos* and *ratio*, we must substitute African symbolism. Starting with the ecclesial furrow where language of faith germinates, we must restore the gospel's power to speak to Africans through the primordial symbol of their existence.

As I have my ears to the ground, I have a sense that religion of one kind or another is of significance for people in South Africa. I have a sense that churches would profess theology in their blood and life stream. However, do they own theology and theological education in truth on the ground? To own it will go with honouring in reality the principles of viability and contextuality of the institutions.

This symposium is a rich and careful articulation of issues in theological and ministerial formation. Bringing together in one volume relevant bibliography makes it that more invaluable.

Bibliography

Bonhoeffer, D., 1967. *Letters and Papers from Prison*. London: SCM.
Bria, L., 1996. *The Liturgy after the Liturgy*. Geneva: WCC.
Ela, JM., 1988. *My Faith as an African*. New York: Orbis.
Frostin, P., 1988. *Liberation Theology in Tanzania and South Africa. A First World Interpretation*. Lund: Lund University Press.
Greensclade, S.L., 1964. *Schism in the Early Church*. London: SCM.
Mofokeng, T., 1983. *The Crucified Among the Cross-Bearers: Towards a Black Christology*. Kampen: Uitgeversmaatschappij J.H. Kok.
Mosala, J., 1989. *Biblical Hermeneutics and Black Theology in South Africa*. Grand Rapids, Michigan: William B. Eerdmans Publishing Company.
Niblett, W.R., 1955. Neutrality or freedom of Faith. In: *Science and Freedom – The Proceedings of the Conference for Cultural Freedom*. London: Martin Secker and Marbury.
Pobee J.S., (ed.), 1979. *Towards Africa Theology*. Nashville: Abingdon.
Pobee J.S., (ed.), 1997. *Towards Viable Theological Education, Ecumenical Imperative, Catalyst for Renewal*. Geneva: WCC.
Pobee, J.S., 2011. Identity, Religion and Nation. *Journal of African Christian Thought*. 14(5). 1-5.
Rahner, K. and Vorgrimler, L. (eds.), 1965. *Theological Dictionary*. New York: Herder and Herder.
Villa-Vicencio, C., 1992. *A Theology of Reconstruction*. Cambridge: COP.
Waliggo, J., 1988. *Inculturation. Its Meaning and Urgency*. Kampale: St Paul's Publications.
Weigel, G., 2013. *Evangelical Catholicism Deep Reform in the 21st Century*. New York: Basic Books.

Acknowledgements

The idea for this book came from the previous edited volume *Between the Real and the Ideal: Ministerial formation in South African churches* (2012, Unisa Press), where problematic issues within the ministerial formation process were flagged in the final chapter. It was seen as important to have a deeper discussion on each of these contested issues, especially as these issues shape and profoundly impact theological training in South Africa. Academics from both the public and private theological education were approached to share their critical insights on selected issues. Sincere thanks goes to each contributor for their cooperation, for making time to reflect on their issue and then working through drafts to ensure excellence in their essays and alignment of the book.

Grateful thanks goes to the National Research Foundation for supplying funds towards this book project which forms part of an empirical research project on "Culture and Formation in Theological Education" (2013-2015). Thanks also goes to SUN MeDIA MeTRO for their extremely efficient service in the peer-review and the editorial stages of the publishing process.

And, finally, I am particularly grateful to Prof. John Pobee, professor emeritus in the Department for the Study of Religions at the University of Ghana, Legon, and fellow of the Ghana Academy of Arts and Sciences. His many publications on African theology and culture remain unmatched in his generation. He retired as the Director for the Programme on Ecumenical Theological Education at the World Council of Churches, Geneva, and was once also Academic Dean at the Ecumenical Institute, Chateau de Bossey, Switzerland. I thank him for his advice regarding this project and feel honoured that he agreed to write the foreword of this book. Although he is the only contributor who is not a South African, his very extensive involvement in theological education in Africa makes him more than capable to comment on the needs of theological education in our time. He has created models for the training and scholarships of those engaged in theological studies of the African continent, in addition to various regions around the world. His involvement with South Africa began in 1973 and his calling remains the same – the agenda for the renewal of theological education, to dare to grow out of tunnel vision, to embrace new times and, therefore, to seek a new vision.

Contributors

Dr Anita Cloete is a lecturer at the Faculty of Theology, Stellenbosch University. Her research areas are youth culture, spiritual formation and digital culture. She published and supervised several postgraduate students in these areas.

Prof. Ernst Conradie is a professor in the Department of Religion and Theology at the University of the Western Cape where he teaches Systematic Theology and Ethics. His field of specialisation is Christian ecotheology.

Dr H. Mvume Dandala is the president of the Seth Mokitimi Methodist Seminary in Pietermaritzburg. He has served as presiding Bishop of the Methodist Church, President of the South African Council of Churches, and General Secretary of the All Africa Conference of Churches.

Prof. Chris L. de Wet is associate professor of New Testament and Early Christian Studies in the Department of Biblical and Ancient Studies at the University of South Africa, and editor of the *Journal of Early Christian History*.

Revd Craig Dunsmuir is an Anglican minister and an executive director of the Theological Education by Extension College, based in Johannesburg.

Prof. Philip Higgs is emeritus professor and research fellow in the College of Education, University of South Africa. He holds two doctorates in the areas of Philosophy of Religion (University of Natal) and Philosophy of Education (University of South Africa).

Dr Lyzette Hoffman is research fellow in the Department of Practical Theology at the University of the Free State. She is executive editor of *Acta Theologica* and minister in the Dutch Reformed Church, Bloemfontein.

Dr John Klaasen is a lecturer at the Department of Religion and Theology, University of the Western Cape. An Anglican minister, he serves on the Provincial Advisory Board for Theological Education and Training, Anglican Church of Southern Africa.

Revd Michael McCoy is an Anglican minister who is also the principal of the Anglican School of Ministry, the open and distance learning project of the College of the Transfiguration in Grahamstown.

Prof. Marilyn Naidoo is associate professor in the Department of Philosophy, Systematic and Practical Theology, University of South Africa. She teaches Religious Education and Empirical Research with a research focus on spirituality and theological education.

Revd Canon Janet Trisk is an Anglican minister and has taught Systematic Theology at the College of the Transfiguration. She is an honorary lecturer at the University of KwaZulu-Natal and also the editor of the *Journal of Theology for Southern Africa*.

Dr Johannes P. van der Walt is working at the Centre for Contextual Ministry (CCM) at the Faculty of Theology, University of Pretoria. His focus is on formalising community-based training facilities in sub-Saharan Africa.

Introduction

MARILYN NAIDOO

With great passion church leaders, theological educators, administrators, students and congregations debate whether theological education is providing the right kind of formative training for leaders of the Church. On the one hand there is an assumption that theological institutions in South Africa ought to be shaping and forming church leaders who can serve the almost insurmountable social needs of our country, be visionary with moral integrity, and be able to attend with competence to the many pastoral tasks at a local church level. On the other hand, theological institutions must determine how to take on the difficult task of forming leaders with fewer resources available within the changing landscape of higher education in South Africa. In the middle of these well-intended struggles there is once more the question of the vision and purpose of theological education. To what end should theological education be undertaken in South Africa to 'equip people for ministry'? What view of the present and the future needs to drive it to situate it historically and practically in the challenges facing the Church and its ministry? Precisely what are we forming pastors to be and do as we attempt to meet the needs of church and society in the changing South African context?

This book is an attempt to answer these questions by taking cognisance of the challenges that influence, impact and profoundly shape the possibility of training ministers in South Africa. This is a volume presenting eleven contested issues that attend to the concerns related to processes, structures, knowledge and practices within theological education. These controversial issues of accreditation, spirituality, diversity, gender, worldview, morality, church partnerships, technology, leadership and the curriculum are called into question in the education process. Contributors have offered keen insights about how to think differently and more complexly about these matters. It is an attempt to turn the soil of South African theological education, to highlight how we attempt to understand theological education within our contextual realities.

The complexity of the South African theological praxis calls for an approach to take on a diversity of perspectives of cultural, public and Christian life. As we know, South Africa is politically, economically and culturally a contested space in itself, filled with many contradictions and paradoxes. We also know that institutions of higher education continue not only to be intensely contested, but also continue to be sites of substantive, meta-theoretical, methodological and political/institutional contestations. Our context is filled with diversity on the level of race, class, gender, sexuality, denominational identity and language, to name a few. And, at the same time, any reference to all things African would have to be partial, provisional and contextualised. To essentialise theological education as 'theological education in Africa' would be a disservice. To propose a generic representation of training which covers all its instances in this part of the world would be to homogenise the experience. Instead this book is an affirmation of the multiple voices, locations, identities and positions within South African theological education, as a starting point for transformative theological education. To envision a transformative theological education requires one to seek fundamentally to reconstruct and re-imagine theological discourse, curriculum, pedagogy and institutional systems from a perspective of the geopolitical context. The importance of context is crucial as it influences the way we theologise and also provokes a seriousness with which we attend to cultural expressions of Christianity. Doing theology involves a multi-perspectival understanding that is shaped by different, interacting cultures and perspectives. The challenge within this book is for us to form our own meanings of sustainable theological education for our own time and place. As Maluleke (1996:17) suggests, we need to drink from our own wells. It is a way to assert our identity in this region, as location and positionality makes a difference.

This vision is not a description of the future, but rather an orientation in the present, a point of entry, a beginning, a departure but not always a final solution. The reason for the latter is that this orientation is mediated by our limits and the limitations of our theological institutions. These essays are a practice in truth-saying; to see ourselves as we are, with theological education institutions striving to be places of truth in church and society as part of its commitment to self-critical accountability. By engaging the impact of these contested issues within theological education, we develop a critical consciousness through attentive discernment and contextual evaluation. Through this sort of imaginative theological work, informed by educational research and practice, we can come to practical wisdom (Warford 2007:12). This wisdom can enable future ministers to confront the question of how to *be* in the world with the required competence, integrity and professional identity to meet the needs of church and society.

Ministerial training and formation

The Church in South Africa faces the task of reconstructing its congregational life, its educational institutions, and its witness in the world amidst an increasingly globalised society where people's desires are more often shaped by consumer culture than by the grace of God. It is a society where conviction is often shaped by state power rather than the cross, and where activities are often shaped by habits of division and violence rather than reconciliation (Jones 2002:190). To make sense of its changing role, the Church remains heavily dependent upon its ordained ministers for the vision and inspiration which are to motivate both its worship and mission. At the same time there is an acknowledgement that a new paradigm is needed for doing theology, and a new kind of Christian leadership is needed that is able to lead churches towards meaningful engagement in society. As the formational mandate becomes more a part of theological training (Foster et al. 2006), it is imperative to develop a more nuanced discussion regarding the relationship of ministerial formation to theological education. Thus, it is important to reflect on the character, activities and teaching of ministerial candidates so as to reconsider how to better 'form' pastoral leaders who can create, renovate, sustain and extend religious institutions.

The period of training is an important time to encourage a mature development of occupational and personal identity and to foster a coherent understanding of role and function in ministry. Ministerial formation is viewed as a multi-faceted activity involving critical thinking, the acquisition of knowledge, skills development, religious identity formation and the development of ministerial and spiritual maturity expected of church ministers (Overend 2007). This concept is embedded in the *habitus* model in which the Church, as a distinctive and historical community, fosters values through corporate worship and shared discipleship, forming a "disposition of the heart" (Ballard and Pritchard 1996:69). Theology as *habitus* is personal, self-engaging and constantly active. This formational notion of theological education is what Farley labels as *theologia* rather than 'theology' in order to underline that it is a kind of personal wisdom, a way of being human. However, *theologia* requires a disciplined reflection in order to achieve this purpose, and this comes through the modes of theological reflection, theological understanding and theological knowledge (Farley 1983:156-158). Here we see an ecclesiological understanding of formation concerning more than the object of study: It is a model of learning in which faith, study and tradition inform one another, and thereby foster the development of the person.

The goal is to help the student undergo a deep kind of formation – a personal appropriation of knowledge about God, the self and the world where learning is not just a personal matter but is done for the sake of public life, ecclesial life and Church leadership. This is a process which is viewed not simply as something that is done to students, but rather as a cooperative and intentional journey which engages the interests, time, skill and creative energies of the students and congregations. It furthermore enlists the enabling resources of theological educators who carry a mandate to provide the link between the education and ministry foundation. Ministerial formation must involve the training and equipping of pastoral leaders to *do* theology by involvement on a grassroots level. This implicates developing responsiveness to historical, biblical and pastoral dimensions within its context so as to be relevant.

Education for ministry is tied to exploration of vocation to ordination (Neuhaus 1992:3-4). This immediately distinguishes theological education from other professional education, since vocation to ordained ministry involves a call from God to the inner self as well as a call from the Church. Both must be present for authentic vocation. It requires that the ordinand explicitly and publically affirms that he or she is willing to let the Church play a large role in the shaping of the self. Ordained ministry has a unique character (Heitink 1993: 317-324) that focuses on the identity of the minister. This identity is not reduced to the external trappings and privileges of the office, but depends on the profound sense of conforming oneself as a servant of the Gospel.

At the same time, theological education no longer refers to university or seminary education alone, but to efforts on the part of the whole Church to learn from its rich traditions. There has been a reappraisal of the status and the role of laity in many Christian traditions. The realignment of Christian vocation as the task of the whole Church signalled a realignment of the nature of ministry (WCC 1982). Ministry is no longer solely equated with the activities of ordained ministry, but rather something exercised by the entire people of God, in church and around the world. There are now many different locations and agendas associated with theological education. Local ministry development and the education associated with it will increase in importance and quantity, and theological education must be a part of it. With this comes the challenge of envisioning and embracing the whole, of providing education which equips leaders for many different contexts. As can be seen within the goals of theological education, there are tensions between a sense of the whole, with a focus on inclusivity and hospitality and the ministry of *all* the baptised, and a push towards particularity and special identities shaped by ethos and context. Whatever 'we' do, it must include both the particular and the universal, the whole church.

With this brief introduction into ministerial training and before observations are made about the scope of this book, it is necessary to make a few general remarks relating to where theological education is currently situated within the South African context.

Changed landscape of theological education

Theological education and ministerial formation have globally been in a state of uncertainty for a number of years. This has been precipitated by the impact of globalisation on theological education, the process of rationalisation within educational and ecclesiastical institutions, the competing and sometimes adversarial interests of liberal, radical and conservative theological establishments, and the crisis in the vocation with regard to the ordained and lay ministry within the Church (Van der Water 2005:203). Whether in crisis or merely in painful transition, the fact remains that many church denominations in South Africa, Christian groupings and theological institutions have engaged in a radical review of their theological education and ministerial formation programmes.

In the changing South African scene, theological education has faced significant developments. Due to the restructuring of higher education over the past decade, which co-existed with demands for social and economic justice (Levy 2007), theological faculties at public universities across the country have been restructured as part of the Human and Social Sciences, as schools, departments or units of theology and religion (Dreyer 2012). Programme rationalisation, to increase efficiency and harmonise curricula, also led to fewer theological courses in some faculties. For Bible colleges and seminaries, the instability in theological education was impacted more strongly by the issue of accreditation and quality assurance. New institutions and mechanisms were put into place to deal with accreditation and authorisation, such as the South African Qualifications Authority (SAQA) with its National Qualifications Framework. These private providers had to apply anew for accreditation, which had a domino effect for seminaries – some, which could not apply for accreditation for various reasons, were unable to attract students, forcing closures and merges. Furthermore, it became increasingly difficult for mainline churches to keep residential training programmes running due to changing patterns of commitment and community which result in shrinking church membership and fewer ministerial candidates. On the other hand, the declining pool of candidates for ordained ministry has brought about an increase in programmes to equip laity for positions of leadership and service.

The nature of theological curricula and the quality of theological education varied greatly amongst different theological institutions. Therefore, accreditation was an important consideration – especially in the case of students who wanted to study further at different or at public theological institutions. Positively, accreditation forced theological institutions to be accountable to government, the Church and the general public, which, in turn, could result in greater effectiveness. However, this new accreditation process did not provide for any accrediting bodies other than itself. Theological institutions also had to resolve the tension between the status of institution as autonomous authority with statutory recognition and as serving local Christian communities and churches (Moodie 2008).

These higher education changes created instability from which churches and seminaries are only now recovering. Each institution's struggle with identity – the definition, purpose and mission, the creation and abandonment of programmes, and the search for fiscal stability – profoundly affected the practice of teaching and learning. While restructuring and closure have been some of the responses to the crisis, some Bible colleges have spawned a variety of emphases and new degree programmes, and found partnerships amongst universities. The positive effect of these movements is, hopefully, stronger ecumenical cooperation amongst the various churches that have collaborated. However, some have legitimate fears that the wheeling-and-dealing has led to a 'lowering of standards' in theological education (Maluleke 1998).

At the same time, we are aware that the very contours of historic Christianity are changing as a result of the phenomenal growth of Pentecostal and independent churches in the global South (Werner 2010). Indeed, Christianity itself is far more variegated and divided today than at any previous time in its history. In South Africa there has been a dramatic increase in demand for general higher education due to a younger and dynamic population, which is also reflected in a growing demand for theological education, especially amongst the African Independent Churches, Pentecostals and Charismatic networks. It would seem that the need for leaders far outstrips the ability of Bible colleges, seminaries and correspondence programmes to supply them. The mushrooming of new theological training institutions has, in turn, created tensions between public and private providers of theological education as they compete for students. The entrepreneurial marketing of theological education, valuing the students in terms of what they can consume or produce and the supermarket of theological offerings, brings the commodification and commercialisation of theological education into focus. The sudden growth in private theological education was partly because some traditions wanted to retain their specific identities and values which they perceived to be under threat (Levy 2007). At the same time, some church traditions have established their own ministerial training rather than looking to the traditional theological college or university. While it may be argued that most churches are not in a position to provide theological education at an appropriate post-secondary level, this developing pattern demonstrates that the needs of the Church have changed and may require different types of training. It is evident from these changes that there is a resurgence of denominationalism in theological education (Naidoo 2012) which is not a good sign for the integrity of Christian witness within the Protestant family.

Theological education in South Africa currently reflects the deep divides of the context within which it is situated – South Africa itself is a contested space and theological education is equally diverse and complex. Currently the spectrum of offerings includes accredited denominational/interdenominational Bible schools and seminaries, university faculties of theology serving particular denominations that are ecumenical, university departments of religious studies, unaccredited Bible schools, apprenticeships, short-term courses offered by well-meaning global partners, outright sale of certificates, moving courseware across borders, and a host of other strategies. Also, despite the widening digital-divide in South Africa there has been a surge of interest in new technologies that has caused an eager population to become further connected, though still to varying degrees. Many theological institutions have now moved into distance (correspondence) education, seen as a solution to the financial viability of institutions.

The approach to theological education within the various theological institutions is markedly different, ranging from confessional and critical correlation with social sciences, to contextual approaches. There are shifting expectations and denominational differences as to what the ordained ministry and church leadership should entail, which makes the task that more challenging. The curriculum in our context has mostly followed the 'clerical paradigm' and prepared students to enter traditional church leadership roles, while the growing need is for ministers to interpret the socio-economic, cultural, political and spiritual contexts of the majority with the aim of transforming these contexts. Most of the theological reflection remains captive to a Western model of theologising, reflecting the tension between African communal culture and the tendencies towards isolation, individualism, and the competitive characteristic of Western culture. The focus in the curriculum has been on the academisation of theological education with administrative and disciplinary silos, while integration is the actual requirement. University faculties have become so diversified that theological disciplines are no longer able to converse meaningfully with one another. Each discipline has its own methodology and, hence, its own language. And because of this it loses its capacity to reflect on a common goal for ministerial formation. The practical, pastoral or the clinical side of the curriculum tends to be equally remote from personal appropriation and internationalisation. The goals of the traditional intellectual approach, shaped by its Western views of rationality found in universities, often omit personal formational elements, despite evidence that students in these courses often enrol for formational reasons. The inner coherence and church-related responsibility of theological education cannot be exercised if the structural framework, especially at public universities, does not allow a formational emphasis. Furthermore, the openness of the over-crowded curriculum itself aids the 'consumer mentality' of our culture, thus reinforcing the character and values of students and frustrating the faculty's attempt to become involved.

This overview highlights the many realities and challenges faced in training ministers, and requires a commitment from all critical and transformative theological educators to articulate the responsibility of Christian witness in relation to these shortcomings. There is no doubt whatsoever that the task and challenge of transforming ministerial formation in this context is an ongoing and dynamic one.

Scope of the book

In a country with a significant percentage of Christians (Statistics South Africa 2001), the focus of training ministers is strategically important as religion plays a critical role in supporting human rights, democracy and development (Piper 2009). In doing this, churches are trying to make sense of their new role in terms of culture, political profile and social influence as social and cultural systems that once held religious identity and traditions together, fragment. As church ministers become more and more involved in increasingly polarised and unpredictable church communities, there needs to be a deliberate strategy within professional training to equip ministers. However, to make this a reality involves the recognition of the many challenges in the educational process that impacts on the training of ministers. Since church denominations themselves have been challenged by internal pluralism and the erosion of the theological particularities, theological institutions have sometimes found it difficult to articulate a focused and coherent stance of their own. Hence there is little consensus about what pastoral identity should look like and questions of competence, excellence and standards are difficult to resolve. The aim of the book, then, is to provide a critical discussion of ministerial training and formation, being cognisant of the complexities that shape the education process in South Africa.

This volume is written from an ecumenical perspective, focusing on issues impacting both public and private theological education. Each contributor has offered a significant contested issue, varying from processes, structures, knowledge and practices, and has problematised this issue with detailed description, discussion and analysis (be it theological, denominational, historical, social, economic, political or structural) within South African theological education. Although contributors' areas of expertise are numerous, it is suffice to say they are sufficiently sensible and modest to recognise that there are no simple solutions to these complex problems, and that solutions can be thoughtful provoking, helpful and imperfect. While trying to maintain a common focus to the book, authors have expressed the kind of diverse interpretation that adds to the complexity in understanding the South African context. A concerted effort was made to invite contributions representing diversity, different theological traditions, younger academics, female academics and racial diversity to allow for the richness of perspective.

This book has three parts:

Part One

This section is a spread of five essays that are critical to the way theological education is currently structured and shaped in South Africa. The first chapter begins with the perennial problem of the lack of integration within the curriculum with its specialisation and fragmentation. This has shaped the 'product' of theological education – leaders who possess advanced degrees, but correspondingly lack advanced spiritual wisdom, maturity, and ministry competence. The second chapter unpacks the problematic role of government accreditation requirements in setting adequate criteria for Christian ministry, and church traditions note that not all prices asked in the marketplace of academic recognition should be paid. This points to the deeper debate of how theological education fits into the secular underpinnings of higher education. The third chapter is a challenge to the cultural dominance of the West. It is a bold attempt in reconstructing theological education for our context, which aims to give indigenous African knowledge systems their rightful place. The fourth chapter highlights that the normative gender role expectation of our society is very strong, and rightly argues that a relevant theological education must be 'engendered'. The latter involves a transformation of both the structures of theological institutions as well as mainstreaming gender studies. The last chapter of this section looks at the neglected issue of managing diversity in theological education, and asks the deeper question of whether South Africans can un-think old categories of citizenship and refine themselves as a nation in order to move beyond racial categorisation (as an example) and their own political bondage.

Part Two

This section has three chapters which attend to issues in the ministerial formation process, namely spiritual and moral formation which is difficult to realise and highly contested, and the required partnership between the Church and training institution in shaping a formational mandate. The focus on the formation of future Christian leaders is duly set on the development of a deeply-rooted spirituality and the disposition of integrity, but not without its challenges. The first two chapters of this section explores contested issues in the educational process and highlight the important role of communal practices as key to forming future leaders. The last chapter explores the problematic tensions created between the theological institution and the church denomination in meeting each other's expectation in training ministers. It explores the potential turf wars or competing notions of education, ministry and mission, and how this relationship needs to be managed constructively.

Part Three

This section has three chapters; the focus is on innovation and emerging developments in training ministers. The first chapter considers the new type of entrepreneurial leader that is developing especially amongst the Pentecostal-Charismatic traditions. This chapter explores the implication of this type of leadership, highlighting the need to pay more attention theologically to the issue of leadership. The second chapter explores the emerging reality of technology in our context as it raises questions of formation, community, assessment and quality in the training process. Technology can bring people together and also isolate; hence the limits of its use must be carefully determined. Finally, since there will never be enough training institutions to assist in the task of leadership development, the last chapter deals with the problematic need to diversify theological training. This chapter speaks of a new initiative – a professional body for ministry training focused on lay leadership.

With the focus on contested issues, this book will surely stimulate further discussion, reflection and debate, and prompt readers to clarify their own thinking and practice as they confront the complexities of training ministers. It is hoped that this more complete description of the South African scene can inspire a transformative vision for the training process, encourage the ability to affirm difference, to learn from each other, and to dare to cross theological boundaries for the sake of common mission and ministry.

Bibliography

Ballard, P. and Pritchard, J., 1996. *Practical theology in action: Christian thinking in the service of church and society*. London: SPCK.

Dreyer, J.S., 2012. Practical theology in South Africa. In: Miller-McLemore, B.J. (ed.). *The Wiley-Blackwell Companion to Practical Theology*. Oxford: Wiley-Blackwell. 505-514.

Farley, E., 1983. *Theologia: The fragmentation and unity of theological education*. Philadelphia: Fortress.

Foster, C., Dahill, L.E., Golemon, L. and Tolention, B.W. 2006. *Educating clergy: Teaching practices and pastoral imaginations*. San Francisco: Jossey Bass.

Heitink, G., 1993. *Practical theology – history, action, domains: Manual for practical theology*. Grand Rapids, Michigan: William B. Eerdmans Publishing Company.

Jones, G.L., 2002. Beliefs, Desires, Practices and the Ends of Theological Education. In: V. Miroslav and D.C. Bass (eds.). *Beliefs and Practices in Christian Life*. Grand Rapids, Michigan: William B. Eerdmans Publishing Company. 185-204.

Levy, D., 2007. A recent echo: African private higher education in an international perspective. *Journal of Higher Education in Africa*. 5:197-220.

Maluleke, T., 1996. Black and African theologies in the new world order: A time to drink from our own wells. *Journal of Theology for Southern Africa*. 96:3-19.

Maluleke, T., 1998. *Africanization, liberation and transformation in Theological Education*. Johannesburg: NICTE Publication.

Moodie, T., 2008. TEE College of South Africa. In: Ross Kinsler (ed.). *Diversified Theological Education: Equipping all God's people*. Pasenda: William Carey International University. 47-80.

Naidoo, M. (ed.), 2012. *Between the Real and the Ideal: Ministerial Formation in South African churches.* Pretoria: Unisa Press.

Neuhaus, R.J. (ed.), 1992. *Theological education and moral formation.* Grand Rapids, Michigan: William B. Eerdmans Publishing Company.

Overend, P., 2007. Education or formation? The issue of personhood in learning for ministry. *Journal of Adult Theological Education.* 4(2):133-148.

Piper, L., 2009. Faith-Based Organisations, Local Governance and Citizenship in South Africa. In: D. Brown (ed.). *Religion and Spirituality in South Africa: New Perspectives.* Pietermaritzburg: University of KwaZulu-Natal Press. 54-77.

Statistics South Africa, 2001. *Census.* [Online] Available from: http://www.statssa.gov.za/census01/htm [Accessed: 12 August 2014].

Van der Water, D.P., 2005 Transforming Theological Education and Ministerial Formation. *International Review of Mission.* 94(373). 203-211.

Warford, M.L. (ed.), 2007. *Practical wisdom: On theological teaching and learning.* New York: Peter Lang.

World Council of Churches, 1982. *Baptism, Eucharist and Ministry.* Faith and Order Paper No. 111. World Council of Churches, Geneva.

PART 1

STRUCTURAL REALTIES OF THEOLOGICAL EDUCATION

Is the re-integration of theological education viable?

ERNST CONRADIE

The fragmentation of theological education in South Africa

Theological education in South Africa reflects the deep divides of the context within which it is situated. These social divisions obviously shape the identities of theological students. While all Christians may be involved in 'doing theology', very few have the opportunity to engage formally in 'studying theology', which is by definition done at theological institutions. Although studying theology is at best aimed at deepening the process of doing theology through critical reflection, there is, for many students, a further divide between the exposition of doctrinal identity (apparently derived from foreign soil) and actual daily life – whether in the secular world of business, industry and consumer culture, or in traditional African villages (Mugambi 2013).

In theological education itself one has to reckon with a number of further divides. Firstly, theological education may be focused on ministerial formation for future (ordained) church leaders. However, there are also theological programmes aimed at lay leaders with ministries either in the Church itself or in various spheres of society, including counselling, education, community development, ethical leadership, and so forth. Secondly, theology may be studied at very different kinds of institutions, ranging from denominational seminaries, non-denominational Bible schools and training centres, faculties of theology, departments of religion and theology or of religious studies. The kinds of programmes that students would encounter in such institutions are markedly different. Confessional differences play a role in this regard, but the deeper divide is between theological education in the so-called mainline churches (member churches of the SACC) and in the large number of evangelical, Pentecostal and independent churches. Ecumenical theological education has been on the agenda from well before 1910 but remains rather elusive in South Africa (Werner et al. 2010). Thirdly, there is a divide between university-based theological institutions (programmes in Christian theology are still offered at 8 of the 23 public universities in South Africa), a significant number of accredited private providers (the list of 90 institutions on the Register of Private Higher Education Institutions includes no less than 20 institutions offering theological education),[1] and other non-accredited private providers (the number is difficult to establish). Elsewhere in Africa one also has to reckon with private Christian universities (Mugambi 2013:118). Again one would encounter confessional differences and conflicting perceptions on quality, but descriptors such as 'evangelical', 'conservative',

---

[1] See http://www.dhet.gov.za/LinkClick.aspx?fileticket=XX%2bGiC6kQYo%3dandtabid= 36 (updated 28 November 2013, accessed 7 January 2014). A further two institutions offering theological education are provisionally registered. There are seven theological institutions for which cancellation or lapse of registration has come into effect.

'ecumenical', 'liberal' and 'contextual' provide better insight in understanding the rather tangible divides in this regard. Divisions in theological education may be found not only between but also within each of the many undergraduate programmes that are offered. The fragmentation of theological education is related to methodological conflict between the various theological sub-disciplines. Such fragmentation and the possibilities of an integrated curriculum aimed at ministerial formation will be the focus of this essay, but have to be understood within their larger social and institutional contexts.

One may safely say that all the accredited programmes in Christian theology that are offered in South Africa still adhere (admittedly with many variations) to the so-called fourfold paradigm which was first introduced at the Humboldt University through the influence of Friedrich Schleiermacher (Farley 1983, Kelsey 1992). His challenge was to ensure the place of theological education at a research university, deeply influenced by the Enlightenment and aimed at expanding the frontiers of knowledge. He defended the place of theology through the distinction between sub-disciplines, each with its own distinct object of study, and the argument that theological education is aimed at training professionals, i.e. ordained ministers who can occupy influential leadership positions in church and society. Schleiermacher's proposal had far-reaching consequences that need not be investigated here any further (Conradie 1997, Kelsey 1993). The point is that, in one form or another, all programmes in Christian theology still follow the distinction between Biblical Theology (Studies), Historical Theology (the history of Christianity/Church History), Systematic Theology and Practical Theology. As will become evident below, the names of each of these sub-disciplines have been contested and have often been replaced by something else, reflecting methodological developments in each field. Finer distinctions have also been introduced (e.g. on the place of Ethics, Missiology and Religious Studies), while modules may be labelled and packaged in innovative ways that reflect contextual, existential, sub-cultural or ecclesial needs.

One further observation may be offered in this regard, namely that the deepest tension within theological education may well be between two contrasting tendencies. The one tendency is towards further fragmentation as a result of the need for increasing specialisation. This is obviously related to research agendas in order to extend the frontiers of knowledge and insight. In South Africa this is driven ahead by the quantitative system of government subsidy allocated to accreditable research output and the corresponding corporatisation of universities with far-reaching consequences for understanding the role of universities in society.[2] This research agenda confronts any academics seeking employment at a university. It is abundantly clear that academics in the fields of religion and theology are deeply implicated in this agenda. They (together with research associates) produce more than two accredited journal articles per permanent academic per year – more than double

---

[2] Knowledge is no longer merely a virtue or a source of power. In a consumer society it also becomes a packaged and marketed product used for entertainment. This has far-reaching implications for packaging the theological curriculum, i.e. in 'bite-sized chunks' (Conradie 2011).

the number expected in other fields.[3] This is facilitated by the large number of academic journals in the fields of religion and theology.

The other tendency is related to the aims of ministerial formation involving intellectual, practical and spiritual apprenticeship (Naidoo 2013:755), where some form of integration of the curriculum of theological education is called for in order to do justice to all three widely endorsed aims of spiritual formation, academic excellence and ministerial training in theological education. Here there is an obvious tension between the demands of ecclesial praxis and the more theoretical reflections emerging from the various sub-disciplines. This tension is exacerbated by at least two further factors. Ecclesial praxis (at least in the case of the more affluent macro-congregations) is also characterised by increasing specialisation in terms of a whole host of ministries – so that it is difficult to gear theological education towards each of these fields of specialisation and to allow for practical ministerial training in each area. The curricular agenda is already over-crowded. In addition, there are shifting expectations and denominational differences as to what the ordained ministry and church leadership should entail. These two tendencies cannot be reconciled easily. As a result, the three aims of spiritual formation, academic excellence and ministerial training remain in tension with each other (Conradie 1997). Starkly formulated: An integrative model is possible where spiritual formation (or ministerial formation) is emphasised, but whenever academic excellence or specialised ministerial training are emphasised, this tends to undermine such an integrative model. As a result, the integration of the theological curriculum remains highly contested. In the rest of this essay I will explore different models for the re-integration of theological education, given the tendency towards fragmentation and the methodological disputes involved. I will start by briefly describing the example of the programmes offered in the Department of Religion and Theology at the University of the Western Cape (UWC) where I am based.

Theological education at the University of the Western Cape

The undergraduate programmes in theological education currently offered at the University of the Western Cape (UWC) emerged under very traumatic circumstances. Until 1994, UWC had an influential Faculty of Theology (best associated with the Confession of Belhar) that provided ministerial training mainly within the then Dutch Reformed Mission Church, but also for a number of other churches. It had a Department of Biblical and Religious Studies with approximately 1 000 students as well as departments of Semitic

---

[3] The ministerial report on the evaluation of the 2010 institutional research publications outputs circulated in 2012, includes a table on journal publications by so-called CESM categories. For Philosophy, Religion and Theology (CESM category 18) an output of 2.64 units per capita is indicated. For Social Sciences (CESM category 20) the figure is 1.07 units per capita. See Department of Higher Education and Training (2012:26). A draft report for 2012 research output (circulated by December 2013) indicates that 743.75 units were produced in Philosophy, Religion and Theology (CESM category 18) by the 312 permanently employed academics in these fields (2.38 units per capita). For 2012, this is trumped by the five academics in Military Science who produced 27.42 units (5.48 units per capita).

Languages and Hellenistic Greek. In 1995, these integrated with a Faculty of Religion and Theology which had four departments, namely Biblical Studies and Languages, Christian Studies, Christianity and Society, and Religious Studies. This was quite a strong faculty with nineteen full-time academic members of staff. Between 1995 and 1999, UWC's student numbers plunged from around 15 000 to around 9 000 students. One of the many reasons included the cancellation of scholarships for prospective teachers in order to correct imbalances in teacher-learner ratios. This drop in student numbers made retrenchments inevitable. In 1998, a large number of academic and administrative staff members were indeed retrenched in a process that lacked transparency. These included six of the fifteen academic staff members in the Faculty of Religion and Theology that remained by that time (four posts that became vacant in the interim were not filled). The Uniting Reformed Church subsequently cancelled its contract with the University with two senior academics moving to Stellenbosch University. By 2000, only six members of staff remained (which remains the number of current staff members).

In 2000, the Department of Religion and Theology was established in the Faculty of Arts. At undergraduate level it offers a three-year Bachelors of Theology, the subject Ethics, and a service course in Hermeneutics at first year level. Semitic Languages and Hellenistic Greek could no longer be offered. The subject Ethics started off as a course offered at first year level only, with around 80 students in 2000. It steadily grew in numbers and stature. More than 700 first year students and more than 150 third year students registered for Ethics in 2014. This astonishing growth may be explained in terms of its distinct focus, namely on the moral and religious foundations of society and the formation of a human rights culture. Students from the faculties of Arts, Law, Community and Health Sciences, as well as Economic and Management Sciences take Ethics as a service course, while some also take it as a major towards the B.A., B.Psych. or B.Th. degrees.

The Bachelors of Theology programme has fluctuating student numbers. The subject Theological Studies typically has first year classes of around 50 students and third year classes of around 25 students. This includes a number of B.A. students who also take the subject, as well as a significant proportion of students on the basis of an agreement between UWC and the United Church of Zambia University College. The programme is thoroughly ecumenical in orientation and, therefore, attracts students from a wide variety of denominations, including students from Pentecostal and independent churches. The most significant feature of the B.Th. curriculum is the way in which it is integrated in terms of a hermeneutical understanding of theology, namely to relate the text of the Bible with the contemporary Western Cape, South African, African and global contexts. Put simply, the task of theology is 'to understand the Word of God anew'. The logic of the programme is best explained with reference to an article by Dirkie Smit (1991) in which he describes theology in evangelical terms as an act of attentive listening to the Holy Scriptures in order to hear the voice of Godself speaking to us anew, to understand the meaning of Scripture more fully with the view to the formation of the Christian faith and to the witness and service of the Church in society. This one task is then outlined in terms of three core challenges, namely to understand and do justice to the biblical texts, to understand how contemporary attempts to relate text to context (to understand the Word of God anew) are shaped for better or for worse by Christian traditions, and to understand the complexities of contemporary contexts. A fourth challenge may be added, namely to bring these together in a creative act of correlation. Reflection on this typically takes place in the context of the sub-discipline of practical theology, but also in the fields of apologetics, ethics, community engagement, and missiology.

On the basis of such a hermeneutical understanding of the task of theology, two crucial decisions were made. Firstly, all modules in the field of Christian theology were simply entitled 'Theological Studies'. The distinction between sub-disciplines according to the fourfold paradigm remained in the description of the various modules, but that was no longer visible in terms of the module codes. Students eventually began to see the subject as one single, if differentiated, task to which various building blocks (modules) contribute. They still had to grapple with the tensions between these modules, but these were included in the same package. Secondly, students were allowed, encouraged and actually forced to include non-theological subjects in the curriculum. The argument is that one has to understand the context in order to relate text to context. Students are required to take 20 credits that focus on the study of religion (at the second year level) and have to do 40 credits at the second and third year levels in subjects such as Ethics, Psychology, Sociology, Women and Gender Studies, Political Studies, and so forth. This leaves room for modules in Theological Studies worth 40 credits (out of 120) at first year level, 60 credits (out of 120) at second year level, and 80 credits (again out of 120) at third year level, supplemented at first year level with 30 credits in Ethics, 15 credits in Hermeneutics (including modules in rhetoric and biblical interpretation), and 15 credits to improve language and communication skills. This yields the following structure:

1	Theological Studies 40 credit	Ethics 30 credits	Hermeneutics 15 credits Language Skills 15 credits	Non-theological subject 30 credits
2	Theological Studies 60 credits	Religious Studies 20 credits	Non-theological subject 40 credits	
3	Theological Studies 80 credits		Non-theological subject 40 credits	

In terms of the distinctions introduced through the fourfold paradigm, the modules in Theological Studies at UWC include some 65 credits in Biblical Studies, alas only 17.5 credits in the History of Christianity, 47.5 credits in Systematic Theology, and 40 credits in Practical Theology. A capstone module on ministerial training at third year level is offered to integrate the full spectrum of modules on the basis of the same hermeneutical understanding of the task of theology.

In addition to the Bachelors of Theology, a Programme for Lay Theological Education (PLATE) was introduced in 2006 through UWC's Continuing Education courses. It is basically the equivalent of the first year of the Bachelors of Theology (120 credits at NQF level 5), with modules in Theological Studies, Ethics, Hermeneutics and Christian Ministry (the only added subject). As indicated in the title, the assumption of this programme is that theological education is not only aimed at formation towards the ordained ministry, but also at the ministries of the laity – not only in the Church, but also in various spheres of society. The programme is offered on a part-time basis, also making use of part-time lecturers, and is spread over a period of two years.

An integrated curriculum?

On the basis of the previous sections I will now explore the contested nature of developing an integrated curriculum for theological education – one that can overcome the presumed divides between ecclesial praxis and theological reflection. One may observe that the need for an integrated curriculum is widely recognised, given the fragmentation of theological education amidst pressing ministerial needs. Integration refers to attempts to synthesise and coordinate the major learning experiences in a programme. It includes the integration of theological disciplines with each other, the integration between theory and praxis, and the dynamic interplay of knowledge, practice and context (knowing, doing and being) (Calahan 2011). However, as I will argue below, one may identify conflicting models as to how such integration may be possible. These models reflect the methodological tensions between the various sub-disciplines. They are reinforced by the pressures of academic life, most notably by the various academic guilds, the journals established to enhance excellence in each field, the need to comply with academic systems of quality assurance, competing schools of theology, and individual interests and ambitions.

It is impossible for any single scholar to follow methodological disputes in all the multiple theological sub-disciplines in South Africa, let alone further afield. At the risk of over-simplification, one may nevertheless say that methodological reflection in the four theological sub-disciplines (according to the fourfold paradigm) developed in opposition to each other. More specifically, all the sub-disciplines managed to liberate themselves from the hegemony imposed by a 'scholastic' approach to systematic theology.

In the field of Biblical Studies, attempts to find proof texts for Christian doctrine in the biblical texts were fiercely rejected in order to allow such ancient texts to speak for themselves in all their radical plurality and moral ambiguity. Instead, the diverse approaches that emerged in the fields of biblical studies modelled themselves on methodological debates in the fields of history, literary studies and/or various social sciences. Biblical theology, at best, articulates the religious views embedded in such ancient texts. Those opting for contextual approaches seek to make such insights relevant for contemporary needs, often by deliberately bypassing the creeds, confessions and liturgical practices found in the Christian tradition. Likewise, studies of the history of Christianity have to do justice to the rigours of historiographic research. This elicits ongoing debates on the distinctive theological nature of church history (or historical theology). Is it only the subject matter that distinguishes it from other areas of historical research?

In the field of practical theology, the obvious need emerged to make Christian convictions relevant for particular ministerial needs. The integrity of the sub-discipline can only be maintained if the focus remains on current ecclesial praxis – how things are done and not only on how they should be done; on what people actually believe and not so much what Christians supposedly should believe. This encouraged empirical investigation, leading to an interest in methodological disputes in the various social sciences. Since practical theology also involves reflection, it may itself become highly theoretical. Systematic theology (at least in some institutions) also liberated itself from a scholastic approach where the focus is on refining elaborate systems of Christian doctrine. Typically, this led to a hermeneutic approach to theology where the emphasis is on understanding the content and the significance of the Christian faith – in conversation with philosophy, various social sciences and, more recently, also the natural sciences. The task is one of making sense of Christianity in a context that is markedly different from the ones in which it first emerged.

Six conflicting models

Although an integrated curriculum for theological education may be desirable, any proposal in this regard would be vulnerable to the charge of hegemony. Re-integration is not viable unless the underlying methodological disputes between the various sub-disciplines can be resolved. Nevertheless, one may find a number of distinct attempts to develop such an integrated curriculum. In each case, this implies some form of imperialism of a particular sub-discipline in the sense that aspects of other sub-disciplines are incorporated on the basis of assumptions held in a particular theological discourse. Such imperialism is hardly surprising and may be found in disciplines such as philosophy, literature, linguistics, sociology, history, economics, development studies, biology, and so forth. In each case, courses of an inter-disciplinary nature may be offered under the rubric of an established discipline. I will not discuss particular examples or contributions to the literature in the discussion below, and will thus, hopefully, avoid stepping on any toes. Instead, a brief description of various models of integration may suffice. My aim is to indicate how these models are indeed deeply in conflict with each other.

1. Inter-cultural biblical hermeneutics

Biblical scholars recognise several different axes of communication, especially in narrative texts, including the events narrated in the text, the production of the text in and for a particular context (decades or centuries later), subsequent revisions (and reinterpretations) of that text for later contexts, the history of interpretation of a text in and for different historical contexts, and contemporary ways of reading the text. Each of these contexts is shaped by particular languages, cultures, economies and worldviews. Inter-cultural biblical hermeneutics is based on the assumption that, given cultural differences, some contemporary readers may recognise cultural assumptions in the layers of the text that others would fail to see. They may also associate themselves with different characters in the narrative (e.g. in the parable in Luke 10, with the man who was assaulted, the Samaritan, the innkeeper, the priest, the Levite or the Pharisees). To juxtapose different contemporary readings of the same text may, therefore, illuminate the text, but may also help readers to understand and assess their own contexts and their ways of appropriating the meaning of the text.

Note how all the other sub-disciplines are assigned a role here: One may find an empirical investigation of how contemporary readers appropriate the text in their lives. On the other hand, the beliefs of culturally diverse contemporary readers are juxtaposed with those of the characters, authors and later editors of the biblical texts. Yet the focus remains overtly on reading the text so that expert outsiders (biblical scholars) who are setting up the hermeneutical experiment, maintain a privileged position. The agenda is framed by biblical scholars and driven by their research and, perhaps also, their political agendas.

2. Act, see, judge and act

In contexts influenced by liberation theology, theology is typically understood as a critical reflection on Christian praxis. On this basis a particular methodology has been developed that is best known as the 'See, Judge, Act' method of doing contextual theology. It is sometimes described as the 'pastoral cycle' of theological. I add the term 'act' here in order to emphasise that this is a spiral that starts with action, prompts reflection (given problems encountered), and inevitably leads to further action, for better or for worse. In terms of this action-reflection model there can be no tension between theory and practice. Theories are born from reflection on action that is always prior to such reflection, but that can in turn inform action (praxis). Yet, without such reflection, action will soon degenerate into an activism that loses its way. In the context of liberation theology, the assumption is that critical reflection on current practices will lead to emancipating praxis under certain conditions that include appropriate interlocutors to ensure that the voices of the poor and oppressed (where God may best be found) are not only heard, but are privileged epistemologically. Again, this approach to doing theology includes all the sub-disciplines. A certain priority is given to social analysis (seeing) and the role of various social sciences. The element of 'judging' would draw on selected biblical texts, but would also be done with reference to particular values, virtues and beliefs. A crucial question is how 'seeing' and 'judging' are related. Does judging not shape what is seen? Or does a particular (Marxist) form of social analysis determine the eventual judgement (leading to a form of inverse hermeneutics – Bosch 1991)? It has to be noted that the focus is on 'Christian' and not only on 'ecclesial' praxis. What is at stake is the ministry of Christians in society, while the role of the institutional church may well be questioned or marginalised. Due to the scandal of particularity, the emphasis on 'Christian' praxis may be replaced by religious, spiritual or emancipatory praxis in general. It may also be noted to what extent this method allows for the influence of a particular theological school that shapes the selection of biblical texts, the form of social analysis, and the emphasis on certain values and convictions. The hermeneutical circle may well, but need not necessarily, become a vicious one. Although this approach emerged in the context of liberation theology, the same approach may also be employed in very different theological schools (including apartheid theology), as is evident in the next model.

3. A practical ecclesiology

If doing theology may be understood as critical reflection on Christian praxis, it may also be understood more narrowly as Christian reflection on ecclesial praxis. This would privilege the Church as the primary 'public' of Christian theology – above the university or various spheres of society as the other potential 'publics' (Bosch 1991, Conradie 1997). This may be developed towards a comprehensive programme for theological education that may be termed a 'practical ecclesiology', given the emphasis on congregational studies. The point of departure is indeed current ecclesial practices. This requires careful description, demographic analysis, sensitivity for denominational differences, and local patterns of pastoral ministry. Of course, theological reflection is prompted by an awareness that current ecclesial praxis does not conform to the 'true' calling of the Church – hence the need for a fully developed ecclesiology. Such an ecclesiology may draw on biblical foundations, considerations in systematic theology, historical examples, liturgical theology, and so forth. The emphasis on 'Christian' reflection is important in order to ensure that such reflection would contribute to the formation of Christian communities. Theological reflection cannot take place in academic isolation but needs to be rooted in the life of the Church (or would otherwise become destructive). Theological reflection is, therefore, best embedded in the formation of Christian virtues, disciplines, habits and practices in Christian communities (under some form of authority). The *habitus* of doing theology is best understood not as the knowledge of God, but as knowing God, intimately and personally (Farley 1983, Wood 1985). Theology entails a life of prayer. It describes the process and mode of reflection, its aptitudes and dispositions, and not so much the views or beliefs that are held. The real interest is, nevertheless, in ministerial formation and competency-based training to which various sub-disciplines are asked to contribute. This may be reduced to coaching in order to attend to various ministerial tasks. However, it is best understood as the ability to engage in ongoing theological reflection as a local theologian (De Gruchy 1994).

Although the roles of all the other theological sub-disciplines may, therefore, be acknowledged, it is striking how they are assigned a particular place, namely in terms of the texts, history, beliefs and practices of the Church. The Bible is the 'book of the Church' (Bird 1982) and is read because it is kept by the Church. The Christian faith cannot be studied in isolation but only in terms of what Christians actually believe and experience. In terms of this model, Christian ministries and vocations in society are indeed important (also for the spiritual and numerical growth of the Church), but would only be authentic if understood as 'ecclesial' ministries. Likewise, any missionary activities should

4. A missionary dimension to all theological education

This model is hypothetical in the sense that obvious examples would be hard to find. It does, however, help to illustrate the conflicting ways in which the integration of the curriculum for theological education may be conceived. In *Transforming Mission*, David Bosch (1991:490-498) discusses the place of studying missiology. He notes that missiology is sometimes introduced as a distinct subject – which allows it some room to flourish, but may also lead to self-marginalisation. It may be incorporated under practical theology or the history of Christianity, but that would tend to underplay a theology of mission and a theology of religions. Alternatively, one may argue that all the other sub-disciplines have a missionary dimension, if not intention. If so, a distinct institutional basis for the sub-discipline of missiology is not required – at the risk that the missionary dimension may well be lost (to their own detriment) in fields such as biblical studies or systematic theology. Bosch (1991:511-512) also discusses the notion of pan-missionism, i.e. that mission touches on all aspects of Christianity and not only of the institutional church. Bosch prefers to err on the side of the danger of adopting an all-inclusive instead of a limited notion of mission. It is here that the distinction between a missionary dimension and an explicit missionary intention is helpful. He insists that a missional agenda for theology is needed and not only a theological agenda for mission (Bosch 1991:494). One is left to wonder how a pan-missionist curriculum for theological education could be constructed. It might well ensure a certain dynamism in reminding all other disciplines of the stark hermeneutical challenges of relating text and context, church and society, gospel and culture, faith and science. It would certainly highlight the 'creative tension' between these pairs and would re-describe such tension in terms of God's mission (*missio Dei*) to the world, in terms of the various offices of Christ (Bosch 1991:512-518), or as the field in which the Holy Spirit is at play. Reflection on an engaged missional praxis would certainly ensure an orientation towards the world in theological education, also, and especially for, ministerial formation (De Gruchy 2010:42).

5. A Trinitarian theological hermeneutics

Systematic theologians may welcome the emphasis on hermeneutics found in each of the above models. Although one may describe the process, object and goals of understanding in quite different ways, some form of interpretation, including appropriation, is clearly involved. The act of understanding is investigated in disciplines such as philosophy, literary criticism, jurisprudence, and in all the sub-disciplines of Christian theology. It may, therefore, be described in different ways. The discipline of theological hermeneutics would draw on such insights in order to describe what understanding specifically entails in a Christian context. Systematic theologians would insist that the act of Christian understanding is itself best understood in terms of the category of faith (or hope and love). This offers them a privileged position as overseers, given the task of systematic theology as critical reflection on the content and significance of the Christian faith. All the other sub-disciplines are assigned a place accordingly, namely to reflect on the text that is understood, the history of interpretation, new acts of appropriation, and also the challenges related to the contemporary context. It is systematic theology that ensures the integration of theological inquiry (Wood 1985:51,62).

Note that Christian faith here refers not so much to the object that is interpreted, but rather to the act of understanding. Faith seeks understanding (*fides quaerens intellectum*), but is itself a form of understanding. The object that is interpreted (in each case through faith) may then be described as the Bible, the Word of God, the Gospel, the Christian tradition, Christian doctrine, and so forth. However, a *theo*logical hermeneutics would need to remind other sub-disciplines that such interpretation is ultimately about God. The focus of theology is on knowing God. If God is indeed the object of interpretation, one may need to confess that knowing God is best understood as God's work. The 'logos' in theology thus refers to being taught by God, not so much to the study of God.

A Trinitarian theological hermeneutics would build on this insight to re-describe the entire task of doing theology in thorough Trinitarian terms. The focus of the biblical witnesses (including the Christian Old Testament) is on what God in Christ has done 'for us and our salvation'. The contemporary context is nothing but the triune God's own beloved, yet distorted, creation. The history of Christianity demonstrates that God sustained loyalty to this creation, while faith (the act of appropriation embedded in various Christian practices) is the work of the Holy Spirit. The creative tension in theological hermeneutics is best understood as the tension between sin and grace, or even better, in terms of God's economy (*oikonomia tou theou*), i.e. God's acts of creation, salvation and the expected consummation of God's work (Conradie 2013). The identity and character of the triune God (the immanent Trinity) can only be derived from such an understanding of the economic Trinity. Where the various theological sub-disciplines (including systematic theology itself) are not subservient to this task, it would yield nothing but heresy.

6. *Christianity as a world religion*

Such a way of integrating the theological curriculum will undoubtedly elicit considerable resistance. Many would argue that such integration would come at the cost of the quest for specialisation and academic excellence allowed for by the emergence of the fourfold paradigm. It would underestimate the rejection of any imposed theological (or Trinitarian) hegemony. The obvious alternative is to regard Christianity as one influential albeit controversial example of a world religion, best studied in a department of religious studies. As with all other religious traditions, it needs to be studied with sensitivity and on its own terms. Admittedly, it also needs to be placed within the wider context of the emergence of life on earth, the evolution of the human species, the phenomenon of religion, and the history of religious traditions. On this basis one may study the sacred texts of Christianity with specific reference to the Bible, the history of its various traditions, earlier and contemporary belief systems in various contexts, rituals, and various Christian practices. Such a secular understanding of the study of Christianity has become internalised, at least to some degree, in all the theological sub-disciplines, including systematic theology. If so, the object of theological investigation is understood as the texts, belief systems, and ecclesial praxis found in various Christian traditions. Knowing God may still play an integrative function in ministerial formation, but no longer in theological education.

Here integration poses no difficulties, albeit attention to debates on the theory of religion would be required. One may simply identify various dimensions of a religious tradition and then study its institutions, ethos, rituals, religious experiences, myths (and sacred texts) and belief systems (Smart 1996). This way of studying Christianity still entails a form of hermeneutics. Christianity may be studied merely for the sake of academic interest, to enhance the self-understanding of insiders, to enable outsiders to come to terms with this tradition, to call for respect for various religious traditions, to preach tolerance, to guard against religious fanaticism, or to muster churches as development agents in order to address social issues around education, health, conflict, justice or the environment.

Conclusion

The discussion in the previous sections suggests three conclusions. Firstly, there is a widely recognised need for the re-integration of the curriculum in theological education in South Africa for the sake of ministerial formation. This is not only due to the divide between theological reflection and ecclesial praxis, but also related to the fragmentation associated with specialisation and to the deeper divides manifested within the South African society. Secondly, this need for integration is recognised in each institution where programmes in (Christian) theology are offered. This is illustrated by the example of the Bachelors of Theology offered at UWC which is based on a particular hermeneutical model. Thirdly, the re-integration of the curriculum will not be viable unless the underlying methodological disputes between the various sub-disciplines can be resolved. This is unlikely, given the conflicting models according to which the integration of theological education may be approached. The best way forward seems to be to at least acknowledge the imperialist tendencies that may be found in each of the theological sub-disciplines.

Bibliography

Bird, P., 1982. *The Bible as the church's book*. Westminster: Philadelphia Press.

Bosch, D.J., 1991. The nature of theological education. *Journal of Theology for Southern Africa*. 77. 3-17.

Bosch, D.J., 1991. *Transforming mission: Paradigm shifts in theology of mission*. Maryknoll: Orbis Books.

Calahan, K.A., 2011. Integration in Theological Education and Ministry: Initial Findings from the Collegeville Institute Seminars. Unpublished report to the International Academy of Practical Theology.

Conradie, E.M., 1997. An ABC in theological education? *Nederduitse Gereformeerde Teologiese Tydskrif.* 38(4). 349-361.

Conradie, E.M., 2011. Knowledge for sale? The impact of a consumerist hermeneutics on learning habits and teaching practices. *Koers.* 76(3). 423-447.

Conradie, E.M., 2013. *Saving the Earth? The Legacy of Reformed views on 'Re-creation'*. Berlin: LIT Verlag.

De Gruchy, J.W., 1994. The nature, necessity and task of theology. In: J.W. De Gruchy and C. Villa-Vicencio (eds.). *Doing theology in context. South African perspectives.* Cape Town: Davis Philip. 2-14.

De Gruchy, S., 2010. Theological education and missional practice: A vital dimension. In: D. Werner et al. (eds.). *Handbook of theological education in World Christianity.* Pietermaritzburg: Cluster Publications. 42-50.

Department of Higher Education and Training (DHET), 2012. *Ministerial report on the evaluation of the 2010 institutional research publications outputs.* Pretoria: DHET.

Farley, E., 1983. *Theologia: The fragmentation and unity of theological education.* Philadelphia: Fortress Press.

Kelsey, D.H., 1992. *To understand God truly: What's theological about a theological school?* Westminster: John Knox Press.

Kelsey, D.H., 1993. *Between Athens and Berlin: The theological education debate.* Grand Rapids, Michigan: William B. Eerdmans Publishing Company.

Mugambi, J.N.K., 2013. The future of theological education in Africa and the challenges that it faces. In: I.A. Phiri and D. Werner (eds.). *Handbook of theological education in Africa.* Oxford: Regnum Books. 117-125.

Naidoo, M., 2013. Spiritual formation in theological education. In: I.A. Phiri and D. Werner (eds.). *Handbook of theological education in Africa.* Oxford: Regnum Books. 755-770

Smart, N., 1996. *Dimensions of the sacred: An anatomy of the world's beliefs.* Berkeley: University of California Press.

Smit, D.J., 1991. The challenge of theological studies for evangelical students. *Apologia.* 6(2). 48-57.

Werner, D. et al. (eds.), 2010. *Handbook of theological education in World Christianity.* Pietermaritzburg: Cluster Publications.

Wood, C.M., 1985. *Vision and discernment: An orientation in theological study.* Atlanta: Scholars Press.

Accreditation and ministerial formation: Serving two masters?

Craig Dunsmuir and Michael McCoy

Introduction

For centuries the Church has taught and formed those who would serve as its ministers – those who equip its members to carry out its vocation and mission. Thus the Church itself has set the standards and requirements of theological education and ministerial formation. The global trend in recent years, however, has been for formal accreditation to become one measure of such standards and requirements. In some instances this is optional, but in South Africa it is mandated by law and implemented through government agencies. This raises a critical question: should the Church surrender to secular third-party entities the final responsibility for determining and judging what is offered as 'acceptable' theological education for church training purposes within South Africa's higher education sphere? This is the contested question addressed in this chapter. Accreditation is about measuring 'minimum standards'; however, the Church seeks to accomplish much more than minimum standards through theological education. This chapter will review how South African churches handled standards for theological education before the introduction of the Higher Education Act in 1997, provide an overview of the current statutory environment, highlight contested issues and dilemmas this raises for theological education and formation, and consider some alternative accreditation processes.

The way we were

Until the implementation of the Higher Education Act of 1997, theological institutions (including church seminaries, independent or ecumenical institutions, and university faculties) were largely left to their own devices in delivering theological education programmes. Given the significance of theological education programmes for the churches, these programmes were usually offered in partnership, or in a relationship of recognition, with denominations for the development of church ministers. Concerted co-operation and effort amongst churches also saw some unique ecumenical developments in South African theological education.

With the legislative changes from 1997 onwards (outlined below), the churches, and the theological educational entities serving them, faced a dilemma: would theological education continue primarily to seek to be true to church needs and mandates for training future ministers, or should it be reshaped to comply with the law of the country? Debate on the issue considered whether the two were mutually exclusive, and to what extent the former might be held captive by the latter.

There is a strong desire amongst theological institutions for some form of accreditation in order to uphold academic respectability, transparency, and academic parity across divergent institutions and contexts (Chatfield 2005:28-29). This, in turn, generates confidence in the institution and its work with church authorities as well as with the general public, and allows comparability across similar institutions and programmes. Students can then transfer locally and internationally, and progress with further study at other institutions. Such a situation enables the churches to access a variety of educational resources in producing their future pastors, teachers, leaders, and theologians (Chatfield 2005:29).

In the 1960s and 1970s, several churches affiliated to the South African Council of Churches entered into ecumenical cooperation in theological education. The Federal Theological Seminary (commonly known as 'Fedsem') was established as an ecumenical residential seminary (Denis 2009:5-6); the Joint Board for the Diploma in Theology (commonly known as the 'Joint Board') was set up to award an ecumenically-recognised and peer-reviewed qualification (Richardson 2007:144-145); and the Theological Education by Extension College (TEEC) was formed to offer ecumenical theological education in distance mode (Mouat in Lombaard 1999:227-228).

These institutions were established for diverse reasons, including issues of financial and resource efficiency, student mobility and institutional access in the restricted era of the Group Areas Act 41 of 1950 (Government of South Africa 1950), and educational disadvantage and disparity under the Bantu Education Act 47 of 1953 (Government of South Africa 1953). The two ecumenical colleges, together with other independent denominational colleges, were members of the nineteen-member Joint Board (Richardson 2007:145). These ecumenically-related, peer-reviewed structures brought together diverse expertise and resources from various quarters, and also strengthened the institutional work of all the seminaries and colleges participating in the Joint Board.

The Diploma in Theology offered by the Joint Board was recognised by the participating churches as an appropriate qualification for authorising people for ordained ministry. The qualification was recognised across denominational boundaries, facilitating the transfer of ministers or in the establishing of united congregations. Furthermore, it was recognised and accepted as a competent undergraduate preparation for higher study at universities.

As required by the law, the Joint Board sought to obtain registration and accreditation on behalf of all its member colleges, with the intention of continuing with the framework for theological education that had served South African churches so well for four decades. However, the restructuring of the higher education landscape required that colleges register independently and in their own right, and that they each own the qualifications that they offer. By 2005, the larger colleges had withdrawn from the Joint Board, and were preparing their own programmes and pursuing their own registration and accreditation (Massey 2005).

Faculties of Theology at universities had the benefit of their newly-established Quality Assurance departments to ensure compliance with the new system of accreditation and registration. For private institutions that were neither subsidised nor profit-motivated, this was onerous to implement. Thus some church training authorities formed partnerships with public institutions through which church ministerial candidates could enjoy preferential rates and also benefit from participating in state-subsidised universities. This approach now placed theological education firmly within the ambit of largely secular institutions (Richardson 2007:150, Duncan 2004:42).

An evolving statutory environment

In response to the educational disparities of the apartheid era, the introduction of the Higher Education Act 101 of 1997 initiated dramatic and far-reaching changes that are still being put into effect. The Council on Higher Education was established in 2000 with two responsibilities: to advise the Minister of Higher Education and Training, and to oversee "quality promotion and quality assurance, specifically, the auditing of the quality assurance mechanisms of higher education institutions and the accreditation of higher education programmes" (Council on Higher Education 2010:1). This is the lens through which the work and purpose of institutions of higher education are viewed, and it is applied across all fields of study. The National Qualifications Framework (NQF) Act 67 of 2008 entrusted the work of the Higher Education Quality Committee (HEQC) to the Council of Higher Education (CHE) with the added responsibilities of developing the Higher Education Qualifications sub-framework (HEQSF) (Government of South Africa 2014), and the development and implementation of policy and criteria relating to qualifications in the HEQSF. The NQF Act deliberately integrated the previously disparate systems and policies around higher education qualifications, thereby "improving the coherence of the higher education system and facilitating the articulation of qualifications" (Government of South Africa 2007:5).

A new development is the fact that the Higher Education Act applies the new educational structure "to all higher education programmes and qualifications offered in South Africa by public and private institutions" (Government of South Africa 2007:6). For the first time, private institutions such as seminaries and colleges are now subject to formal government educational registration and regulation requiring State accreditation. This affects admission requirements for studies, and determines what programmes can be offered, how the content is to be structured educationally, and how the institution is to function.

Theological education, if it is to function legally, needs to offer programmes that have been through three distinct processes: (1) They have been formally assessed and accredited by the HEQC through the CHE; (2) they have been registered with the Department of Higher Education and Training (DHET) for delivery from specific and pre-approved sites; and (3) they have been formally registered on the NQF through the South African Qualifications

Authority (SAQA). Theological education institutions may not offer training programmes leading to a tertiary qualification unless they have completed this process.

The NQF describes the requirements for the permitted qualification types. Institutions wishing to award these qualifications need to design programmes that conform, which are then reviewed, accredited, and registered. The fundamental building blocks of programmes are their credit values and the NQF 'level' at which those credits are offered in relation to the qualification design. The CHE's *Criteria for Programme Accreditation* document describes the requirements for submitting a programme for accreditation, including the "minimum standards" (CHE 2004). The measure applied is "quality assurance in higher education through [the CHE's] permanent sub-committee, the HEQC" (CHE 2014:13). The question arises: is a programme leading to a qualification in theology able to both fit this framework and to meet the requirements of preparing people for ministry roles? While the HEQC is measuring compliance with generalised minimum standards, the churches are looking beyond this for programmes that prepare and develop candidates in ways that go well beyond the official criteria. Neither the delivery nor the success of such programmes is easily quantified in terms of the official minimum standards. What, then, is actually being assured through official accreditation?

What is being accredited?

Farley (1983) explores the historical development of theological education through to its current expression within subject areas and academic disciplines. What began as the revealed knowledge of God through faith (*theologia*) becomes systematised through rational reflection, study and argument. Farley calls the original pursuit of theological wisdom *habitus* – the "cognitive disposition and orientation of the soul, a knowledge of God and which God reveals" (Farley 1983:35). The work of faith and the work of reason both form the believer, and both are the focus of theological education. From this perspective, to focus through accreditation only on the academic 'programmatic' aspects of ministerial training distorts the value and significance of the whole formation process, and often elevates formal academic ability over the broader competencies and values required for ministry in a complex world.

Farley laments the strong shift to scientific method in theological education in later periods, where 'un-prove-able' theology fell by the wayside and *habitus* was abandoned with it. He further explores the attempts to make theology scientifically credible that led to its fragmentation into independent disciplines, losing its original internal unity. Thus theological education becomes largely functional, training ministers for ministerial tasks, focusing on strategic and technical knowledge (Farley 1983:131-132), with reduced emphasis on the broader goals of ministerial formation "involving critical thinking, the acquisition of knowledge, skills development, religious identity formation, and the development of ministerial and spiritual maturity expected of church ministers" (Naidoo 2012b).

Recent denominational and ecumenical documents on ministerial formation agree that Christian ministers need to be shaped in holistic and integrated ways. For example, Werner (2008) identifies five competencies required for Christian ministry in the 21st century; and Forster, Dahill, Goleman and Tolentino (2006:100-126) describe the pedagogy of formation – echoing the notion of *habitus* (Farley 1983; Ballard and Pritchard 2006:73-76).

The landmark Hind Report in the Church of England emphasised that in ministerial formation the Church looks not just for personal development, but for transformation:

> The purpose of the early stages of ministerial formation should not be to provide the knowledge and skills which will be necessary throughout ministry, but to establish the patterns of learning, piety and competence which will sustain an appetite for continued growth. (Hind 2003:29, 3.10)

However, the desire for theological education to be a science has focused on critical and technical aspects rather than on personal and pastoral formation. Also, the more measurable aspects, which might be secondary to the core focus, receive attention – for example, teaching and assessing exegetical competence rather than knowledge and understanding of the scriptures themselves. The *locus* of theological education has also shifted: where once theological knowledge and education was the "wisdom of Christians" (Farley 1983:130), it is now the vehicle for specialist professional training, and is largely bound to tertiary institutions. While the study of theology is often regarded as the preserve of a ministerial or academic class of person, it is in fact integral to the life, message and mission of the Church.

Was the prior situation deficient?

As noted earlier, accredited programmes can only be offered by registered institutions. However, theological institutions take many forms, complicating the situation. Aleshire's discussion of three stages in the development of the identity and purpose of an institution for theological education helps us to appreciate this (Aleshire 2008) – although here we focus only on the first two stages. First, he argues, comes the 'Abbey' – the in-house training centre that serves denominational or constituent needs. The foundational essentials and personal formation are the focus, and students rub shoulders with experienced practitioners who also embody and pass on the ethos and practice of the Church. This resonates with Kelsey's 'Athens' and with Farley's *habitus* (Forster et al. 2006). The new requirements for higher education institutions in South Africa push institutions towards Aleshire's second stage, namely the 'Academy'. The tasks of the Abbey now have to conform to the frameworks and regulations of either secular authorities, or peer-review mechanisms. Quality assurance is often the driver, and the 'measurable' takes centre stage – particularly when generic or secular frameworks are used, as peer-review processes usually handle this better through broader measures and better understanding of the institution and its goals. *Paideia* gives way to *wissenschaft*, while *habitus* is abandoned for provable 'science' (Forster et al. 2006:47-49).

The nineteen-member institutions of the Joint Board varied greatly in terms of Aleshire's typology (2008), yet the Joint Board provided them with a common standard and platform for cooperation and engagement. Diverse institutions were drawn into a common space for a mutual goal without requiring them to become what they did not intend to be. In this respect, the Joint Board served the churches well. It also provided a common core and framework for content and assessment while allowing the individual institutions freedom to include denominational distinctives in their teaching format and curricula. It permitted students to move between residential 'contact' mode and home- or work-based 'distance' mode while remaining registered on the same programme. And it allowed students to move between training institutions – whether denominational, ecumenical, or cross-denominational – and to remain registered on the same programme.

Under the new dispensation, however, this ecumenical basis for maintaining the standards and quality assurance of theological education, including ministerial formation, has largely disappeared. The closure of Fedsem (Duncan 2004), together with the requirement that Joint Board colleges be registered and accredited in their own right apart from the Joint Board, was a major blow for ecumenical cooperation in theological education. The last remaining enterprise from the initial ecumenical collaboration in theological education, TEE College, now sees two of its major denominational clients – the Methodist Church of Southern Africa and the Anglican Church of Southern Africa – setting up their own distance-mode programmes.

Denominational authorities have moved to creating independent institutions and programmes, to resort to unaccredited short course programmes, or to partner with universities to use their programmes. This sees much duplication of effort with multiplied expense, and the loss of regional collegiality and standards for theological education in Southern Africa.

It has been suggested that ecumenical cooperation in earlier years was rooted in expediency and as part of a united, prophetic response to major national issues in the apartheid era. The ecumenical track record has not been without its problems and difficulties, and even the lack of resolution in the closure of Fedsem – despite stated intentions to remain ecumenically committed – has created a very real hesitation to commit to future ecumenical endeavours in theological education (McCoy 2013, Duncan 2004:65). With the ecumenical mat largely pulled from under the feet of theological education institutions, the current statutory process remains the only viable route for offering accredited programmes.

Questions raised by a move to accredited programmes

The above situation raises several key questions. If theological education embraces ministerial formation with *habitus* at its heart, how do we measure and accredit that? How do we define the purpose, structure, and content of this process within standard and generic higher education frameworks? "A prescribed path might not lead to the desired destination – and may even miss the crucial aspects" (Allais 2009:29), particularly when the Church's goal is that people formed for ministry would have theological wisdom in addition to technical knowledge or skill.

Should theological education be reserved primarily for those who will be 'specialist operators' or office-bearers in the Church? The majority of theology students are primarily intending to engage in some form of ministerial practice, usually within a particular denominational context. As such the place of denominational distinctiveness in theology, ethos and practice is an important part of the formational journey. Is this then to be engaged outside of accredited study programmes, or can it be accredited and credit-bearing within higher education?

Is it helpful to limit theological education largely to tertiary institutions, removed and isolated from local communities of faith? Students embarking on theological study as part of ministerial preparation anticipate Farley's *habitus* and Aleshire's 'Abbey', yet they are confronted with the 'Academy'. For some this results in a separation of the spiritual from academic activity, with a dualistic and disconnected approach to personal faith and ministry in relation to theological knowledge and learning. This creates an existential crisis for some individuals whose personal faith struggles to cope with debates around belief, faith, and the Christian scriptures, thus reinforcing the disconnect between theological studies and the community of faith.

Contested issues raised by accreditation

Accreditation – particularly by a body not related to the Church – is not easily or readily accepted (Chatfield 2005:29-30), and raises several issues for those who govern theological institutions. A number of subtle but significant shifts occur with the requirement to change to a regulated and accredited environment – even more so when accreditor and institution hold differing worldviews with regard to higher education in general and theological education in particular. We identify some of these shifts:

- The commercialisation and 'commodification' of theological education. This causes a shift from study that has a societal and social value to that which has credit value that can articulate into other academic domains. This can distort the student's goal, which began with a desire to serve in response to God's call to ministry.
- The required 'independence' of private institutions as registered companies frustrates relationships with parent church bodies. Many such institutions are governed and funded by church bodies, their work is sanctioned or authorised by them, their students are sourced from there, and the institution is staffed by church 'insiders'. Yet, denominational theological institutions are now to be viewed independently of their denominational parent body, and the criteria for admission as to who may study in a theological institution are now determined by 'outsiders'.
- The relationship between peer institutions has been affected. Where there may have been cooperation between such institutions in the past, they are now more easily

viewed as commercially-orientated and in competition. There is also the division between institutions that are registered and accredited and those that are not. Of the nineteen colleges participating in the Joint Board at the time of its dissolution in 2005, only two[4] are registered and one[5] is provisionally registered (Government of South Africa 2014).

- The imposition of political control by the State and its agencies, in the form of imposed goals or requirements, or of enforced ideological or methodological inputs, raises deep concerns (Chatfield 2005:30).

A number of critical issues arise from the process of accreditation.

Flexibility in delivery: Institutions and programmes are linked to registered sites of delivery. This limits alternative educational or delivery models in response to regional contexts and student needs. Internships and placements for ministerial formation, for example, take place away from the registered site of delivery, and 'blended learning' by definition involves diverse and dispersed modes of delivery (Kinsler 2008). Such initiatives will not necessarily be appreciated or understood by evaluators external to the situation.

Market responsiveness: Private higher education institutions respond to market needs and changes that are themselves uncertain and usually less-regulated. Responsiveness to dynamic contexts while carrying a non-responsive bureaucratic burden, is not easy. To attempt to formally offer multiple or varied programmes for these different contexts also increases the regulatory, administrative, and cost burden.

Prescribed programme structure: Institutions seek to develop programmes in response to need; however, they are required to conform to a fixed, prescribed pattern regulated by the NQF and HEQSF through the authorised qualification types. This inflexibility leads to academic inflation: Either coursework is extended to meet the requirements of a higher qualification, or it is abbreviated to meet the requirements of a lower qualification.

The issues described above are quite crucial to those who design and deliver programmes in the private sphere. The *Criteria for Programme Accreditation* document provides a comprehensive checklist that any institution can use to evaluate itself and ensure that the basic issues related to the delivery of higher education are adequately and appropriately addressed (CHE 2004:6-7). Where institutions seek more than mere compliance with minimum standards, they are improved and strengthened. However, there are some requirements that, while intended to be positive, have negative consequences instead.

Access: The intention of the Higher Education Act is to broaden access to higher education. This is, however, often strongly curtailed and complicated by the current regulatory requirement that students have a proper and adequate secondary education. Many theological students are mature people who suffered under inadequate and

---

[4] The Theological Education by Extension College (ecumenical) and the Seth Mokitimi Methodist Seminary.
[5] The College of the Transfiguration (Anglican).

disparate educational systems, and have been left without the now required certification of secondary schooling. Unfortunately, the current Recognition of Prior Learning (RPL) provision is insufficient for alternative access, and in reality it is a hit-and-miss affair which varies considerably across institutions. Creating alternative access mechanisms is both expensive and time-consuming for institutions and students. The ongoing crisis in both primary and secondary education means that this issue will affect many more generations of school leavers.

Affordability: Institutions that are adequately functional and productive are easily considered 'under-resourced' in terms of standardised external criteria. Requirements such as annual health and safety inspections are a cost burden, while providing student computers in libraries might not be relevant for every site of delivery. The required documentation, recordkeeping and reporting, are administrative burdens that also translate into an increased salary bill or the high cost of using outsourced expertise. These requirements might be out-of-scale for the size of the institution. All of this translates into increased delivery costs and increased student fees.

Accountability: To whom is the theological institution accountable – to the Church that establishes the institution and usually provides its governance and funding? To the students whom it primarily serves? To external criteria established independently of the context in which theological institutions operate? To an industry 'standard' comprising a certain grouping or alignment of particular parties? To a statutory body? Additionally, does one rate staff on their research and writing output, or on their nurture and support of students? Is the institution rated by its reputation and resources, or by the performance of its students and graduates? Are those graduates measured by ministerial competence or by their final marks at graduation? Institutional practices, values and effectiveness go beyond what can be easily measured.

Is accountability a one-way street? Institutions that are denied accreditation are also denied access to the reports or minutes of meetings that describe their programmes as 'not accreditable'. Similarly, the names and affiliations of those 'peers' who make these judgements against the institution are not revealed, which is problematic in the increasingly commercialised environment of higher education. This is a top-down approach that places 'peers' over one another rather than maintaining their relationship with each other.

Conformity to a single national standard: The validating authority (or its participants, where these are co-opted 'peers') might not agree with or seek to understand issues specific to the institution under review, such as its values or educational methodology. The requirement to conform may reduce or undermine institution-specific solutions or time-tested and established practices within that educational context.

How, then, do we meet the challenge of applying an appropriate accreditation framework alongside the goal of equipping people for ministry through diverse models of theological education? The aims of the Higher Education Act are laudable. However, with compliance only possible through the imposition of a single, limited framework, does this not compromise the goals, credibility, and coherence of theological education?

Is this way the only way?

While legislation creates the framework that applies to the accreditation of theological institutions in South Africa, this is not the case everywhere. There is a broad diversity in the models used for accrediting purposes. We now consider some of these models for their appropriateness to the Southern African context.

Church of England – a State-endorsed entity that operates independently

The Church of England – which, as the established Church in that country, has a distinctive relationship with the State – regulates its own institutions and programmes of ministerial formation. Theological education and training is offered by training institutions that have been recognised by the House of Bishops. The training institutions are subject to the quality assurance and enhancement framework of the Church, which includes regular inspection. The quality assurance includes checking the quality of education and formation being offered to the ministers of the future, and helping training institutions to enhance what they offer.

The Church of England publishes its inspection reports on ministerial training institutions. Every training institution, both Church of England and ecumenical, is fully inspected once during each six-year cycle in line with the published programme of inspections.

Association of Theological Schools – a non-State agency in partnership with the State

The United States of America and Canada use a three-legged approach to accreditation that involves the institution to be accredited, the Federal government, and a non-governmental organisation that serves as the accrediting body. For theological institutions this is the Association of Theological Schools (ATS), which currently accredits 270 theological schools across a broad range of Christian traditions (ATS 2014a). Its goal is "to promote the improvement and enhancement of theological schools to the benefit of communities of faith and the broader public" (ATS 2014a). It achieves this by providing (1) a resource base, both administrative and educational, to support the work of theological institutions, and (2) accrediting services, particularly for degree programmes. In this context theological education is commonly offered at a graduate level.

In this tripartite relationship, the State authorises the institution as a company, establishing it as a legal entity. However, the State makes no determination about the quality of the institution. The accrediting body assesses institutional and educational quality, but it confers no legal status on the institution. The two goals of this accrediting process are the standards of institutional and educational quality, as well as ongoing improvement (ATS 2014b). For Southern African institutions we see each of these dynamics in the provisions of the Companies Act (overseen by the Companies and Intellectual Property Commission, etc.) and the Higher Education Act (overseen by the CHE and DHET). A three-tiered membership structure allows new member institutions to work towards, obtain, and then maintain accredited status.

Theological Education for the Anglican Communion – non-institutional, but operates across institutions and is multi-national

Many ecclesial polities have developed checklists or outcome statements for ministerial or ordination candidates entering into, progressing through, and emerging from their ministerial formation. One example is the set of outcomes for theological education for laity and clergy developed by a global working group known as Theological Education for the Anglican Communion (TEAC) (Theological Education for the Anglican Communion 2008). Commonly referred to as the 'TEAC grids', these five sets of outcomes – each focused on a specific aspect of ministry, ranging from baptised church members to bishops – lay out the anticipated outcomes in twelve areas of life and ministry. For deacons and presbyters, for example, criteria are defined for when they candidate for ordination, when they are ordained, the three years following ordination, and their ongoing ministerial formation. Within the Anglican Communion it is a relatively simple matter to adapt the TEAC grids for local conditions, and then use them as the basis for designing teaching opportunities from Sunday School to Catechism to theological college, as well as measuring progress and improvement ('quality assurance'). While the TEAC grids were developed specifically for the Anglican Communion, their value lies in being a common expression and in being highly adaptable for context and culture. As such they have the potential to inspire something similar for ecumenical or inter-denominational contexts, or through agencies such as the Ecumenical Theological Education desk of the World Council of Churches.

In these examples we see national and supra-national non-governmental systems dealing with the same issues of quality assurance and educational credibility as do our own Quality Councils. As theological institutions often exist in a space between academia and institutional church, so these alternative accrediting bodies are better positioned to engage, critique and assess these institutions, and, additionally (as in the case of ACTEA and ATS), to supply appropriate resources and expertise specific to the institutions in this domain.

Association for Christian Theological Education in Africa – a peer-reviewed association with no State relationship

The Accrediting Council for Theological Education in Africa (recently renamed 'Association for Christian Theological Education in Africa', ACTEA) has a primary focus on theological institutions with an evangelical ethos. Its mission "is to promote quality evangelical theological education in Africa, by providing supporting services, facilitating academic recognition, and fostering continental and inter-continental cooperation; serving theological education in Africa for excellence and renewal" (ACTEA, n.d.). This is a voluntary peer-reviewed process that uses perceptive self-evaluation reports combined with site visits (ACTEA 2014).

These networked accrediting associations are not only concerned with academic integrity and questions of quality, resourcefulness or competence, but also hold a light to institutional accountability in their consistency of ethos and mission, regional contextualisation, collegial cooperation, and issues that are beyond the curriculum. This approach understands ministerial formation within the context of delivering formal theological education, and consequently such associations provide categories of membership for institutions that are formally accredited through other agencies, yet also seek an informed peer endorsement.

This work is similar to, yet broader and more comprehensive than, that of the former Joint Board. This raises the question of whether a similarly structured association might be founded upon the ethos of the Joint Board for the purposes of peer-reviewed accreditation for South African theological institutions.

Are we trying to serve two masters?

The reorganisation of higher education rightly demanded a firm, centralised (and, some might say, ideologically-driven) framework, such as that of the NQF, to address past fragmentation and disparity. This process included several institutions through the Standards Generating Bodies in establishing Unit Standards and national qualifications. However, fifteen years later, while many challenges remain, it could be argued that, ironically, the churches' institutions and programmes have been weakened, not strengthened, by the onerous demands of the State-regulated system. If, as Naidoo (2012a:157) argues, theological education is "a key indicator of the character of today's Christianity," then the churches in South Africa are at a crossroads.

The drive for quality assurance in higher education seeks to ensure that institutions of higher learning produce people who are competent in their fields. The churches can have no quarrel with that basic aim. Yet the current accreditation framework's strong focus on issues other than holistic personal formation and transformation – *habitus* – sets some theological institutions at odds with their primary goal. Is there another way? In terms of current legislation, the HEQC (through the CHE) is the only body authorised to accredit higher education programmes, and any attempts at alternatives would be illegal.

However, the focus in theological education, and especially in ministerial formation, is (or should be) on forming people in mind and heart for a life of faithful discipleship and leadership. And such qualities or outcomes are difficult, if not impossible, to measure, let alone to guarantee. Ultimately, therefore, theological education, and ministerial formation in particular, can only seek to form and shape a Christian community – and especially those who are called to lead it – in the knowledge, skills, and values that will best serve its mission in the world. While such outcomes can be measured to some extent, there is also an element of the unpredictable and the intangible in the formation of character. Authentic education and formation is a journey, not a predetermined destination.

We have seen that the South African churches had initiated and upheld a decades-long commitment to ecumenical participation and academic standards for theological education that maintained denominational distinctives and autonomy while providing high standards and support through ecumenical institutions and programmes. Internationally we see associations that understand the theological education domain and its goals, and the integral relationship with churches. These expert teams of peer reviewers, as used by many accrediting associations around the world, best serve the work of critiquing institutional and educational quality with insight, while also realistically challenging institutions continually to improve.

The CHE's Accreditation Committee already receives reports and recommendations from their appointed 'peer' evaluators before forwarding their own recommendation to the HEQC for a final decision regarding accreditation. Could the 'evaluator' role not be performed by a peer-reviewed association? Previously, the South African Council for Theological Education (SACTE) had played a similar role until its demise.

This would assist the CHE with the kind of precision and specialisation for theological education that other accrediting associations around the world provide. It is, therefore, highly likely that the churches and institutions seeking accreditation would overcome past ecumenical struggles and support, and resource a collective initiative: One that ensures that institutions offering theological education (or that are partners in preparing people for Christian ministries) offer the best possible programmes in and for the Southern African context.

It may be that the churches of South Africa will have to learn to live in that uncomfortable space 'between the real and the ideal' (to borrow the title of Naidoo 2012a). The 'real' is the current regime of State-sponsored accreditation; the 'ideal' is the churches' passionate commitment and unconstrained freedom to craft ways of forming their leadership for mission and ministry. Between those two, we need to find the space to negotiate and make changes so that we meet the legitimate requirements of our society while also being, and doing, the best we can.

Bibliography

Aleshire, D., 2008. *Earthen vessels: Hopeful reflections on the work and future of theological schools.* Grand Rapids, Michigan: William B. Eerdmans Publishing Company.

Allais, S.M., 2009. *Quality Assurance in Education.* Johannesburg: CEPD.

Association for Christian Theological Education in Africa (ACTEA), [n.d.]. *Projects.* [Online] Available from: http://www.aeafrica.org/projects/accrediting.htm [Accessed: 14 February 2014].

Association for Christian Theological Education in Africa (ACTEA), 2014. ACTEA *Standards and Guide to Self-Evaluation*. [Online] Available from: http://www.theoledafrica.org/actea/Standards/ [Accessed: 14 February 2014].

Association of Theological Schools (ATS), 2014a. *About ATS*. [Online] Available from: http://www.ats.edu/about/overview [Accessed: 29 January 2014].

Association of Theological Schools (ATS), 2014b. *Handbook of Accreditation*. [Online] Available from: http://www.ats.edu/accrediting/handbook-accreditation [Accessed: 29 January 2014].

Ballard, P. and Pritchard, J., 2006. *Practical theology in action: Christian thinking in the service of church and society*. 2nd edition. London: SPCK.

Chatfield, A., 2005. The question of accreditation and academic standards in TEE. *The T.E.E. Journal*, 5. 27-38.

Church of England, [n.d.]. *Quality assurance in ministerial education*. [Online] Available from: https://www.churchofengland.org/clergy-office-holders/ministry/ministerial-education-and-development/quality-assurance-in-ministerial-education.aspx [Accessed: 19 January 2014].

Council on Higher Education (CHE), 2004. *Criteria for programme accreditation*. [Online] Available from: http://www.che.ac.za/sites/default/files/publications/CHE_accreditation_criteria_Nov2004_0.pdf [Accessed: 19 February 2014].

Council on Higher Education (CHE), 2010. *Communiqué 1. The functions of the Council on Higher Education as a quality council: Higher education qualifications framework*. Pretoria: CHE.

Council on Higher Education (CHE), 2014. *The higher education qualifications sub-framework*. Pretoria: CHE.

Denis, P., 2009. Unfinished business: The painful closure of the Federal Theological Seminary of Southern Africa. *Missionalia*. 37(1). 5-19.

Duncan, G., 2004. A crisis in mission and unity: The closure of the Federal Theological Seminary of Southern Africa. *Missionalia*. 32(1). 39-67.

Farley, E., 1983. *Theologia: The fragmentation and unity of theological education*. Philadelphia: Fortress Press.

Forster, C.R., Dahill, E.L., Goleman, L.A. and Tolentino, B.W., 2006. *Educating clergy: Teaching practices and pastoral imagination*. San Francisco: Jossey Bass.

Government of South Africa, 1950. *Group Areas Act (41 of 1950)*. [Online] Available from: http://www.historicalpapers.wits.ac.za/inventories/inv_pdfo/AD1812/AD1812-Em3-2-011-jpeg.pdf [Accessed: 19 February 2014].

Government of South Africa, 1953. *Bantu Education Act (47 of 1953)*. [Online] Available from: http://www.disa.ukzn.ac.za/webpages/DC/leg19531009.028.020.047/leg19531009.028.020.047.pdf [Accessed: 19 February 2014].

Government of South Africa, 1995. *South African Qualifications Authority Act (58 of 1995)*. [Online] Available from: http://www.acts.co.za/south-african-qualifications-authority-act-1995/ [Accessed: 19 February 2014].

Government of South Africa, 2007. *Higher Education Act (101 of 1997)*. The Higher Education Qualifications Framework. Government Gazette (No. 30353) [Online] Available from: http://www.acts.co.za/higher-education-act-1997/ [Accessed: 19 February 2014].

Government of South Africa, 2008. *National Qualifications Framework (NQF) Act (67 of 2008)*. [Online] Available from: http://www.acts.co.za/national-qualifications-framework-act-2008/ [Accessed: 19 February 2014].

Government of South Africa, 2014. *Higher Education Qualifications Sub-Framework (HEQSF)*. [Online] Available from: http://www.che.ac.za/sites/default/files/publications/HEQSF%202013.pdf [Accessed: 19 February 2014].

Government of South Africa, 2014. *Private Higher Education Institutions Register (July 2014)*. [Online] Available from: http://www.dhet.gov.za/Registers_DocLib/Private%20Higher%20Education%20Institutions%20Register%20July%202014%20.pdf [Accessed: 15 August 2014].

Hind, J., 2003. *Formation for ministry within a learning church*. London: Church of England.

Kinsler, F.R., 2008. *Diversified theological education: Equipping all God's people*. Pasadena: William Carey International University Press.

Lombaard, C. (ed.), 1999. *Essays and exercises in ecumenism*. Pietermaritzburg: Cluster Publications.

Massey, J., 2005. *Joint Board meeting* [E-mail] Message to James Massey. 7 November 2005.

McCoy, M., 2013. *Track 3: Co-operation in the training of students for ministry and the post-ordination training of ministers*. Report to Church Unity Commission Central Committee, 16 June 2013.

Naidoo, M. (ed.), 2012a. *Between the real and the ideal: Ministerial formation in South African churches*. Pretoria: Unisa.

Naidoo, M., 2012b. Ministerial formation of theological students through distance education. *HTS Theological Studies*. 68(2). 9.

Richardson, N., 2007. Ministerial training and theological education in the Methodist Church of Southern Africa: The road ahead. *Missionalia*. 35(2). 131-148.

Theological Education for the Anglican Communion (TEAC), 2008. *The ministry grids*. [Online] Available from: http://www.anglicancommunion.org/ministry/theological/teac/grids/index.cfm [Accessed: 19 February 2014].

Werner, D., 2008. *Magna charta on ecumenical formation in theological education in the 21st century – 10 key convictions*. Geneva: ETE/WCC.

THE AFRICAN RENAISSANCE AND THE DECOLONISATION OF THEOLOGICAL EDUCATION

PHILLIP HIGGS

Introduction

Theological education during the colonial period in Africa was hegemonic and disruptive to African cultural practices, indigenous epistemologies, and ways of knowing. The centuries old subjugation of Africa to colonial exploitation, ranging from slavery to the creation of socio-economic structures during the colonial era which were designed to achieve maximum extraction and exportation of raw materials, wreaked serious damage that still remain palpable years after the demise of colonial rule. This was accomplished, as Nkomo (2000:52) notes, by a whole range of arrangements, including educational philosophies, curricula and practices of which the context corresponded with that of the respective colonial powers. This meant that with the advent of colonisation, traditional African epistemologies started disappearing due to cultural repression, misrepresentations and devaluation (see Higgs 2012).

Theological education in Africa in the 21st century has to operate in both a post-colonial and globalising context. However, theological education in post-colonial Africa is still to a large extent confronted by the legacy of colonial forms of theological education that remained in place decades after political decolonisation. As a result, theological education in Africa, despite the advent of decolonisation, still in many instances, mirrors colonial models inherited from the West and Europe. The voices of African indigenous populations are, therefore, greatly negated in theological education discourses. Consequently, there is an existential and humane need today to decolonise theological education in Africa by means of post-colonial forms of theological education that will reclaim indigenous African voices through curriculum reforms and the transformation of theological discourses.

This chapter is an attempt to explore the need for the reconstruction of theological education in an African context in the light of Africa's colonial past, and the call for an African Renaissance on the African continent. In reflecting critically on this educational issue, I understand education as a social and epistemic practice which is concerned with the cultural and social conditions that underpin the construction of knowledge (Luckett 2010). In this endeavour, I argue that through the implementation and integration of indigenous African epistemologies in theological education in Africa, Africans can reclaim their voices in the continent's spaces of theological education, including South Africa. Ministerial training in such a context will allow ministers in training to understand and acquire a voice that resonates with and acknowledges a decolonised African identity. Such an African identity is highly contested in South African theological education, especially in the training of church ministers. The reasons for such contestation are many and varied.

However, a major factor remains the ever-present duality of Western/European forms of theological education, while the training of church ministers in an African context should actually be informed by indigenous African knowledge systems. In addressing this problem, I will reflect critically on the question of indigenous African knowledge systems and the problem of an African identity. In doing so, I will attempt to deconstruct this dualism in claiming that the African notion of communalism and the *ubuntu* ethic can lead to an African-based theological education in the training of church ministers throughout the continent, and, indeed, in South Africa as well. My argument that follows is rooted in the call for an African Renaissance in theological education in its many manifestations in Africa in pre- and post-colonial periods.

The African Renaissance and theological education

The call for an African Renaissance has been present in the period marking the nearly four decades of African post-independence. The process of decolonisation that unfolded during this period, saw Africa assert its right to define itself within its own African context in the attainment of independence. Wa Thiong'o (2009:21) claims that independence was about people's struggle to claim their own space, and their right to name the world for themselves rather than be named through the colour-tinted glass of the Europeans (Zenawi 2012).

In the context of education, Hoppers (2001:1) describes this continuing struggle in the following way:

> The African voice in education at the end of the twentieth century is the voice of the radical witness of the pain and inhumanity of history, the arrogance of modernisation and the conspiracy of silence in academic disciplines towards what is organic and alive in Africa. It is the voice of 'wounded healers' struggling against many odds to remember the past, engage with the present, and determine a future built on new foundations. It invokes the democratic ideal of the right of all to 'be', to 'exist', to grow and live without coercion, and from that to find a point of convergence with the numerous others. It exposes the established hegemony of Western thought, and beseeches it to feel a measure of shame and vulgarity at espousing modes of development that build on the silencing of all other views and perceptions of reality. It also seeks to make a contribution to the momentum for a return of humanism to the centre of the educational agenda, and dares educators to see the African child-learner not as a bundle of Pavlovian reflexes, but as a human being culturally and cosmologically located in authentic value systems.

What this means in the context of theological education, is that the latter is founded on the perception that the overall character of much of theological education in Africa is overwhelmingly Western and Eurocentric. In other words, it is argued by advocates of an African Renaissance in theological education, such as Boesak (2005) and Botman (2008), that much of what is taken for theological education in Africa is, in fact, not African, but rather a reflection of Europe in Africa. The African Renaissance has also taken on a much greater significance in recent days, with the call for the recognition of indigenous African knowledge systems by scholars such as Gigaba (2011). The inference here, when applied to theological education, is the distorted view that Africans possess little or no indigenous knowledge of value that can be utilised in theological education. It is also believed that theological education in Africa is context-bound by Western European culture, where the English language is sacralised and internalisation of bourgeois European values are seen as the index of progress (Sefa Dei 2013). This situation is compounded by globalisation which has corrupted African culture through its progressive technological changes in communication, political and economic power, knowledge and skills, as well as cultural values, systems and practices. Shizha (2011:2) notes that globalisation promotes the epistemological and ontological realities and experiences of the most powerful in the world. In doing so, globalisation has, as Maweu (2011:36) observes, catalysed the colonisation of African ways of knowing. And it is in response to this state of affairs that the call for an African Renaissance in theological education goes out – a call which insists that all critical and transformative theological educators in Africa embrace indigenous African epistemologies and root their theological and educational paradigms in indigenous African socio-cultural and epistemological frameworks. This implies that all educational discourses in Africa, including those in theological education, should have Africa as their focus, and as a result be indigenous-grounded and orientated. Failure to do so will mean that theological education becomes alien, oppressive and irrelevant. Thus, in order to debunk the belief that Western Eurocentric knowledge in Africa is the only viable knowledge when it comes to theological education, it is vital to decolonise the misconception of its superiority.

The call for an African Renaissance in theological education seeks to demonstrate how indigenous African epistemologies can be tapped as a foundational resource for theological education in Africa. However, in assuming the indigeneity of culture, the call for an African Renaissance in theological education does not connote a detachment from political radicalisation and mobilisation. In fact, proponents of the African Renaissance in theological education (Boesak 2005, 2006, Botman 2008, Bowers 2007, Carney 2010 and Steinke 2011) would rather claim that the influence of Western Eurocentric culture on Africans needs to be forcefully arrested by all critically conscious African theological educators in the struggle for the establishment of an African identity in theological education. This will entail countering the colonisation of the African mind by forces emanating from the excessive mono-cultural domination of Western and European forms of knowledge and languages, as well as the asking of critical questions about the knowledge included in theological education and the languages spoken and used as mediums of instruction.

Such a critical questioning about knowledge included in theological education will be evidenced in, what I call, transformative education discourses. Such discourses examine the sources of the knowledge that is imposed on or prescribed for Africa, as well as how theological education in Africa is implicated in the universalisation of Western and

European experiences. These discourses will also ask which ways of knowing theological education in Africa it validates and promotes, and which ones it ignores, invalidates, and why. By this means, transformative education discourses in theological education will help to decolonise theological education and will also seek to integrate indigenous African epistemologies with the content and practices of theological education in Africa. Theological education will thus provide for the construction of an empowering knowledge that will enable communities in Africa to establish their own African identity within theological education.

Theological education and the problem of an African identity

The issue of an African identity in theological education requires that attention be directed towards the questions:

- Who is an African, and what does the term 'African' denote?
- In what way does African philosophy provide African identity with distinctive content?

The responses to these questions will suggest what needs to be focused on in attempting to decolonise theological education by divesting it of any undue influences emanating from the colonial past. The appropriation of an African identity in theological education is given voice by a number of scholars (see, for example, Maluleke 2006). However, the question of what an African is and what it means to be one, is not unproblematic. In the light of Africa's colonial past, African philosophy is confronted with the problem of establishing its own unique African order of knowledge. Or as Nabudere (2005:12) states, "The struggle for African authentic development is about an epistemological revolution and struggle for knowledge production that satisfies the demands for cultural identity."

What it means to be African

The question of cultural identity in an African context directs attention at what meaning we attach to the adjective 'African', and is a crucial debate in attempts at establishing a uniquely African order of knowledge (see Masolo 1995).

LeBeau and Gordon (2002:218) contend that the African Renaissance universalises African identities towards a single African culture. Thabo Mbeki (in Lotter 2007:13) concurs in promoting African pride, but does not call for a multi-cultural South Africa to achieve the goals and objectives of the African Renaissance. Rather, Mbeki contends that to be truly 'African' one must participate in the African Renaissance. In other words, as Boesak (2005:42) states, "… to be a true African is to be a rebel in the cause of the African Renaissance." Nehusi (2004:22) maintains that:

> An Afrikan is a person who shares with others a common geographical origin and ownership of, and spiritual attachment to their ancestral land known as the continent of Afrika. A proper definition of a people must be clear about who they are as well as about whom they are not. Some Afrikans believe that anyone who lives

in the continent of Afrika is an Afrikan. Nothing could be further from the truth. Arabs and Europeans have established themselves in Afrika with much physical and cultural violence. There is a widespread tendency to over emphasise this nationality to the exclusion of identity. The answer to the problem is a redefinition of 'Afrikan' by Afrikans to place more emphasis upon similarities and commonalities of origin, values, history, heritage, and interests.

Nehusi's definition of an 'African' has clear reference to the basis of identity as having to do with skin colour. This raises a serious ontological issue for theological education on the African continent: Do the prospects of the inclusion of indigenous African epistemologies in theological education in Africa include a place for all races and cultural groups? However, Appiah (1994:2) is critical of all assertions of a united, homogeneous African voice, Africa identity and what he calls radical Pan Africanism, declaring that Africa is like "… my father's house in which there are many mansions … meaning that there are, and should be, many and various ways of being African."

Ramose (2003:114-116) argues that the term Africa(n) is contestable on at least two grounds. One is that the name is not conferred by the indigenous people of Africa on themselves. The other is that the name Africa(n) does not by definition refer to the particular histories of the indigenous peoples inhabiting various parts of the continent from time immemorial. In other words, the term is geographically significant although, historically, its meaning is questionable from the point of view of indigenous African peoples. Other African philosophers, for example Houtondji (1996), regard an intellectual product as African simply because it is produced or promoted by Africans. In other words, if an African is a person who shares with others a common geographical origin, ownership of, and spiritual attachment to their ancestral land known as the continent of Africa, then 'African' includes members of all races and cultural groups.

African philosophy and an African identity

The struggle for an authentic African epistemic is taken up in African philosophy. This involves, as Nabudere (2005:12) states, "The … struggle for knowledge production that satisfies the demands for cultural identity." With regard to the term 'philosophy', two conceptions of philosophy have become prominent in debates about an African identity for African philosophy. Firstly, the definition of philosophy as a rational, critical activity. Those who adopt this definition of philosophy, for example Appiah (1989a), Hountondji (1996), Oladipo (1989), and Ramose (2003), frown at the attempt to equate African philosophy with traditional African world epistemologies. In doing so, they make a distinction between philosophy in the popular sense, and philosophy in the academic sense. In the first instance, philosophy is regarded as being concerned with traditional African epistemologies, whereas in an academic sense, philosophy is a theoretical discipline like physics, algebra and linguistics, with its own distinctive problems and methods. Scholars in Africa who view philosophy in this academic sense are referred to as universalist African philosophers since they emphasise reason as a universal human phenomenon. Secondly, there are other African philosophers such as Gyekye (1997), Kaphagawani and Malherbe (1998), and Motshega (1999) who maintain that traditional African epistemologies constitute an authentic African philosophy. They insist on a definition of philosophy that is broad enough to accommodate these epistemologies. Recourse to traditional African epistemologies is taken up in the practice of what is called ethno-philosophy.

These two mentioned conceptions of philosophy that have become prominent in debates about an African identity in African philosophy, are distinguished by:

- those who insist on a strict definition of philosophy on a purity of form – they are out to defend the professional integrity of their discipline against the popularisation by cultural nationalists; and
- those who give a rather broad definition of philosophy and emphasise the specificity of the content of whatever is produced by African philosophers in the practice of ethno-philosophy.

The concern of identity – be it with regard to definitions of 'African' or 'philosophy' – is considered by some, for example Oladipo (1992) and Appiah (1989b), to be misguided and distracting. Oladipo (1992:22) argues that there are no definitions that capture the essence of either the terms 'African' or 'philosophy'. No one definition can be credited with a universal application, because both these terms are linked with a social history that impacts upon their meaning. In responding to the preoccupation with definition, Appiah (1989b:12) points out that:

> There are other issues for philosophers in Africa to explore now, which require not preliminary anxieties as to whether our work fits existing labels, but confident examinations of some of the questions for which our training happens to have equipped us.

In the light of these remarks, it would seem that the problem surrounding African philosophy is not the problem of anything meeting the criteria for being both 'African' and 'philosophical'. It is rather the problem of the extent to which African philosophers have been able to put their intellect in the service of the struggle and destiny of Africans. In other words, the issue is not that of whether a contributor to a debate is African-born or whether the question under consideration is authentically African in the cultural sense. It is not even the issue of whether what they are doing is pure philosophy, applied philosophy, ethno-philosophy, social criticism, etc. In fact, as said in the words of Oladipo (1992:24):

> ... it is the issue of the extent to which African philosophers have been able to use whatever intellectual skills they possess to illuminate the various dimensions of the African predicament.

This sentiment is taken up in part by African scholars, such as Serequeberhan (1994), who adopts a hermeneutical perspective on the term 'African' in African philosophy. Rooting themselves in what is traditional to Africa, such scholars seek to escape an enslavement to the past by using that past to open up the future. They contend that African philosophy properly construed must move beyond a preoccupation with universalist abstractions and ethnological considerations, and call into question the real relations of power in Africa. In this regard, Serequeberhan (1994:43) states that:

> The discourse of African philosophy is indirectly and historically linked to the demise of European hegemony (colonialism and neo-colonialism) and is aimed at fulfilling/completing this demise. It is a reflective and critical effort to rethink the indigenised African situation beyond the confines of Eurocentric concepts and categories.

To appreciate the distinctive features of African philosophy, it is also helpful to compare its method and execution with other systems of philosophy. Appiah (1994:144) elucidates the difference between African and Western philosophy being mindful of the condescending attitude of the West towards Africa. For Appiah (1994:145), the West considers the issue of what philosophy is 'for' – that is, its social meaning and relevance – with intellectual and academic contempt. Undoubtedly, the West does philosophise in a different style and method than Africa. This, however, may be attributed to enormous resources and funding. The West is concerned with perfecting philosophical discourse for its own sake, while Africa wants to use philosophy in a particular sense to address social issues.

Central to the issue of philosophy in Africa, therefore, is the question of relevance and usefulness. Africa, perhaps owing to its level of development at this point, wants philosophy to contribute towards the political, economic, ethical and general upliftment of people. In Africa, philosophy is expected to be pragmatic and to render a 'service'. It must contribute effectively towards the amelioration of the human condition, the lived and existing human condition. Wiredu (as quoted by Anyanwu 1989:127) concludes in saying that "… we will only solve our problems if we see them as human problems arising out of a special situation." Thus, Anyanwu (1989:127) affirms that African philosophy "… invites people to take a stand on the issue of reality as experienced." This experience of an African reality gives rise to a sense of commonality in an enunciation of indigenous African knowledge systems which find expression in certain general themes in African philosophy – one of these being the discourse of community in Africa, also referred to as 'communalism', the other being the African ethic of *ubuntu*.

In the light of this sense of commonality in indigenous African knowledge systems evidenced in communalism and the African ethic of *ubuntu*, what then are the implications for attempts at decolonising theological education in Africa? I turn my attention firstly to the notion of communalism.

Theological education and communalism

Despite the diversity and extraordinary dynamism of the African continent as emphasised by Appiah (1994:47), it is argued by many (see, for example, Gyekye 1997:158) that there are commonalities which unite the African experience. In the words of Diop (1962:7), "… there is a profound cultural unity still alive beneath the deceptive appearance of cultural heterogeneity present in Africa which gives rise to certain commonalities in indigenous African knowledge systems."

One such commonality which is highlighted by Letseka (2000:181-187), is communalism. According to Letseka (2000:181), the importance of communality to traditional African life cannot be overemphasised. This is because community and belonging to a community of people constitute the very fabric of traditional African life. Unlike the Western liberal notion of the individual as some sort of entity that is capable of existing and flourishing on its own, unconnected to any community of other individuals, not bound by any biological relationships or socio-economic, political and cultural relationships, obligations, duties, responsibilities and conventions that frame and define any community of individuals, the communal conception of the individual in most traditional African settings is described by Mbiti (1970:108) in the following way: "Whatever happens to the individual happens to the whole group, and whatever happens to the whole group happens to the individual. The individual can only say, 'I am, because we are; and since we are, therefore I am'."

This, Mbiti (1970:109) claims, is a cardinal point in the understanding of the African view of man. Commenting on traditional life in Kenya, Kenyatta (1965:297) echoes similar views:

> According to Gikuyu's ways of thinking, nobody is an isolated individual, or rather, his uniqueness is a secondary fact about him; first and foremost he is several people's relative and several people's contemporary.

Menkiti (1979:158) concurs when he states:

> A crucial distinction thus exists between the African view of man and the view of man found in Western thought: In the African view it is the community which defines the person as a person, not some isolated static quality of rationality, will or memory.

In traditional African life then, a person depends on others just as much as others depend on him or her. In fact, in terms of an African communitarian view, the individual's life and fulfilment is only to be found in community with others. My concern in noting the discourse of community in Africa has been directed at highlighting the role of community knowledge in theological education in Africa. It is evident from the discourse of community in Africa that:

- Theological education in Africa should be sensitive to the double role of individuals in African societies (see Kaphagawani and Malherbe 1998:214). Elders and other 'epistemic authorities' in communities should not only be perceived as important informants, but also as research colleagues with critical perspectives on theological practices in theological education. Also, in that learning is an individual endeavour, it will be important to open the necessary spaces for individuals in African community-based theological education.

- The communal nature of African societies indicates that community-based education needs to be taken into consideration by theological education if it is to be relevant in an African context.

I would, therefore, argue that the significance of indigenous African knowledge systems for theological education in Africa is centred in the question of communalism. In other words, if we can speak of indigenous African knowledge systems which are characterised by discourses of community, I would argue that theological education, if it is to be relevant in its outreach in Africa, then not only needs to take into account indigenous African knowledge systems, but also needs to direct attention towards the needs of local African communities. The argument here is one of advocating an appropriate and relevant theological education for a given set of circumstances, because the logical implication of the significance of indigenous African knowledge systems for theological education is that theological education should be closely linked to communal values. This means that theological education should take cognisance of the values which strengthen communal behaviours, and regard these values as fundamental to its outreach to African communities. In other words, African community-based theological education should take cognisance of indigenous African knowledge systems and values present in the community for purposes of fostering the communal discourses of that community. In doing so, African community-based theological education becomes a kind of theological education that is conducted by, with, and for the community. Such an African community-based theological education is evidenced, for example, in the work of the Ujamaa Centre at the University of KwaZulu-Natal. The centre has worked extensively throughout South Africa and across the African continent, and has an international reputation for its community-based work and research. The core characteristic of African community-based theological education is, what I call, a participatory involvement – that is, a form of involvement that seeks to enhance the capacity of the community members to participate in the process that shapes theological education and intervention strategies. The active co-operation and participation of members within the community are the essential components of African community-based theological education. This allows for the community to become an active agenda setter for theological education rather than just be a passive recipient of such an education. In this sense, theological education is applied democratically to respond to the needs of the community. African community-based theological education will, therefore, give theological education in Africa a communal basis by linking theological education with community needs and experiences. Indeed, I would argue that African community-based theological education can play a significant role in theological education in an African context, since it forces the inclusion of grassroots perspectives on theological education, and contributes to a desalination of theological education as being solely Western and Eurocentric.

However, also to be noted in African community-based theological education is what I refer to as its trans-traditional vantage. This means that it is important for African community-based theological education to acknowledge the validity of other non-African knowledge systems in theological education, and, at the same time, integrate indigenous African knowledge systems with these (see also Hoppers 2002). If this is not done, attempts at the indigenisation of theological education in Africa will itself become hegemonic and be guilty of a universalistic intent. However, in considering the decolonisation of theological education in Africa, cognisance also needs to be taken of the other commonality revealed in African indigenous knowledge systems, namely the African ethic of *ubuntu*.

Theological education and *ubuntu*

There is an extensive literature on the African ethic of *ubuntu* – see, for example, Appiah (1998), Gyekye (2004), Louw (2010), Higgs and Smith (2010a, 2010b), Letseka (2000), Metz (2010), and Waghid (2007). Letseka (2000:182-184) observes that traditional African morality is known for its concern with human welfare and that this finds expression in the African ethic of *ubuntu*, which means 'humanness'. *Ubuntu*, therefore, has to do with the essential humanness of the individual where "… the inner being is understood to be the centre of human personalities, feelings, thought and will" (Mafunisa, in Nicholson 2008:116). Gyekye (1997:158) argues that:

> … if one were to look for a pervasive and fundamental concept in African socio-ethical thought generally – a concept that animates other intellectual activities and forms of behaviour, including religious behaviour, and provides continuity, resilience, nourishment, and meaning to life – that concept would most probably be humanism as given expression in the *ubuntu*. Humanism is used here to refer to a philosophy that sees human needs, interests and dignity as of fundamental importance and concern.

Letseka (2000:184) points out that the expression *umuntu ngumuntu ngabantu* (I am a person through other persons) captures the underlying principles of interdependence and humanism in African life. It illuminates the communal embeddedness and connectedness of a person to other persons, and highlights the importance attached to people and to human relationships. As Sindane (1994:8-9) suggests, "*Ubuntu* inspires us to expose ourselves to others, to encounter the difference of their humanness so as to inform and enrich our own."

In other words, to be human is to affirm one's humanity by recognising the humanity of others. Teffo (2000:45) argues that *ubuntu*, as one of the commonalities identified in African experience, indicates that there is a way of thinking, of knowing and of acting that is peculiar to the African. For Africans, what they know is inseparable from how they know it in the lived experience of their African culture. This sense of African-ness is, in other words, born out of a deep socio-ethical sense of cultural unity that provides African identity with its distinctiveness. In the light of such a striving for an African identity, what then are the implications for theological education when it comes to a consideration of the African ethic of *ubuntu*? Briefly, it means that theological education in post-colonial Africa needs to:

- ensure that the values and principles enshrined in the African ethic of *ubuntu* which concern a person's integrity and dignity, are acknowledged and respected;
- embed its content and activities in the values of *ubuntu*; values such as compassion, kindness, benevolence, helpfulness, forgiveness, understanding, caring, sharing, wisdom, humility and godliness (Ng'weshemi 2002:23);
- recognise that the core value of *ubuntu* in African ethics is the community; and
- fundamentally concern itself with *ubuntu* in the service of the community and personal well-being.

In this sense, theological education in an African context will be characterised not only by its concern with the person, but also by its interweaving of social, economic, political, cultural, and educational threads into a common tapestry. As a result it will be distinguished by the importance attached to its collective nature, as well as its intimate tie with communal life. Theological education, in an African setting, cannot, and indeed should not, be separated from life itself if it is to be inspired by a spirit of *ubuntu* in the service of the community.

Communalism and the African spirit of *ubuntu* represent the resources for the decolonisation of theological education in Africa in the search for a theological education that will speak to the continent's local communities. However, these resources, as Maluleke (2000:24) reminds us, should "adopt a critical gaze which takes seriously the ambiguities of intercultural discourses and the elusive character of meaning."

Conclusion

The need to construct an African hermeneutic for theological education has been acknowledged by a number of theologians, both in South Africa and abroad (see, for example, Khumalo 2008, Poling 2004, and West 2012).

In similar vein, this chapter has attempted to explore the need for the reconstruction of theological education in an African context in the light of Africa's colonial past, as well as the call for an African Renaissance on the African continent. Such a re-imagining of theological education in Africa is necessary since theological curricula across the continent have followed Western and European models – a situation still persisting well into the 21st century.

Indigenous African epistemologies, I have argued, provide a framework that can contribute to the decolonisation of theological education in Africa – primarily because these epistemologies respect diversity, acknowledge lived experience, and challenge the hegemony of Western Eurocentric forms of universal knowledge. Furthermore, such community sensitive frameworks, as articulated in indigenous African epistemologies, can also contribute to the construction of empowering knowledge that will enable communities in Africa to participate in their own theological education development. In turn, such a liberating context will lead to the rediscovery of what Maluleke (2000:36) refers to as the "agency of Africans" in theological education in Africa.

Bibliography

Anyanwu, K.C., 1989. The problem of method in African Philosophy. In C.S. Momoh (ed.). *The substance of African Philosophy*. Washington DC: Brooking Institute. 125-132.

Appiah, K.A., 1989a. *Necessary questions: An introduction to philosophy*. New Jersey: Prentice-Hall.

Appiah, K.A., 1989b. Thought in a time of famine. *Times Literary Supplement*. 29 July 29-4 August. 17-18.

Appiah, K.A., 1994. *In my father's house: Africa in the philosophy of culture*. New York: Oxford University Press.

Appiah, K.A., 1998. African ethical systems. In E. Craig (ed.). *Routledge encyclopaedia of philosophy*. London: Routledge. 15-28.

Boesak, A., 2005. *The tenderness of conscience: African Renaissance and the spirituality of politics*. Glasgow: Wild Goose Publications.

Boesak, A., 2006. African Renaissance and spirituality. *International Journal of Renaissance Studies*. 1(1). 175-183.

Botman, H.R., 2008. *Good governance – the role of the churches: A South African perspective*. [Online] Available from: http://www.3.gkke.org/fileadmin/files/publikationer/2008/spierworkshop-beitrag.pdf [Accessed: 6 July 2012].

Bowers, P., 2007. Theological education in Africa? Why does it matter? AIM-SIM Theological Education Consultation, 19-23 March 2007. Honeydew, South Africa.

Carney, J.J., 2010. Roads to reconciliation: An emerging paradigm of African Theology. *Modern Theology*. 26(4). 550-569.

Diop, C.M., 1962. *The cultural unity of Negro Africa*. Paris: Presence Africaine.

Gigaba, M., 2011. Statement by Mr Malusi Gigaba, Minister of Public Enterprises, addressing the African Renaissance Conference on 'The Role of state-owned enterprises in African infrastructure development in Durban'. [Online] Available from: http://www.info.gov.za/speech/DynamicAction%3Fpageid%3D461%26sid%D20540%26tid%3D38875 [Accessed: 4 August 2011].

Gyekye, K., 1997. Person and community in African thought. In P.H. Coetzee and A.P.J. Roux (eds.). *Philosophy from Africa*. Cape Town: Oxford University Press. 154-160.

Gyekye, K., 2004. *Beyond cultures: Perceiving a common humanity*. Washington D.C.: The Council for Research in Values and Philosophy, 2004.

Higgs, P. and Smith, J., 2010a. *Rethinking our world*. Cape Town: Juta.

Higgs, P. and Smith, J., 2010b. *Rethinking truth*. Cape Town: Juta.

Higgs, P., 2012. African philosophy and the decolonisation of education in Africa: Some critical reflections. *Education Philosophy and Theory*. 44(2). 22-34.

Hoppers, C.A., 2001. Poverty, power and partnerships in educational development: A post-victimology perspective. *Compare*. 31(1). 21-38.

Hoppers, C.A., 2002. *Indigenous knowledge and integration of knowledge systems: Towards a philosophy of articulation.* Braamfontein: New Africa Books.

Hountondji, P.J., 1996. *African philosophy: Myth and reality.* Bloomington: Indiana University Press.

Kaphagawani, N.D.N. and Malherbe, J., 1998. African epistemology. In P.H. Coetzee and A.P.J. Roux (eds.). *Philosophy from Africa.* Johannesburg: Oxford University Press. 212-220.

Kenyatta, J., 1965. *Facing Mount Kenya: The tribal life of the Gikuyu.* Gikuyu: Vintage Books.

Khumalo, R., 2008. Teaching community with others: A transformation centred approach to Christian Education. *Journal of Constructive Theology.* 15(1). 24-32.

LeBeau, D. and Gordon, R., 2002. Challenges for anthropology in the African Renaissance: A Southern African contribution. *African Studies Review.* 47(1). 218-220. [Online] Available from: http://www.jstor.org/stable/1514803 [Accessed: 14 April 2014].

Letseka, M., 2000. African philosophy and educational discourse. In P. Higgs, N.C.G. Vakalisa, T.V. Mda and N.T. Assie-Lumumba (eds.). *African Voices in Education.* Cape Town: Juta. 181-187.

Lotter, K., 2007. *African Renaissance: The renewal and rebirth of a continent.* [Online] Available from: http://africanaffairs.suite101.com/article.cfm/African_renaissance [Accessed: 8 April 2014].

Louw, D.J., 2010. *Ubuntu and the challenges of multi-culturalism in post-apartheid South Africa.* [Online] Available from: http://www.phys.uu.nl/_unitwin./ubuntu.doc [Accessed: 8 April 2014].

Luckett, K., 2010. Knowledge claims and codes of legitimation: Implications for curriculum recontexualisation in South African higher education. *Africanus.* 40(1). 4-18.

Mafunisa, J.M., 2008. Ethics, African societal values and the workplace. In R. Nicholson (ed.). *Persons in Community.* Pietermaritzburg: University of KZN Press. 110-118.

Maluleke, T.S., 2000. The rediscovery of the agency of Africans. *Journal of Theology for Southern Africa.* 19-38.

Maluleke, T.S., 2006. The Africanisation of theological education: Does theological education equip you to help your sister? In E.P. Antonio (ed.). *Inculturation and postcolonial discourse in African Theology.* New York: Peter Laing Publishing. 46-55.

Masolo, D.A., 1995. *African philosophy in search of identity.* Nairobi: East African Educational Publishers.

Maweu, J.W., 2011. Indigenous ecological knowledge and modern Western ecological knowledge: Complimentary, not contradictory. *Thought and Practice: A Journal of the Philosophical Association of Kenya.* 3(2). 35-47.

Mbiti, J.S., 1970. *African Religions and Philosophy.* London: Heinemann.

Menkiti, I.A., 1979. Person and community in African traditional thought. In R.A. Wright (ed.). *African philosophy: An introduction.* Washington: University Press of America.

Metz, T., 2010. The African ethic of *Ubuntu/Botho*: Implications for research on morality. *Journal of Moral Education.* 39(3). 273-290.

Motshega, N., 1999. *The dawn of the African century: The African origin of philosophy and science.* Halfway House: Kara Publishers.

Nabudere, D.W., 2005. Imperialism, knowledge production and its use in Africa. *Global security and Cooperation Quarterly.* 14. 21-30.

Nehusi, K.S.K., 2004. *Who is an African?* [Online] Available from: http://www.hollerafrica.com/pdf/vol1AfricanRenSep_Oct_2004.p df#page=18 [Accessed: 8 April 2014].

Ng'weshemi, A.M., 2002. *Rediscovering the human: The quest for a Christ-Theological anthropology in Africa.* New York: Peter Laing.

Nkomo, M., 2000. Educational research in the African development context. In P. Higgs, N.C.G. Vakalisa, T.V. Mda, and N.T. Assie-Lumumba (eds.). *African Voices in Education.* Cape Town: Juta. 46-54.

Oladipo, O., 1989. Towards a philosophical study of African culture: A critique of traditionalism. *Quest: Philosophical Discussions.* 3(2). 24-35.

Oladipo, O., 1992. *The idea of African philosophy: A critical study of the major orientations in contemporary African philosophy.* Ibadan: Molecular Publishers.

Poling, J., 2004. Understanding cultural differences in spirituality and culture. In J.F. Foskett and E. Lartey (eds.). *Pastoral Care and Counselling: Voices from Different Contexts.* 3-13.

Ramose, M.B., 2003. I doubt, therefore African philosophy exists. *South African Journal of Philosophy.* 22(2). 110-121.

Sefa Dei, G.J., 2013. Learning culture, spirituality and local knowledge: Implications for African schooling. *International Review of Education.* 48(5). 335-360.

Serequeberhan, T., 1994. *The hermeneutics of African philosophy: Horizon and discourse.* New York: Routledge.

Shizha, E., 2011. Reclaiming our indigenous voices: The problem with the postcolonial sub-Saharan African school curriculum. *Journal of Indigenous Social Development.* 2(1). 1-9.

Sindane, J., 1994. *Ubuntu* and nation building. Pretoria: *Ubuntu* School of Philosophy.

Steinke, P., 2011. Theological education: A theological framework for renewed mission and models. *Dialog: A Journal of Theology.* 50(4). 363-367.

Teffo, L.J., 2000. Africanist thinking: An invitation to authenticity. In P. Higgs, N.C.G. Vakalisa, T.V. Mda and N.T. Assie-Lumumba (eds.). *African Voices in Education.* Cape Town: Juta. 40-48.

Waghid, Y., 2007. Education, responsibility and democratic justice: Cultivating friendship to alleviate some of the injustices on the African continent. *Educational Philosophy and Theory.* 39(2). 182-196.

Wa Thiong'o, N., 2009. *Something torn and new: An African Renaissance.* Philadelphia: Basic Civitas Books.

West, G., 2012. After the missionaries: Historical and hermeneutical dimensions of African appropriations of the Bible in sub-Saharan Africa. *Studies Historiae Ecclestiasticae,* XXXVIII. 1. 111-130.

Zenawi, M., 2012. *Africa: The African Renaissance is beginning.* [Online] Available from: http://www.poptel.org.uk/mozambique-news/ [Accessed: 8 April 2014].

Choosing the better part: Engendering theological education

JANET TRISK

Introduction

In Luke 10:42 we read how Mary of Bethany placed herself as a student at Jesus' feet, challenging the exclusively male rabbinical circles of her time. Jesus commends her for 'choosing the better part'. Two thousand years later, many women still struggle to break into that circle – whether as students or teachers of theology. This chapter explores the contested nature of training female ministers, those issues that weigh against women trying to choose this better part, as well as how practices of theological education might be altered to draw women into the circle as students and teachers of theology.

About 25 years ago, when I commenced my formal theological education at what was then St Paul's College in Grahamstown, I recall one of the male students praying in chapel that the Anglican Church of Southern Africa (then the Church of the Province of Southern Africa) would not change its stance and introduce the ordination of women to the priesthood. Open hostility to the ordination of women was not uncommon. Other students and teaching staff members were not so much hostile as uninformed. It was assumed, for example, that women students were just a female version of the male students; that we had no different interests, concerns or aspirations from the men. At that time, too, we had no female teachers or role models. None of us had seen a woman preside at the Eucharist – the principal service in Anglican liturgy. The only hint we had of feminist insights into our studies was a short introduction to feminist theology as one of a range of theologies of liberation. Women barely appeared on the pages of our history books, except as wives and mothers. Feminist liturgies, including those ritualising women's experiences of childbirth, miscarriage or menopause, were never considered. We had no introduction to feminist hermeneutics. Gender-based violence, one of the most pressing social issues, was never mentioned.

Several years later, I came back to teach at The College of the Transfiguration (formerly St Paul's College, hereafter referred to as 'CoTT'). By then I had been ordained. In the twelve years I served on the teaching staff at CoTT, I had a number of women colleagues – both lay and ordained. I taught courses in feminist or women's theologies during those twelve years. I fondly hoped that the presence of women on the teaching staff, leading services in the chapel and the introduction of courses which examined gender issues, feminist theologies and feminist hermeneutics, might make a difference to the Church and, especially, to the lives of women in the Church. The Anglican Church of Southern Africa, the denomination of which I am a part, now has two women bishops. However, the diocese in which I served, although being one of the first dioceses to ordain women, has less than 20 full-time paid female clergy out of a total of just over 100 stipendiary clergy. Other denominations which ordain women, such as the Methodist, Presbyterian and Lutheran churches, appear to have similar statistics. The Roman Catholic, Orthodox and some Pentecostal churches still do not ordain women at all.

Sunday by Sunday the experiences of women – and even their existence – is frequently denied. For example, although some worship leaders attempt to use more inclusive language when referring to humanity (and God), there has been no attempt to revise the language of the Anglican Prayer book, which refers to God only in male metaphors. Clergy men continue to be addressed as 'father' as if little difference has been made in the Church. Although we have female leaders in the political arena and, to some lesser degree in the business world, South Africa, shamefully, has one of the highest incidences of gender-based violence in the world. This is all the more astonishing given the fact that just short of 80% of the population self-identifies as being Christian.[6] We still seem not to draw connections between what Van Klinken (2010:5) terms the "dangerous and deadly" constructions of patriarchy, and the violence directed at women and girl children. In the light of the extraordinary levels of gender-based violence, any statistics regarding the number of women ordained, in training or holding academic positions is rendered almost meaningless. If the purpose of theological education is to develop the whole person and produce transformational leaders (Naidoo 2012), then certainly, insofar as gender issues are concerned, we, the churches and theological educators, appear to have a long way to go.

This chapter will focus on theological education in the formal institutions of learning – universities, colleges and seminaries. However, it is important to note that by far the vast majority of theological education takes place in churches (and perhaps in the home). The first site of engendering theological education, therefore, needs to be the Church. Sadly, that is precisely the place where most women, and some men, experience the greatest imbalances of power and the abuse of patriarchal privilege. As Ryan and Shefer point out, in church women are frequently excluded from leadership, most liturgy and church pronouncements are couched in sexist language, God is almost exclusively imaged in male metaphors, and scripture is interpreted uncritically and androcentrically (2007:85-86). I shall return to these concerns below.

Even where women hold positions of responsibility or leadership, too often the model of leadership exercised is patterned on patriarchy. For example, in the Anglican Church, the Mothers' Union is often led by the wife of the priest or bishop. Not only do women's organisations model themselves on patriarchal power and privilege, some even go so far as to conceal marital rape or family violence. Mombo (1998:221) suggests that the Mothers' Union's strong emphasis on traditional family values underlies this practice. The intersecting of patriarchal cultures in (South) Africa and the practices of the Church, serve to reinforce one another in the denial of the full dignity and worth of women

---

[6] http://www.indexmundi.com/south_africa/demographics_profile.html

(Oduyoye 1995, Rakoczy 2004). Kanyoro (2001:36) notes: "The status of women within their church is a microcosm of their status within the society of which the church is a part." These sexist and patriarchal cultural and ecclesial attitudes and practices militate against the theological education of women, their participation as teachers of theology, and against gender justice more broadly, as we shall explore below.

There are, however, glimmers of light – examples of how one might engender theological education at the 'grassroots' level. One such example is the Umtata Women's Theology Group described by Isaac, Kretzschmar, Pigott and Thelin (1991). Initially, this study group was formed and material prepared so that a group of women might educate themselves about liberating possibilities in reading the Bible. Emerging out of their study together, other transformational activities developed, such as the assistance given to children fleeing from violence. As liberating and exciting as this fundamental theological education may be, this chapter will, however, pay attention to theological education in universities, seminaries and colleges.

My own practical experience of formal theological education has been as a student and teacher at CoTT, as a part-time lecturer at Rhodes University, before it closed its Theology department, and also at the University of KwaZulu-Natal. While not using these experiences as case studies, I shall refer to them for their illustrative value.

Women in theological education

Mercy Amba Oduyoye suggests that, "In Africa, the very idea of a 'free woman' conjures up negative images" (1995:4), whilst, at the same time, male propaganda asserts that "our women are not oppressed" (1995:13) and "feminism is a non-issue" (1995:13). Not content to rest with this injustice, Oduyoye and others established the Circle of Concerned African Women Theologians (hereafter referred to as 'the Circle') to "call the church to account" (Oduyoye 1995:172) and to develop and promote the voices of African women theologians. Isabel Phiri, in a paper reflecting on ten years of the work of the Circle, identifies the challenges facing African women who wish to enrol for theological education (2009:126). These include the relatively poor education for women at secondary school level (thus rendering them ineligible for entry to university), the lack of scholarships available to women, and the fact that most theological education is geared towards ordination, while many churches do not ordain women or prefer not to do so.

Phiri notes, in the same article, the problems in getting women appointed to the permanent teaching staff of universities in religious studies and theology departments (2009:127). She observes that on the African continent, more than half of the universities do not have women on their theological teaching staff – even in those universities where women are recruited, they are often teaching non-theological subjects. Of the women who are employed to teach theological subjects, the majority are employed part-time, leading, amongst other things, to the difficulty of finding time to research and publish, thus further marginalising them in the 'publish or perish' milieu.

Rebecca Chopp (1996) theorises about this separation of women from the formal teaching and learning of theology. In modernity, knowledge in the public sphere is generated through science and the intellect, whilst in the private sphere – where religious experience is located – such religious experience is pre-rational, even pre-linguistic, confined to the experiential. This separation is gendered, with men inhabiting the public, intellectual sphere, and women the domestic, non-rational sphere. "… in public the citizen of modernity is the labourer, the master of history, while in private, the individual is the consumer of cultural values such as art, religion, tradition and family." (Chopp 1996:361) This "patriarchal codification of knowledge" (1996:362) precludes women from being teachers or students of theology, though they may be 'religious'. Although this is an interpretation of theological education in the West, the western approach to religious education is the model which has been adopted in Africa.

The Circle seeks to address the separation of women from the formal, public sphere, and the challenges faced by potential female students and teachers of theology by building capacity and promoting the teaching of gender issues in theology (Phiri 2009). Several books and collections of essays have emanated from the Circle.[7] However, there is only one accredited journal dealing with theology and gender in South Africa.[8] How might we address this situation? We now turn towards considering the engendering of theological education.

Engendering theological education in context

It should be made clear that 'engendering theological education' does not equate to feminist, womanist, mujerista or any other women's theologies of liberation. Nor is the idea of engendering theological education the same as gender studies; although, as Gross (2004:24) suggests, very often the "whole field of women and religion has been identified with and collapsed into Christian feminist theology." In the context of engendering theological education, Priscilla Singh (2001:25) describes gender as:

> … an analytical tool to help women as well as men to understand the local contexts, structures and systems in the world through which classism, racism and sexism entrenches and operates. These result in imbalance in and control over resources …

Engendering theological education flows from a recognition of these imbalances and seek ways to transform them in the process of theological education. What is implied in the 'engendering' of theological education is, unsurprisingly, contextually driven. For example, in Kenya, where women's ordination is not often recognised, and even when it is, "female candidates often face tougher interviews as their call to ministry is often tied with other

---

[7] See, for example, N.J. Njoroge and M. Dube (eds.), 2001. *Talita cum!: Theologies of African women*. Pietermaritzburg: Cluster Publications; I.A. Phiri, D.B. Govinden and S. Nadar (eds.), 2002. *Her-stories: Hidden histories of women of faith in Africa*. Pietermaritzburg: Cluster Publications; I.A. Phiri and S. Nadar (eds.), 2003. *African women, religion and health: Essays in honour of Mercy Amba Ewudziwa Oduyoye*. Pietermaritzburg: Cluster Publications.

[8] *Journal of constructive theology: Gender, religion and theology in Africa*.

notions such as their age, marital status and cultural demands and expectations" (Galgalo and Mombo 2008:39), engendering theological education firstly means simply extending education to both women and men, lay and ordained people (Galgalo and Mombo 2008:38). Only then does engendering theological education imply a re-formulation of the curriculum to make theology relevant to women and men (Galgalo and Mombo 2008:40). Even in places such as South Africa, where many churches accept the ordination of women ministers, there is still an expectation that women should marry, bear children and be homemakers. (See, for example, Jacobsen 1991:242.)

In other contexts, where women's ordination is not challenged (at least *de jure*), the engendering of theological education includes, as Ellen Blue describes, entirely separate classes to specifically address women's issues. In her article 'Should theological education be different for clergy women?'(2008), she describes a course which she set up specifically for clergy women in training. Men were not excluded from taking the class, but its specific focus was on the issues faced and concerns of women in training. Blue (2008:65) states the goal of the course as a way to "help women form their identity as women ministers." She describes how she invited a range of women ministers to address the class through the course of the semester. The class members were free to structure their questions and discussions with each guest speaker. Thus there was no pre-ordained decision about the content of the course, although the guests were invited according to their areas of expertise. Texts written by women were used. In this engendering of theological education, not only the content of the course but also the pedagogical methods reflect a commitment to changing patriarchal, androcentric and hierarchical ways of teaching and learning.

There is another aspect relating to the context of theological education to consider. As David Bosch (1991) describes, there are significant differences between theological education in the university, on the one hand, and in seminaries and theological colleges, on the other. Theology in the university tends towards the analytical, rational study of religions or theology, with little attention paid to spirituality and practice. "Generally, university theology is done outside the control of the Church" (Bosch 1991:4). Seminaries and theological colleges, on the other hand, are usually geared towards training ministers, are often denominationally organised, and have as one of their goals the formation of the potential minister for service in the particular denomination (Bosch 1991:8). Engendering theological education in these two different institutions may very well take rather different shapes. For example, the seminary- or college-trained student may be assisted in the process of gender awareness and even transformative practice, if the *habitus* of the institution is one of equal participation of women and men and the fostering of gender justice. However, if the *habitus* is one of patriarchal leadership and androcentric practice, this will work against the attempts to engender the curriculum. The university, on the other hand, with its focus on the transmission and generation of knowledge (Bosch 1991:6) but with no commitment to maintaining the status quo of a denomination, might be able to better conscientise students about gender issues, but have less opportunity to form its students in the practices of gender justice. In the late 1990s, I taught a course in feminist theology at

Rhodes University. Although we could explore the writings of feminist theologians and discuss the implications for our own praxis, this was just one course amongst many taken by the students. A similar course offered at CoTT – where students and staff not only shared a classroom but also daily chapel services, meals and community life – enabled us to deepen the lessons of the classroom in a broader context, for example by exploring the use of non-male terms for God in prayers.

Mainstreaming gender studies

There are three aspects to the mainstreaming of the issue of gender in theological education, namely (a) the inclusion of gender issues in all courses, such as Biblical hermeneutics, theology, pastoral theology, church history, etc.; (b) the introduction of specific courses dealing with gender issues, for example a course in womanist theologies; and (c) the introduction of an entire programme of undergraduate and post-graduate studies in gender and religion (Phiri 2009).

In the first years that CoTT actively pursued a practice of engendering its theological education, it decided to follow option (b) – the introduction of a course in feminist theology. When I was offered an opportunity to return to CoTT to teach this new course, I leaped at the chance. After several years of offering the course, I was somewhat discouraged by the fact that very low numbers of students took this elective. This was not simply due to the fact that not many students enrolled for the course, but also that those who did enrol (especially male students) were teased by their colleagues. Similarly, Phiri notes that at the University of KwaZulu-Natal, where a complete programme in gender and religion is offered, some students fear having their degree certificates endorsed with the words 'gender and religion' (Phiri 2009:129). These two illustrations demonstrate the difficulties of even attempting to introduce mainstreaming of gender into theological education. As Kaunda (2012: 141) observes, gender mainstreaming is

> not the mere addition of a few new courses dealing with gender issues within an existing theological programme, but reformulating a gendered core curriculum, theological ethos and structures for gender justice.

If a course dealing with women's theologies is offered without changes being made to the rest of the curriculum – and, in fact, to the entire ethos of the academic institution – the course itself will probably have little impact.

A comparison of the way in which CoTT was dealing with the crisis presented by the HIV/AIDS pandemic, is instructive. In addition to introducing a specific course on theological, Biblical and pastoral responses to HIV/AIDS, issues of HIV and AIDS were included in other courses such as Biblical Studies, Pastoral Theology and Systematic Theology. Furthermore, the College also developed policies regarding stigmatisation and the position of students and staff who live with the virus. When it came to gender issues, although there were bursaries identified to support women students, there was no policy regarding the appointment of women on the teaching staff, nor a quota system stipulating the minimum number of female students in each year's intake. There was no provision made for the specific needs of women. For example, there was no provision of a crèche for the young children of students and staff. Although HIV and AIDS began to be seen as everyone's issue – not just the issue of people living with the virus – gender issues, even if recognised, were seen as a women's issue to be addressed by women and not a matter for the entire College.

However, a different perspective is offered by Mary Ryan and Tamara Shefer (2007) on using just one gender course in training. Their research explored the impact of a single course in assisting women develop a gendered consciousness in regard to religion and spirituality. They offered a module in feminist theology for post-graduate women at the University of the Western Cape. Working at both the theoretical and the experiential levels, the course involved critical readings, seminar discussions, practical as well as written assignments, and also a weekend retreat (Ryan and Shefer 2007:84). The researchers note that all the women who took the course expressed that "some measure of healing or integration in themselves had occurred" (Ryan and Shefer 2007:93). They conclude that "an exposure to feminist spirituality through a critical feminist pedagogy ... has made a difference to the development of the religious discourse of the participants ..." (Ryan and Shefer 2007:98).

It should, of course, be noted that the women who participated in this research were post-graduate students who were already aware, at an academic level, of gender issues. At an undergraduate level and working with men and women who may not be aware, theoretically, of the issues of gender discrimination, a single course in isolation from the other changes – identified as necessary by Kaunda above – would perhaps not have the same impact. Ryan and Shefer (2007:98) do indeed identify the need for a "community of practice which can help women sustain those shifts in consciousness..."

It is also important to note that the course was taken at a university and not a seminary or theological college, by people from a range of different church denominations. As noted above, theological study in a university is, in some respects, freer to explore change since there is not the weight of denominational tradition to be faced.

Whether one is constructing a single course or an entire programme to deal with theology and gender, the three-step process suggested by Longkumer (2006) is appropriate. She firstly describes a "critical deconstruction of texts, translations, personalities, discourses, perspectives, practices and socio-historical conditions," a liberating reconstruction of these texts, and highlights the need to make women's voices and faces visible in church and society.[9]

---

[9] http://cca.org.hk/home/ctc/ctc06-01/ctc06-01g.htm

It should, furthermore, be noted that not all those working for gender justice support mainstreaming of gender issues in theological education. As Haddad (2001:70) points out, some women fear that gender mainstreaming will simply lead to the bureaucratisation of women's issues, leading to further invisibility of women rather than foregrounding gender justice. However, she observes that this danger is alleviated when, instead of simply changing the content of programmes, there is also an active attempt to reorganise the institutional practices. I shall refer to some examples of this in considering pedagogical practices below. Before doing so, however, it is important to note the relatively new and complementary discipline of masculinities studies, which we now consider.

Men and masculinities studies

An interesting development in recent years has been the inclusion of masculinities studies in academic courses and programmes. Recognising that gender is a social construct, and drawing deeply on feminist theology, the newer discipline of men and masculinities explores redemptive or reconstructed notions of maleness.[10] Chitando and Chirongoma, the editors of *Redemptive Masculinities*, recognise the potential problems in even naming their topic. 'Redemptive masculinity' can conjure up the idea (again) of a male saviour of women (Chitando and Chirongoma 2010:1). However, for various reasons they dismiss other possibilities such as 'liberating' masculinities, 'progressive' masculinities, 'troubling' masculinities and 'transformative' masculinities (Chitando and Chirongoma 2010:1-2). Whatever the nomenclature, the focus on the role of men and male gender constructions has become vital, particularly in the light of the HIV/AIDS pandemic and the pandemic of gender-based violence, both of which obviously have deep connections with gender and theological studies.

Exactly how constructions of masculinity need to be transformed is neither obvious, nor agreed upon. Van Klinken (2010), in an instructive article, contrasts the transformation of masculinities in academic theological circles and in a local Pentecostal church. Theologians, he suggests, seek to deconstruct cultural masculinities so as to bring about gender justice. The churches, on the other hand, seek to reform masculinities within the patriarchal framework – for example, by promoting responsible leadership/headship. The male is still the leader or head. It is just that he should not abuse his position. This reformed masculinity "reminds men of their 'God-given' responsibility towards themselves, women, their families and the community" (Van Klinken 2010:15).

Chitando and Chirongoma pertinently ask: "Is this not patriarchy reinventing itself in order to survive?" (2010:25). However, they contend that the need for healthy and transformative constructions of masculinity outweigh the problems. They suggest that in both policies and programmes there is a need for men who do not condone sexual violence or male privilege and who challenge those men who do so (2010:4). I shall explore this a little

---

[10] See, for example, *The Masculinity Studies Reader* (2002), the *Journal of Men's Studies*, and especially the important work of Chitando and Chirongoma, *Redemptive Masculinities* (2014).

further in the section which follows on role models. The authors note the limited dialogue between theorists of masculinities and feminist/womanist theorists (2010:13). Perhaps there is a particular space for the contribution of theological educators who can bring these two partners into conversation around, for example, Biblical hermeneutics – as Gerald West (2012) demonstrates in his article examining a masculine reading of the Tamar text – or in constructing a holistic theological anthropology.

Theological education and issues of power: The need for new models and role models

According to Longkumer (2006), "Feminist pedagogy addresses the very methodology we use for transmitting knowledge in our classrooms."[11] Longkumer in her research into feminist theological pedagogy in Asia, suggests that feminist pedagogy has at its heart a concern for gender justice – teachers are 'political agents', she suggests. This vocation is to make the world more just and includes the claiming of five 'powers' – the powers to receive (that is to listen and reflect), the power to rebel against what is unjust, the power to actively resist oppression, the power to reform, and the power to love (Harris 1987:89-94).

The route to this more just world includes a range of teaching and learning practices. Firstly, feminist pedagogy challenges the traditional banking model of education, where students are seen as empty vessels to be filled. This insight (founded in the practices and teaching of Paulo Freire) has been responsible for shifts in pedagogical practice in a number of disciplines. A shift from the 'banking' model of teaching goes hand in hand with engendering theological education. When it is recognised that learners bring life skills, wisdom and knowledge to education, the experience of women can begin to shape the learning experience. According to Jaison (2008: 44), "feminists' praxis-orientated education includes narrativity, human experience, critical thinking, interdisciplinary and non-hierarchical learning." She goes on to reject models of education such as the banking model, the expert/apprentice model (where the teacher is the trainer who moulds the student), and the consumer model (where the student is 'sold' information by the teacher/sales person) (Jaison 2008:44).

Feminist pedagogy also recognises that all members of the teaching/learning community bring experience, wisdom and pertinent questions to the table. Palmer (1998:101) calls this a 'community of truth' – a teaching and learning community where no one person is the expert and others all amateurs. In the community of truth, all are 'knowers' and have different ways of seeing the subject. Through a complex pattern of communicating insights, the truth (which is not static, but a fluid, shifting set of insights) is discerned. Conflict, rather than competition, characterises the learning environment. A community of truth admits diversity, ambiguity, creative conflict, honesty and humility (Palmer 1998:107-108). Such 'communities of truth' admit different voices and perspectives. Those who learn

---

[11] http://cca.org.hk/home/ctc/ctc06-01/ctc06-01g.htm

in such communities have a much better chance of becoming church leaders who are hospitable to diversity and difference, and also more likely to transform present sexist, racist, tribalist practices (Rakoczy 2004:245).

Thirdly, Haddad (2001:72) suggests modelling different ways of teaching such as team teaching. Team teaching suggests collaboration, dialogue between the teachers, and a complementing of one teacher by another – thus undermining the idea that one expert has all the knowledge and skills. Again, this has implications for the 'one-man-band' model of ministry in churches, suggesting instead a "discipleship of equals and ... a community of liberation" (Rakoczy 2004:247).

Leona English (2008:112) notes the innovations to pedagogical practice through those who have paid attention to women's ways of knowing and learning: The creation of safe learning spaces, reflective learning (through the use of journals), the use of small groups, personal sharing, etc. She suggests that these practices are now commonplace , though many in Africa might contest this. However, her concern is to step back and consider whether these innovations are as useful as we might assume them to be. For example, she challenges the 'essentialising' of women students (English 2008:121), leading to the assumption that one model is appropriate for all women. She proposes that we pay attention to the ways in which power manifests and not simply assume that these feminist practices are an answer in themselves. Similarly, we might question the idea of models that work better for women. Is it not the case that different personalities (male and female) respond differently to different styles and models of learning?

As was noted earlier, the simple addition of a few courses on gender issues will not change the attitudes and practices of an institution. So, too, without appropriate role models, restricting gender issues to academic discussions will not make any lasting or significant difference. For example, learning how feminism challenges clericalism and patriarchy will have little significant impact if the male members of a seminary staff insist upon them being, or allow themselves to be, called 'father'. Institutional churches which in law or practice afford power to clergy over laity, bishops over clergy, will perpetuate the side-lining of those considered to be of less worth to the institution. Even the appointment of women to the teaching staff in educational institutions carries its own difficulties. Masimbi Kanyoro (2001:160) suggests that women theological educators face opposition when they suggest an alternative order. Not only do these trained women theologians face hostility from their male colleagues, but they also face suspicion from other women. Thus the temptation is to follow the old patterns – to study, read and write in the expected way. "But for us in Africa, it does not matter how much we write about our theology in books, the big test before us is whether we can bring change into our societies" (Kanyoro 2001:160). There is a double bind here. Women educators who do not work actively for change in the community, fail Kanyoro's test. Those who do participate actively in community transformation will be under pressure to complete the usual academic tasks of research and publishing.

My own experience of getting through almost all of my undergraduate theological training without ever seeing a woman preside at the Eucharist, is perhaps more unusual now in Southern Africa, but it is not unheard of. And for many women in other parts of the continent, where women's ordination is rarer, or for women who do their training by means of distance education, there is every possibility that they will complete their degree without ever seeing a woman preside. It is a small wonder, then, that some women clergy seem only to emulate male models of clericalism.

It seems harsh to place an additional burden on theological educators to be good role models, too. However, the need for mentoring as part of the project of transformation towards gender justice cannot be ignored. This role is one not only for women, but also for men – particularly those men who are able to disrupt the prevailing patriarchal models in education. As Longkumer observes, feminist theological pedagogy is characterised by "cordial relationship" and a "collaborative and mutual learning environment."[12]

Conclusion

Engendering theological education is a multi-faceted enterprise including the content of courses and programmes, the context in which teaching takes place, the way in which teaching and learning occurs (pedagogy), and institutional support for women teachers and learners. As I have tried to demonstrate, it is not simply about adding courses or teaching programmes. It also seeks to incorporate women's experiences in a sexist and patriarchal context. It is also not simply about 'adding women' – whether as students, teachers, or ordained minsters. Its central concern is gender justice, which includes making a place for women inside the circle of teaching and learning, giving them space to choose the better part for which Jesus commended Mary of Bethany.

Bibliography

Blue, E., 2008. Should theological education be different for clergy women? Doing women's work in a mainline Protestant seminary. In: I. Jones, J. Woolan and K. Thorpe (eds.). *Women and Ordination in the Christian Church*. London and New York: T and T Clarke. 64-75.

Bosch, D.J., 1991. The nature of theological education. *Journal of Theology for Southern Africa*. 77. 3-17.

Chitando, E. and Chirongoma, S., 2010. Introduction: On the title. In: E. Chitando and S. Chirongoma (eds.). *Redemptive Masculinities*. Geneva: WCC Publications. 1-38.

Chopp, R., 1996. Emerging issues and theological education. In: J. Astley, L.J. Francis and C. Crowder (eds.). *Theological Perspectives on Christian formation: A Reader on Theology and Christian Education*. Grand Rapids, Michigan: William B. Eerdmans Publishing Company. 359-373.

English, L., 2008. Revisiting voice, subjectivity and circles: Feminist pedagogy in the twenty-first century. *Journal of Adult Theological Education*. 5(2).112-125.

Galgalo, J. and Mombo, E., 2008. Theological education in Africa in the post 1998 Lambeth Conference. *Journal of Anglican Studies*. 6(1). 31-40.

---

[12] http://cca.org.hk/home/ctc/ctc06-01/ctc06-01g.htm

Gross, R., 2004. Where have we been? Where do we need to go? Women's studies and gender in religion and feminist theology. In: U. King and T. Beattie (eds.). *Gender, religion and diversity: Cross cultural perspectives*. New York and London: Continuum. 17-27.

Haddad, B., 2001. Engendering theology. What does it entail? In: *Report of a Consultation at Montreux, Switzerland, 5-8 November 2001*. [Online] Available from: http://193.73.242.125/What_We_Do/DMD/DMD-Documents/DMD-Engendering-Theol_Education.pdf [Accessed: 4 January 2013].

Harris, M., 1987. *Teaching religious imagination: An essay in the theology of teaching*. San Francisco: Harper.

Isaac, J., Kretzschmar, L., Pigott, M., and Thelin, N., 1991. A case study: The Umtata women's theology group. In: D. Ackerman, J. Draper and E. Mashinini (eds.). *Women hold up half the sky: Women and church in Southern Africa*. Pietermaritzburg: Cluster Publications. 64-75.

Jacobsen, W., 1991. Women and vocation: The 'if' question. In: D. Ackerman, J. Draper and E. Mashinini (eds.). *Women hold up half the sky: Women and church in Southern Africa*. Pietermaritzburg: Cluster Publications. 241-253.

Jaison, J., 2008. *Women training in Protestant theological institutions: A critical appraisal of contextual challenges in Kerala, India*. PhD thesis, The Queens University of Belfast. [Online] Available from: http://theologicaleducation.net/articles/view.htm?id=103 [Accessed: 4 January 2014].

Kanyoro, M., 2001. Engendered communal theology: African women's contribution to theology in the twenty-first century. *Feminist theology: The journal of the Britain and Ireland school of feminist theology*. 27. 36-56.

Kaunda, C.J., 2012. Towards an African theological education for gender justice and peace: An African theological reflection on the concept of just-peace. *Journal of gender and religion in Africa*. 18(1). 137-153.

Longkumer, L., 2006. *Feminist theological pedagogy for ministerial formation*. CTC Bulletin. XXII (1) [Online] Available from: http://cca.org.hk/home/ctc/ctc06-01/ctc06-01g.htm [Accessed: 20 August 2013].

Mombo, E., 1998. Resisting *vumilia* theology: The Church and violence against women in Kenya. In: A. Wingate, K. Ward, C. Pemberton and W. Sitshebo (eds.). *Anglicanism: A global communion*. London: Mowbray. 219-224.

Naidoo, M., 2012. Introduction. In M. Naidoo (ed.). *Between the real and the ideal: Ministerial formation in South African Churches*. Pretoria: Unisa Press. 1-14.

Oduyoye, M.A., 1995. *Daughters of Anowa: African women and patriarchy*. New York: Orbis, Maryknoll.

Palmer, P., 1998. *The courage to teach: Exploring the inner landscape of a teacher's life*. San Francisco: Jossey-Bass.

Phiri, I.A., 2009. Major challenges for African women theologians in theological education (1989-2008). *International Review of Mission*. 98(1). 116-134.

Rakoczy, S., 2004. *In her name: Women doing theology*. Pietermaritzburg: Cluster Publications.

Ryan, M. and Shefer, T., 2007. An exploratory study of the impact of a postgraduate module on feminist theology on the consciousness and practice of a group of church-going women. *Journal of theology for Southern Africa*. 129. 82-98.

Singh, P., 2001. Engendering theological education: Some explorations. In: The Lutheran World Federation. *Engendering theological education for transformation: Report of a consultation at Montreux, Switzerland, 5-8 November 2001*. [Online] Available from: http://193.73.242.125/What_We_Do/DMD/DMD-Documents/DMD-Engendering-Theol_Education.pdf [Accessed: 4 January 2013].

Van Klinken, A. S., 2010. Theology, gender, ideology and masculinity politics: A discussion on the transformation of masculinities as envisioned by African theologians and a local Pentecostal church. *Journal of theology for Southern Africa*. 138. 2-18.

West, G., 2012. The contribution of Tamar's story to the construction of alternative African masculinities. In: E. Chitando and S. Chirongoma (eds.). *Redemptive masculinities*. Geneva: WCC Publications. 173-192 [Online] Available from: http://archived.oikoumene.org/fileadmin/files/wcc-main/documents/p4/ehaia/RedemptiveMasculinities.pdf [Accessed: 4 January 2014].

Dealing with the Other: Managing Diversity in Theological Education

Marilyn Naidoo

Introduction

Theological education faces the same challenges with growing diversity as the rest of higher education in South Africa. In our post-apartheid society, church denominations have gone through a process of reformulating their identity and have restructured theological education for all its members, resulting in growing multi-cultural student bodies (Dreyer 2012). These new student constituencies reflect a wide spectrum of cultural backgrounds, personal histories, and theological commitments, and represent diversity in race, ethnicity, culture, class, gender, age and sexual orientation.

Within theological education, this issue of diversity is theologically complicated and contested as it is attached to religious dogma. In dealing with 'otherness', educators cannot agree whether the goal is to 'understand' or to 'convert', or to bring them 'into the fold' or to explore the 'interconnectedness' (Foster 2002:21). For example, one of the most significant changes in theological education has been the increase in women students, resulting in political leverage for feminist theological education that continues to challenge traditional practices in seminaries (Chopp 1995:iv). Diversity exists both as a threat and promise, problem and possibility (Foster 2002:22). The aim of this chapter is to unpack the contested nature of diversity and diversity management in theological education in South Africa in order to show how this impacts on the training and formation of church ministers.

To begin with, diversity is about understanding each other and moving beyond simple tolerance towards embracing and celebrating the rich dimensions of divisions and differences contained within each individual (Foster 2002:5). As such, diversity represents a mix of characteristics that makes a person or group unique, or assigns them an identity. However, it must be emphasised that social markers of difference and privilege are neither innocent nor innate, but rather the result of socially structured boundaries between individuals or social groups (Cross and Naidoo 2012:229). The boundaries between different categories of social groups and knowledge are a function of power relations, as "power relations create boundaries, legitimise boundaries, reproduces boundaries between different categories of groups, gender, class and race" (Bernstein 2000:5). Attitudes towards diversity have shifted, and in South Africa diversity is valued across the political spectrum. It responds to what is perceived as a future trend towards a multi-cultural, multi-ethnic, multi-lingual, multi-gender and multi-sexual order (Rosada 2006). However, given the apartheid legacy, the pursuit of diversity in South Africa is only meaningful within the framework of human rights and social justice (Cross 2004).

Within theological education, reflections about diversity begin with the exploration of theological visions of the theological institution and its education, or more concretely, the responsibility of the college or seminary to the mission of the Church (Speller and Seymour, 2002:2). Meyer (2009:32) identifies four reasons why faith-based higher education institutions must be concerned about diversity. Firstly, Christian colleges and universities must reckon with the history of discrimination against women and racial/ethnic groups and their participation in discriminatory systems. Secondly, is the concern for students to grow through cross-cultural experiences as they prepare to work in an increasingly diverse world. Valuing difference, developing multi-cultural competence, and being globally minded are essential skills in today's workforce. Furthermore, colleges and universities exist to serve the needs of their constituencies which are changing and becoming more diverse. Finally, diversity is fundamentally a matter of justice.

Attention to diversity is not simply a matter of inviting participation, but a lens in the theological school's "essential task of learning, teaching, research and formation" (Gilligan 2002:9). However, diversity is a challenging, sensitive and often divisive task. In some seminaries the institutional culture only sees the need to adapt some procedures in order to respond more effectively to students' needs, or to include some courses that reflect theological perspectives distinct from those of the dominant culture (Riebe-Estrella 2009). In these cases the fundamental worldview of institutions and of pedagogy remain the same, while some accommodation is made for those who come from diverse cultures and ecclesial experiences. Even though it become unacceptable and politically incorrect for most educational institutions not to take diversity seriously, theological institutions have not done enough to prepare students from different cultural and racial backgrounds for effective ministry in a variety of cultural settings (Foster 2002).

Despite the efforts to increase diversity in theological education during the last three decades in the United States (Cascante 2008:21), some, but not enough, progress has been made. In general, the lenses of race, ethnicity, class, gender and sexuality have only been used as hermeneutical, pedagogical and critical perspectives on the production and function of knowledge in many theological disciplines (Androas 2012:5). According to Riebe-Estrella (2009:19), no new vision of theological education is being proposed in which differences are lifted and divisions are unmasked. Rather the institutional culture remains one of privilege for those who have held the power to maintain their dominance, making the educational enterprise fundamentally reflective of that same group.

In South Africa, there is scarcity of literature on how diversity is managed in theological institutions. One wonders how theological institutions are dealing with diversity while forming students within their institutional cultures, as this kind of socialisation is seen as most formative (Hindman 2002). Religious organisations are mediating institutions between the private and public spheres (Smith, Stones, Peck and Naidoo 2007). As such, churches and theological institutions have the potential to draw people out of their private, racially segregated lives into a social space where human interactions are more intimate than in the public arena. If anyone should be doing something about our racialised society, they say it should be the Christians, as their religion calls for it and their faith gives them the tools and the moral forces needed for change. The new interracial, non-sexist relationships that are created in these institutions can become a model for South African society. However, the reality in many cases is that "churches, the presumed agents of reconciliation, are at best impotent and at worst accomplices in strife" (Volf 1996:36). A church should, by definition, be a place of acceptance and love; however, it is also an arena for subtle racial tension and sexism. Here one may question, for example, how the Church in South Africa is dealing with racism, sexism and homophobia, what kind of Christians will such a church and its accompanying theological training institutions form, and how are future ministers being equipped to deal with this kind of diversity? How will ministers provide the necessary leadership that will enable churches through their outreach to become beacons for the reign or rule of God in which all persons are treated with equity, dignity and respect?

Engaging diversity in higher education

Higher education institutions play an important role as sites where issues of tolerance, inclusion, access, and structural inequities could be addressed effectively. Consequently, 'diversity', 'diversity issues' and 'diversification' have become part of the education debate and policy, and pose new challenges to South African tertiary institutions (Cross 2004:397). Most institutions are attempting to respond to these challenges within the context of a transformation process which impacts on every aspect of academic life – from student access and support, outreach programmes, staff recruitment and retention, to academic programme development, research, scholarship and the social and learning environment on campus. Generally, conceptualisations of diversity converge on or point to the need for integrating the politics of cultural and identity recognition with the politics of social justice and equity, which represents a key strength in South African diversity discourse (Cross 2004:400).

The management of diversity issues are challenging in many institutions. For example, despite the continuing problems related to racism, there are cases – especially in public schools and universities – where few people are talking about race, sometimes even affirming that "we don't have a problem here" (Carrim 2000:33). Schools and universities attempt to conceal negative racial attitudes because, according to Carrim, it is related to at least three kinds of fear: (1) fear of losing privilege; (2) fear of continuing with the ways of the past; and (3) fear of civil strife (2000:33). Stevens corroborates this denial of racism by stating, "Whatever the reasons, South African society's pre-occupation with not being pre-occupied with 'race' and racism provides an initial impetus for continued critical research, theorising and study into these phenomena" (2003:192).

Linked to racism is also gender discrimination or sexism, which legitimises unequal relations of power between men and women, and oppressive patriarchal relations that relegate women to subservient lower status and deny them access to societal rewards. This is not to play down the significance of the ideological manipulation of other forms of difference. Homosexuals are welcomed in the faith community and regarded as devoted Christians, but church councils are officially allowed to exclude homosexuals who are honest about their sexual lifestyle (Dreyer 2008:1236). At the same time the point needs to be made that gender is not just about women and sexuality is not just about gay and lesbian people, although they are often the ones who highlight the issues precisely since they have been defined as not the norm. Here we see that categorisation tends to homogenise groups and create a discursive illusion that members of a category share more in common than they in fact do. This hides the variety of interests, social positions, and identities ascribed to the group by that category (Cross and Naidoo 2012). At the same time it must be noted that individuals have multiple identities and these identities must be understood as they intersect with each other (Smith 2009). Simplifying the complexity of experience makes it difficult, if not impossible, to account for the nature of the intersections of race, class, gender and other forms of difference, and these intersections have yet to be explored and theorised (Cross and Naidoo 2012:231).

It is important to note an instrumentalist view of diversity issues existing in scholarship in our South African context (Makgoba 1999, Goduka 1996). In this sense, the debate on diversity has been dominated more by practical concerns than critical ones. Diversity has emerged as an applied enterprise or problem-solving exercise, more concerned with 'how to' and less with 'why' (Cross 2004:399). Traditional emphasis on the pursuit of diversity knowledge as part of the wider academic programme on race, class and gender studies, are giving way to the workshop-type skills-based programmes on diversity management, diversity awareness, teaching and learning in diverse classrooms, gender sensitivity, etc. Institutional practice has not been accompanied by adequate academic scholarship and intellectual practice grounded in disciplinary knowledge. At the same time, according to Cross (2004:396), the development of campus social/integration programmes are taking a backseat in some institutions: There is a firm belief that programmes that systematically promote social integration represent a form of undesirable 'social engineering' and that 'these things must happen naturally'. This brings into the debate the relative value of 'evolutionary' versus 'managed' change in higher education (Cross 2004:396).

Contestations in managing diversity in theological education

Within theological education, the aim of exploring diversity is to involve the theological community to look at the ways in which difference is constructed, how its significance shifts, how it is operationalised in society, and, most critically, why difference continues to matter. Gilligan (2002:9) takes this definition further by stating that diversity means resisting the homogenising of racial, ethnic, cultural and class differences into uniformity. Gilligan (2002) believes that learning how diverse constituencies use power to control and shape the agenda of theological education and its mission, is critical. The reason for these initiatives related to diversity in theological education is not to ferret out racists or sexists, but to examine the unrecognised ways in which power assumptions embedded in institutional culture might disenfranchise certain groups of students (Riebe-Estrella 2009:19), whether knowingly or unknowingly, and undermine the educational mission of empowering students for work.

A significant part of the challenge in exploring diversity has been the insistence on universalism in the name of Christianity, which all too often has amounted to the eradication of difference in the interest of hegemony of the dominant (Christerson et al. 2005). These very claims were often the reason why Christian churches could avoid dealing in a concerted way, head on, with concerns about stereotyping and racism. Important to note is that dogmatic and fundamentalist adherence to personal beliefs have been positively associated with racist attitudes (Duriez and Hutsebaut 2000:85). "One's creed, per se, does not particularly associate with such prejudice, but the attitude that one's beliefs are the fundamentally correct, essential, inerrant ones, is associated with bigotry" (Altemeyer 2003:19). The relationship between spirituality and racism is, therefore, moderated by the historic-cultural context and by the degree of dogmatism with which the beliefs are held.

In theological circles, differences have been lifted up and celebrated, but only to the extent that Christians could 'tame' it, and only when it was difference that was preferred. Therefore, instead of finding a common matrix upon which to relate serious differences of opinions, many feel they have no place of acceptance, sometimes no sense of identity grounded in the Church's tradition and history (Christerson et al. 2005). Church traditions are filled with polarities and different approaches, with an unwillingness to "sit down at the table and have fellowship, to talk with and learn from one another" (Speller and Seymour 2002:2). For example, within theological education, while there is theological agreement that racism is morally wrong and that seminaries need to address the issue of race, there is less theological agreement about how to do it (Aleshire 2009:2). Theologically, some, like the evangelicals, view sin and salvation as personal, stating that racial prejudice is a personal sin. In this theological worldview, the wrongs of racial discrimination are dealt with by looking inward, dealing with individual prejudice, and can be solved by the repentance and conversion of the sinful individuals at fault (Emerson and Smith 2000:48). This approach comes from relationalism (a strong emphasis on interpersonal relationships) derived from the view that human nature is fallen and that salvation and Christian maturity can only come through a personal relationship with Christ (Emerson and Smith 2000:48). Some other main line traditions perceive sin and salvation as having deeply social dimensions. Racial discrimination is more than the sum of the personal prejudice – it is a function of power, class and systems of domination. In this theological view, social systems and structures must be addressed, which, if corrected, will impact the effects of personal racial prejudices – whether or not individuals become more righteous. These two examples highlight different perspectives in approaching an issue of diversity which further challenges the process of managing diversity.

Nowhere is the failure to see diversity as a unifying force or concept more visible than when Christians speak of God; when Christians think and speak theologically. Indeed, the tendency of such talk to divide is so great that many theological institutions go out of their way not to talk about God or beliefs stemming from a particular theological perspective. Here is another irony: the primary basis of Christian belief and value systems is something Christians do not or cannot share. The implications of this for unity or comprehensive approaches towards education for ministry in churches filled with diversity and difference, are great.

In our context, theological institutions educate students for service in a democratic and pluralistic society, and to engage through scholarship and participation in the issues of that society. From this perspective, the very survival of training institutions is contingent upon adaptation to the current culture. Societal pressure is not the only source of 'push' – there are also forces *within* the institution that push towards this adaptation (McMinn 1998). Scriptural teachings and the missional focus of theological education all direct Christians towards a religious praxis that welcomes diverse peoples as equal partners in faith. Theology courses itself are well-suited for investigating and challenging social inequalities, since theology deals with fundamental beliefs about the self, God, community and society. As these internal and external forces push Bible colleges and seminaries towards greater pluralism, the institutions are also pulled towards greater homogeneity. Thus the need to preserve the institution's core values and beliefs makes it difficult for it to fully embrace those who do not look or sound like the majority of its constituents (Abadeer 2009).

One of the reasons Christian intuitions struggle with diversity, is the fear that embracing diversity will ultimately result in the theological institution's environment becoming contrary to the faith and, in the context of the United States, becomes secularised (Parades-Collins 2009). Locally, Bible colleges maybe fear that an unintentional by-product of incorporating diversity could be that their colleges will become 'politicised'. When institutions do not employ initiatives for diversity or engage in a passive role as it relates to race relations on campus, negative reactions and misunderstandings amongst students are likely to occur. Steele (1995:177) reminds us that "on our campuses, such micro-societies, all that remain unresolved between black and white, all the old wounds and shames that have never have been addressed, present themselves for attention – and present our youth with pressures they cannot always handle." The institution's culture is not really a self-contained culture; it is more accurately a sub-culture of the broader social and religious world outside the school.

Once theological institutions do face the full magnitude of diversity, there could be the temptation to adopt a 'colour blind' position that shields institutions from differences rather than help the seminary community appreciate and learn from their experience. This is exactly where the problem lies: a lack of consciousness of the ways in which institutions are organised that holds direct consequences for students, identity and transformation. This attempt to neutralise cultural particularities in an educational environment maintains the *status quo*, creating an ethos that favours the dominant group as the norm rather than the dynamism of unity within diversity (Hurtado 2005:600). Educators who apply this colour blind approach often try to suppress and gloss over their prejudice against students from racial groups other than their own, by professing not to see colour. Furthermore, what is implied in these practices is the belief that newcomers to institutions come from educationally and culturally inferior backgrounds, and that adjusting the curriculum to meet their needs amounts to lowering the otherwise high standards. Assimilation has proved to be inadequate, as it was premised on absorbing diversity into dominant ways of being and doing. In addition, the multi-cultural educational approach has also been seen as weak by celebrating diverse cultures in isolated events. It is only seen as a benign form of assimilation, but is unable to challenge social structures, processors and attitudes that perpetuate unjust power relations between groups (Cross and Naidoo 2012:237).

To overcome the 'colour blind' stance in theological education, an analysis of power relations between dominant and oppressed groups is done, using theories of critical pedagogy, feminist pedagogy, anti-racist education, critical multi-cultural theories, and post-conflict or reconciliation pedagogies (Androas 2012, Cascante-Gomez 2008, Reddie 2010, Riebe-Estrella 2009). It assumes that structural social change will result when power relations are challenged (Brookfield 1995). As we know, the internalisation of apartheid stereotypes, structures and beliefs has resulted in degrees of resistance, rigidity, and low levels of adaptability of the individual or groups to the changing South African environment and its new value system. Jansen (2008:5) calls this "bitter knowledge" and it represents "how students remember and enact the past." This is a product of intergenerational transmission of spoken and unspoken messages from parents, the Church, school, cultural associations and the peer group (Jansen 2008:5). These messages have not been interrupted over the period of transition, despite the major changes in the formal institutions of democracy. The question remains as to how South Africans can un-think old categories of citizenship and refine themselves as a nation in order to move beyond racial categorisation and their own political bondage.

To sustain learning environments that are welcoming and empowering to all students, for example in the classroom, would involve a reassessment of pedagogy, theological content, methods of communicating and knowledge construction. In *Fighting the Elephant in the Room: Ethical Reflections on White Privilege and Other Systems of Advantage in the Teaching of Religion*, Hill, Harris and Martinez-Vazquez (2009:4) offer a strategy for re-imagining liberating education that takes social justice seriously. They write of the elephant in the room as the complex nexus of systems of advantage, with a special focus on white privilege. In developing models of anti-racist and anti-oppressive practices for Christian ministry, Reddie (2010:96), in the United Kingdom context, speaks of challenging unaware white students to reflect on what privileges and opportunities are accrued by the simple fact that they are white. It begins with an acknowledgement of the unearned privileges that whiteness confers. Whiteness studies is an emergent field that examines "white inflections in which whiteness as a form of power is defined, deployed, performed, policed and reinvented" (Steyn and Conway 2010:284). The point of these practices is to conscientise students to the dynamics of difference, to challenge assumptions, so that difference is not seen negatively but as an opportunity to deconstruct their past with all its attendant behaviours (Lee 2009:21). These reflections are undertaken within a multi-disciplinary framework, similar to the forms of analysis advocated by womanist theologians in that issues of gender, class, sexuality and disability (how many used the terms 'male' or 'heterosexual' or 'able-bodied') are also discussed and reflected upon.

At the same time the perennial dominant Eurocentric approach to teaching and learning needs to be critiqued. These approaches dominant in the field of theology include both the content and method of communicating knowledge. Whether the theology taught in institutions is Christian dogmatics or constructive theologies, it invariably focuses on Western formulations of faith and philosophical thought. The very language of discourse that has developed is inherently racialised as white and normative. The work of unmasking these dominant frameworks of knowledge and their interconnectedness with colonial power in all its forms, past and present, is not new (Androas 2012:6). However, not enough attention has been given to this, because cultural colonisation, which involves colonised minds and education systems, is a deeper and long-lasting form of colonial power. This form of power is more subtle and more difficult to identify, resist and transform.

To transcend the Eurocentrism of theological education, the cultural, religious and theological knowledge represented in the classroom needs to be acknowledged as being *not* equally valued. Using Mignolo's terms, "persons who come from different places and think from different locations," that is from different worldviews, are not interacting mutually (Mignolo 2007:490). There is a hierarchy of systems and sources of knowledge, with the Western perspective at the top of the pyramid which is consistently affirmed in subtle ways as universal. The approach advanced by Mignolo (2007:453) for decolonising knowledge, is described as 'delinking' – understood as a de-colonial epistemic shift leading to other universality and brings to the foreground other epistemologies, other principles of knowledge and understanding. Pedagogical strategies rooted in these discourses, as can be seen from the examples presented above, place emphasis on critical thinking as the foundation for new meaning construction, self-discovery, and self-creation against the legacies of prejudice and alienation. Through exploration and reflection, students are challenged to question the taken-for-granted notion of their rootedness in a culture or a nation.

This dominant Eurocentric universality claim must continue to be dismantled; however, to challenge this worldview is not only to introduce change, but also to threaten the fundamental stability of the educational enterprise. There should be a discussion about maintaining the current theological 'canon' and about widening the dialogue to include other voices. This is more than simply adding black scholars to the syllabi. It has significant implications for the shape of theological discourse, the redefining of who should be the 'gatekeeper' and who should be involved in the 'de-colonialisation' of the curriculum (Andraos 2012).

Impact of diversity management on ministerial formation

Within the theological institution, the content and structures of religious faith are both essential for the student to develop an understanding of the relationships between self, community and God, and for developing character and morality that help them become better leaders. It is important to note that the institutional culture plays a powerful role in how students are actually shaped by institutional culture. This 'culture' is not easily changed or manipulated, and gives meaning to the life of the institution. However, it must be noted that students are not clones of the community (Hindman 2002). Instead they negotiate with it, contest aspects of it, and use it as a tool kit for constructing perspectives that are in varying degrees of agreement or disagreement with the normative core of the culture (Mezirow 2000). In their interactions with the institutional culture, students are, in varying degrees, influenced and moulded by the culture even as they (students) affect the institution's culture. Faculty and students can be helped to understand the formative means that institutional culture employs so that they might find a common theological discourse together.

Within this institutional culture, students are being shaped within diversity and socialised in how to respond to diversity. The way in which diversity is managed could create a source of division, or it could be used as a positive element in religious identity formation. For example, Kleinman (1984) analysed the culture of a Midwestern theological seminary and focused on the way the school's culture has a paradoxical effect in certain ways of de-professionalising its students while, at the same time, equipping them for a professional calling.

The question at play here is, how can students relate theology to their own context while also attempting to understand the other to such an extent that their own presuppositions are challenged and their work in society becomes more effective? This question belongs to the work of formation which is about ongoing development of ministerial identity, of moving towards what may be referred to as greater authenticity, more authentic identity, and authenticity vocation (Palmer 2000). Reclaiming one's race, culture, gender sexuality and other aspects of identity, is part of moving towards greater authenticity.

Parks (2000) explores how community can best challenge and support students in their spiritual development, which also includes identity formation. Fowler (1981) suggests that spirituality is about how people construct knowledge through largely unconscious and symbolic processes manifested through image, symbol, ritual, art and music. These dimensions of spirituality are often deeply cultural, hence the connection of spirituality to cultural identity. To progress towards internalised and autonomous racial identity, for example, students need to cross racial borders of learning and growth. As students meet each other, they reach new levels of engagement either by challenging their development process and forming new values, or by confirming their current values (Parks 2000). Tisdell (2003) believes that in reclaiming their cultural identities, individuals will typically go through a process of unlearning what they have unconsciously internalised (Hurtado 2006). Part of this process is learning from their own histories, reclaiming what has been lost or unknown to them, and reframing what has often been cast subconsciously as negative in more positive ways (Hurtado 2005:605). This encounter of 'otherness' within one's immediate peer group provides opportunities of genuine encounter. Pettigrew and Tropp's (2000) meta-analysis of hundreds of studies of interactions amongst groups and intergroup contact theory, highlights the power of these conditions to reduce prejudice and discrimination. Learning to see the religious dignity and humanity of the other is a first step towards encounter and dialogue (Hurtado 2007).

Since handling diversity in education is so complex, educators need to recognise the validity of differences. This will, in turn, require an appraisal of the educator's personal as well as institutional ideologies and perceptions, and a frank dedication to facilitate and manage student diversity (Meier and Hartell 2009:180). This formative educational process is challenging enough, more so for educators who do not share the same ecclesial or cultural perspectives as students, and are expected to prepare students for ministry. The ambiguity arising from this lack of shared experience is exacerbated by gendered, socio-economic, educational experience and by ideological commitments through which educators understand who they are in relation to students (Foster 2002:24). At a very profound level, people who do work with these issues are engaged in changing people's social identities. It is not enough to merely train teachers and students to understand people's differences at a superficial level. They need to have a deep grasp of their own social and personal contradiction which requires soul-searching and self-reflexivity.

Conclusion

The question is no longer whether to acknowledge or pursue diversity, but to understand the conditions that are needed to make diversity work in different contexts. Smith (2009) argues that a comprehensive approach towards diversity is needed – one that shifts the emphasis from individuals and underrepresented groups to institutions. For Christian institutions, building institution capacity for diversity can be supported through its unique identity, mission and theological foundation as a source of strength. The problem diversity poses is to locate a common intersection amongst and between the ideas, myths and dreams undergirding these identities and cultures, and then to create an educational and conversational space sturdy enough to allow the restructuring of 'what counts' as theological education. In spite of the contested nature of managing diversity by embracing and encountering difference of many kinds, there needs to be an awareness that this profoundly impacts on the spiritual, academic and professional formation of students.

Theological training institutions are gifted with the lenses of faith and values, and are challenged to identify, reinterpret, and dismantle barriers that prevent diversity. This becomes an opportunity to 'live out the Gospel, institutionally'. Once the institutional culture begins to see its own situatedness, it can begin to shed its parochial and paternalistic tendencies (Foster 2002:16). This is only possible when 'whiteness' or 'blackness' or heterosexuality or being male is no longer conceived as the norm, but as one contextual position amongst many, albeit often carrying with it particular privileges and considerable power. It is hoped that the giftedness of diversity in our context can become an opportunity for empowerment, healing of memories, and re-imagining racial, cultural and religious reconciliation.

Bibliography

Abadeer, A., 2009. Seeking redemptive diversity in Christian institutions of higher education: Challenges and hopes from within. *Christian Higher Education*. 8(3). 187-202.

Aleshire, D. O., 2009. Gifts Differing: The Educational Value of Race and Ethnicity. *Theological Education*. 45 (1). 1-18.

Altemeyer, B., 2003. Why do religious fundamentalists tend to be prejudiced? *International Journal for the Psychology of Religion*. 13.17-28.

Andraos, M.E., 2012. Engaging Diversity in Teaching Religion and Theology: An Intercultural, De-colonial Epistemic Perspective. *Teaching Theology and Religion*. 15(1). 3-15.

Bernstein, B. B., 2000. *Pedagogy, Symbolic Control, and Identity: Theory, Research, Critique*. London: Rowman and Littlefield.

Brookfield, S., 1995. *Becoming a critically reflective teacher*. San Francisco: Jossey-Bass.

Carrim, N., 2000. Critical anti-racism and problems in self-articulation forms of identities. *Race Ethnicity and Education*. 3. 26-44.

Cascante Gomez, F.A., 2008. Advancing racial/ethnic diversity in theological education: A model for reflection and action. *Theological Education*. 43(2). 21-39.

Chopp, R.S., 1995. *Saving Work: Feminist Practices of Theological Education*. Louisville: Westminster John Knox Press.

Christerson, B., Edwards, K.L. and Emerson, M.O., 2005. *Against All Odds: The Struggle for Racial Integration in Religious Organizations*. New York: New York University Press.

Cross, M., 2004. Institutionalising campus diversity in South African higher education: Review of diversity scholarship and diversity education. *Higher Education*. 47. 387-410.

Cross, M. and Naidoo, D., 2012. Race, Diversity Pedagogy: Mediated Learning Experience for Transforming Racist Habitus and Predispositions. *Review of Education, Pedagogy, and Cultural Studies*. 34(5). 227-244.

Dreyer, J.S., 2012. Practical theology in South Africa. In: Miller-McLemore, B.J. (ed.). *The Wiley-Blackwell Companion to Practical Theology*. Oxford: Wiley-Blackwell. 505-514.

Dreyer, Y., 2008. A pastoral response to the unhealed wounds of gays exacerbated by indecision and in articulacy. *HTS*. 64(3). 1235-1254.

Duriez, B. and Hutsebaut, D., 2000. The relation between religion and racism. *Mental Health, Religion and Culture*. 3. 85-102.

Emerson, M.O. and Smith, C., 2000. *Divided by Faith: Evangelical religion and the problem of race in America*. Oxford: University Press.

Foster, C.R., 2002. Diversity in Theological Education. *Theological Education*. 38(2). 15-37.

Fowler, James W., 1981. *Becoming Adult, Becoming Christian*. New York: Harper and Row.

Gilligan, M., 2002. Diversity and accreditation: A measure of quality. *Theological Education*. 38(2). 9.

Goduka, I.N., 1996. Reconstructing education to affirm unity and diversity. *South African Journal of Higher Education*. 10(2). 67-74.

Hill, J.A., Harris, M.L. and Martinez-Vazquez, H.A., 2009. Fighting the Elephant in the Room: Ethical Reflections on White Privilege and Other Systems of Advantage in the Teaching of Religion. *Teaching Theology and Religion*. 12(1). 3-23.

Hindman, D.M., 2002. Form splintered lives to whole persons: Facilitating spiritual development in college students. *Religious Education*. 97(2). 165-182.

Hurtado, S., 2005. The next generation of diversity and intergroup relations search. *Journal of Social Issues*. 61(3). 595-610.

Hurtado, S., 2006. Diversity and learning for a pluralistic democracy. In: W. Allen, M. Bonous-Hammarth and R. Teranishi (eds.). *Higher education in a global society: Achieving diversity, equity, and excellence*. San Diego: Elsevier. 203-226.

Hurtado, S., 2007. Linking diversity with the educational and civic missions of higher education. *Review of Higher Education*. 30(2). 185-196.

Jansen, J. D., 2008. *Bearing Whiteness: A Pedagogy of Compassion in a Time of Trouble*. The Fifth Annual Hans Brenninkmeijer Memorial Lecture, Catholic Institute of Education.

Kleinman, S., 1984. *Equals before God: Seminarians and humanistic professionals*. Chicago: University of Chicago Press.

Lee, S.K., 2009. Engaging difference in pastoral theology: race and ethnicity. *The Journal of Pastoral Theology*. 19(2). 1-20.

Makgoba, W.M., 1999. The South African University and its challenges in transformation. In: M. Cross (ed.). *Transforming Higher Education in South Africa*. Cape Town: Maskew Miller Longman. 7-20.

McMinn, L.G., 1998. Enclave adaptation, multi-culturalism and evangelical Christian colleges. *Research on Christian Higher Education*. 5. 23-52.

Meier, C. and Hartell, C., 2009. Handling cultural diversity in education in South Africa. *SA-eDUC Journal*. 6(2). 180-192.

Meyer, A.J., 2009. *Realizing your intentions: A guide for churches and colleges with distinctive missions*. Abilene: ACU Press.

Mezirow, J. and Associates, 2000. *Learning as transformation: Critical perspectives on a theory in progress*. San Francisco: Jossey-Bass.

Mignolo, W.D., 2007. Delinking: The Rhetoric of Modernity, the Logic of Coloniality and the Grammar of De-Coloniality. *Cultural Studies*. 21(2-3). 449-513.

Palmer, P., 2000. *Let your life speak*. San Francisco: Jossey-Bass.

Parades-Collins, K., 2009. Institutional priority for diversity at Christian institutions. *Christian Higher Education*. 8. 280-303.

Parks, S.D., 2000. *Big questions, worthy dreams: Mentoring young adults in their search for meaning, purpose and faith*. San Francisco: Jossey-Bass.

Pettigrew, T.F. and Tropp, L.R., 2000. Does Intergroup Contact Reduce Prejudices? Recent Meta-Analytic Findings. In: S. Oskamp (ed.). *Reducing Prejudice and Discrimination*. Hillsdale: Erlbaum.

Reddie, A.G., 2010. Teaching for Racial Justice: A Participative Approach. *Teaching Theology and Religion*. 13(2). 95-109.

Riebe-Estrella, G., 2009. Engaging borders: Lifting up difference and unmasking division. *Theological Education*. 45(1). 19-26.

Rosada, C., 2006. What do we mean by 'managing diversity'? In: S. Reddy (ed.). *Workforce Diversity. Vol. 3: Concepts and Cases*. Hyderabad: ICAFAJ University.

Smith, D.G., 2009. *Diversity's promise for higher education*. Baltimore: The John Hopkins University Press.

Smith, T.B., Stones, C.R., Peck, C.E. and Naidoo, A.V., 2007. The association of racial attitudes and spiritual beliefs in post-apartheid South Africa. *Mental Health, Religion and Culture.* 10(3). 263-274.

Speller, J.M. and Seymour, J.L., 2002. Reflections on Institutional Issues Relate to Race and Ethnicity in ATS Schools. *Theological Education.* 38(2). 55-70.

Steele, S., 1995. The re-coloring of campus life: Student racism, academic pluralism and the end of the dream. In: J. Arthur and A. Shapiro (eds.). *Campus wars: Multi-culturalism and the politics of difference.* Boulder: Westview Press.

Stevens, G., 2003. Academic representations of 'race' and racism in psychology: Knowledge, production, historical context and dialectics in transitional South Africa. *International Journal of Intercultural Relations.* 27. 189-207.

Steyn, M., 2001. *Whiteness just isn't what it used to be: White identity in a changing South Africa.* Albany: State University of New York Press.

Steyn, M. and Conway, D., 2010. Introduction: Intersecting whiteness, interdisciplinary debates. *Ethnicities.* 10(3). 283-291.

Tisdell, E., 2003. *Exploring spirituality and culture in adult and higher education.* San Francisco: Jossey-Bass.

Volf, M., 1996. *Exclusion and Embrace: A theological exploration in learning and teaching*, New York: Oxford.

Werner, D., 2009. *Challenges and opportunities in theological education in the 21st century.* Geneva: ETE/WCC. Bossey Ecumenical Institute.

PART 2

MINISTERIAL FORMATION CHALLENGES

Contesting spiritual formation in theological education

Lyzette Hoffman

Introduction

Theological study comes with certain expectations that would not normally be found in other fields of study. One of these expectations on the side of the student, is that theological education implies spiritual formation (Glennon et al. 2011:360). Spiritual formation is recognised in the literature as an important aspect of theological training (Kanarek and Lehman 2013; Keely 2003; Naidoo 2008, 2010). However, should this necessarily be the case? Hence spiritual formation is not without contestation. In this chapter, recent spiritual formation practices in South African institutions will be broadly reviewed. Furthermore, possible challenges in spiritual formation will be discussed and, lastly, how spiritual formation influences the pastor in the congregation will be sketched.

What is spiritual formation? Lowe's (2010:2) statement that spiritual formation is a synthesis of a number of factors illustrates why there are so many definitions of spiritual formation. Some descriptions include the following:

- Engaging students in reflecting upon the spiritual life, as well as providing opportunities to deepen their own spiritual journeys (Keely 2003:202).
- Integrating of the intellectual, psychological, social, cultural and spiritual dimensions of life in the educational process (Warford 2007 in Naidoo 2011).
- "A lifelong process of being formed and developed in the likeness of Christ… It is a personal and relational formation which seeks to promote, encounter and cooperate with God and society as a whole" (Naidoo 2010:187).
- "The intentional process by which the marks of an authentic Christian spirituality are formed and integrated" (Naidoo 2011).

For the purpose of this discussion, spiritual formation will be described as the intentional providing of opportunities to deepen the spiritual journey of students (and faculty) through the integrating of the intellectual, psychological, social, cultural and spiritual dimensions of life.

Spiritual formation of the student at seminaries, Bible schools and public universities in South Africa, receives attention in different ways. Some contemporary examples of institutions of theological training referring specifically to spiritual formation, is the Seth Mokitimi Methodist Seminary as well as the faculties of Theology at the University of the Free State and Stellenbosch University. The Seth Mokitimi Methodist Seminary describes itself on its webpage, "Thus, the seminary understood from the start that its task was not merely to produce graduates with strong academic credentials in theology, but also to form individuals of spiritual maturity with impeachable personal values and virtues" (Seth Mokitimi 2014). At the University of the Free State, the Faculty of Theology declares, "The Faculty embraces values that encourage cultural, gender and ethnic inclusivity, promote academic and intellectual excellence and innovation, and support spiritual and ethic integrity" (University of the Free State 2014). The curatoria of the Uniting Reformed Church of South Africa (URCSA) and Dutch Reformed Church (DRC) established a seminary at Stellenbosch University's Faculty of Theology to assist in the ministerial formation of theology students. Spiritual formation is specifically mentioned.

Formation happens through the modes of residential and/or distance-learning, with various combinations of full-time, part-time, online or correspondence training. At public universities, spiritual formation is often left to the churches represented by the students. It is usually not written into the curriculum and not used to assess the preparedness of the theology student for ministry. Regular prayer meetings for students and staff, as well as Bible study groups organised by the theological student organisations, are some of the ways spiritual formation is directly addressed. For example, in the reformed universities, like Stellenbosch, Pretoria and Free State, the Dutch Reformed Church is using a 'curatorium' (a body of ministers elected by a church denomination to oversee theological study) through which a mentor minister is assigned to a student for regular contact sessions. At inter-denominational seminaries and Bible schools, spiritual formation can be addressed more openly as part of their training without being overly sensitive to offend some specific church tradition. In Protestant institutions, spiritual formation happens informally, personally and implicitly with the focus on academic instruction and some practical exposures (Naidoo 2011:121). Githuku (2004:228) warns that it can happen that churches assume the university or seminary will give attention to the spiritual maturity of the theology student, and, on the other hand, the university or seminary might assume that the churches will give attention to this aspect. This may lead to spiritual formation not receiving the proper attention from either institution.

Spirituality is seen differently within various traditions. Naidoo describes four approaches to spiritual formation (2011:225), namely "… speculative/kataphatic – head spirituality, primarily a 'thinking' approach; affective/kataphatic – a heart spirituality, drawing on a charismatic, affective way of connecting with God; affective/apophatic – a mystic spirituality, more interested in being with God than expressing oneself to God, and speculative/apophatic – a kingdom spirituality that is committed to witnessing to God in the world." It poses the challenge as to which approach towards spiritual formation should be chosen by a specific institution. This, in turn, will influence the content and the methods used for spiritual formation.

A study done by Walvoord (2008) showed that students and faculty had different ideas about theological education. While the students expected that they will also be spiritually formed, faculty saw their task as creating critical thinkers (see also Glennon et al. 2011:360). According to research done in South Africa, theology students perceive their training institutions to attend to their spiritual formation (Naidoo 2011:133). Furthermore, it was found that Pentecostal and Charismatic theological institutions working with a vocational model for training, showed greater commitment to the different dimensions of spiritual formation than Reformed and Presbyterian institutions (Naidoo 2011:137). This also coincides with whether it is a denominational seminary, Bible college, or a theological faculty at a public university. The focus of spirituality is often marginalised within higher education. The question can be asked whether theological training should be done within a paradigm of higher education if the critical area of spiritual formation is problematic or overlooked.

Pobee (2010:339) describes spirituality as integral to theological education: "… the subject of theology is God, the Ultimate Reality, and, therefore, spirituality cannot be an extra – it is integral to theological construction." Looking at theology in this light, the 'subject matter' calls for spiritual formation. Through information, formation also takes place. To distinguish between information and formation in education is to use illusory dichotomised language, according to Moore (Glennon et al. 2011). Information leads to formation and in the case of theology, one aspect of this formation is spiritual formation. Furthermore, spiritual formation plays an important role in equipping students for ministry. An essential aspect of a minister's work is the spiritual dimension of human lives (Naidoo 2008:134). Therefore, the theology student needs knowledge and experience of spiritual formation. The experiences of theology students' spiritual life will influence their leadership in church (Keely 2003:202) as well as other aspects of their ministry. Through theological study the student's ministerial identity is shaped, spiritual formation being an important aspect of this identity (Naidoo 2008:141). Marty (2008:321) goes so far as to say that "… (all) of the best thinking and learning in the work of theology will be pointless if it is not at the service of forming lives that matter." Spiritual formation, therefore, seems to be critical to theological education. However, it is not a straightforward issue.

Contestations in spiritual formation

From the brief background sketch, some challenges become apparent. Spiritual formation was earlier described as the intentional providing of opportunities to deepen the spiritual journey of students (and faculty) through the integrating of the intellectual, psychological, social, cultural and spiritual dimensions of life. In the light of the definition and other aspects mentioned above, contestations within spiritual formation will be grouped into four categories: conceptual, institutional, operational and communal. These four categories resemble aspects of spiritual formation as spelled out in the definition.

Conceptual issues

The first category deals with how spiritual formation should be conceptualised. As seen earlier, definitions include terms such as process and content. Which processes are to be included as part of spiritual formation? Giving more attention to either the human or the

Divine aspect of the process, will influence the conceptualisation of spiritual formation. Can spiritual formation take place without human agency (Hess 2008:21)? The role the Divine plays in spiritual formation must be acknowledged in any conceptualisation of spiritual formation. The essential content for spiritual formation is also described in the definition. Content to be included will differ for various church traditions. The aim and goal of the formation process can vary from institution to institution, and church tradition to church tradition. In the Protestant tradition, the expectation the Church has of its leaders is seen as the goal of spiritual formation. The Roman Catholic tradition has a sacramental view of ministry as priesthood and "formation takes place through the provision of programmes and resources organised around clear institutional goals" (Naidoo 2010:186).

Spiritual formation has a developmental agenda which needs to be acknowledged in its conceptualisation (e.g. compare Fowler's stages of faith development in Elias 1983:119-136). The scope of spiritual formation is also a lifelong one which will not be completed during theological training. There are thus limits to what can be achieved during theological education. Scharen (2008:266) expounds on this aspect stating, "No instruction of programme can simply transmit the wisdom and imagination that good pastors seem to have ... these emerge over time." Students are only there for a limited time and their maturity, psychological and emotional growth can all influence their spiritual formation. Due to the wide field of theological studies, including at least six sub-disciplines, students rarely have prolonged contact with one specific lecturer, minimising the possible contact time for spiritual formation by a specific lecturer. Furthermore, students are already formed by different experiences with congregation, family, school, etc. when they come for theological education (Scharen 2008:265). Some students start studying theology directly after school, while others experience a calling to study theology in their later years. This can result in different age groups going through different stages in their lives, studying in one class. Being in different stages of faith development (compare Fowler's stages of faith development) will translate into different developmental needs in this regard. These differences between students will have to be taken into consideration when looking at their spiritual formation.

A distinction is often made between formation and information; however, the one cannot really be seen without the other (cf. Jacobsen and Jacobsen in Glennon et al. 2011:361). This should be taken into consideration in conceptualising spiritual formation. Where spiritual formation is conceptualised as an 'add-on' to theological education, spiritual formation can be left to the students themselves. However, if spiritual formation is conceptualised as integral to formation of the theology student, it will need to be integrated into the curriculum.

Institutional challenges

The debate over whether or not theological training should be done at a public university, has been held in various places (Tolmie and Venter 2012; Venter 2011). In South Africa, theological education takes place at public universities as well as seminaries and Bible schools. For theology to be intellectually rigorous, spiritual formation plays an important role. Hauwerwas (2007:183) describes it in this way: "According to D'Costa, theology can be done with intellectual rigor only in the context of a love affair with God and God's community, the Church." On an institutional level the importance of spiritual formation needs to be recognised as part of the 'love affair with God and His community', influencing the intellectual rigor of the discipline.

Where theological institutions are attached to a specific church tradition, 'spiritual formation' is not as problematic. In these seminaries it is sometimes assumed that the theology student is spiritually formed through the rigorous selection processes in the church. Furthermore, it is expected that the students will take responsibility for their own spiritual formation. This can result in seminaries ignoring this aspect of theological education. Intentionality in spiritual formation is, however, of great importance, as this is a critical component in the growth of theology students (Lowe 2010:9). Spiritual formation cannot be left to take place on its own. According to Githuku (2004:229), the teaching of Biblical studies and regular devotions at a theological institution do not adequately capture the spiritual formation of students. He suggests it should be incorporated into the programme of study.

In theological institutions that form a part of a public university, spiritual formation becomes problematic, although Keely (2003) argues that spiritual formation can be effectively integrated into the curricula of liberal, ecumenical seminaries. Is it possible to think about a 'generic spiritual formation' if some studies show differences between denominational institutions? At public universities, theology students are often from various Christian denominations or may even have different religious backgrounds. Can there be spiritual formation that is acceptable to all denominations? The ethical requirement of academic teaching is to preserve student autonomy, and the overarching goal of a university education to promote critical thinking. This raises the question whether spiritual formation might go against critical scholarship at a university. Martin (2008:213) argues that faith development (which can also be described as spiritual formation) can actually deepen the learning experience of the student, amidst these characteristics of university teaching. Spiritual formation can provide a valuable deepening of pluralism, autonomy, and critical thought in the educational experience of students (Martin 2008:213).

On the institutional level of the university there must be an understanding of the importance of spiritual formation in theological education as a deepening of their educational experience (Martin 2008:213). There must be an 'institutional will' within the institution to integrate spiritual formation into theological education, otherwise spiritual formation will become the responsibility of a few interested people. An institution that decides corporately to give attention to spiritual formation, should supply the resources to do so (Naidoo 2011:125). In the light of many other budgetary needs to be met, this might be a contentious issue.

Another institution that plays a role in spiritual formation is the sending churches. The task of spiritual formation is not only the challenge of the theological institution, but also that of the Church. This is illustrated by the URCSA's policy document of 1997 on theological training. This document states that the purpose of theological training "… (is) to shape and equip candidates spiritually, intellectually and practically for their service in the Church of Jesus Christ" (URCSA 1997:718ff). Palka (2004) found that the local congregation where the theology students were involved had a significant influence on their spiritual formation. The kind of knowing that comes from practising spirituality through different modes (prayer, worship, etc.), is the kind of knowledge which congregational leaders look for in a candidate for ministry (Scharen 2008:266). Where classroom-based formation is not complemented with congregation-based formation, the best theology curricula are wasted (Wood 2008:291). Theological training in all its aspects should be thoroughly discussed and monitored by the different churches involved. This can prevent the criticism by congregations that universities and seminaries turn out students who are skilled in the cognitive disciplines, "… but (are) essentially clueless when it comes to the skills necessary for ministry" (Wood 2008:302). It should especially be discussed with the local congregations of the students. Nevertheless, how this can be monitored is another matter.

Operational issues

Once spiritual formation is conceptualised by the theological institution, the question remains how this can be operationalised in the students' education. The inclusion of spiritual formation in the curriculum is contestable, especially at a public university. As stated earlier, spiritual formation can be included in the academic work of the student and/or through activities aimed at spiritual formation. Classroom worship services can be very meaningful in shaping spirituality. Laytham (2010:110) highlights four aspects which make it a powerful pedagogical instrument:

> (Classroom worship) focuses teaching and learning on God… It positions the entire class in dialogical relation to the divine Thou, in communal relation to each other, the larger church and the wider world, and in personal relations that risk spiritual transformation. Third, it frames theological education as an integrative practice of faith and learning. Finally, it invites teachers to know their students as whole persons and students to trust their teachers as spiritual guides.

The way in which different denominational traditions can be accommodated in these services, will have to be taken into consideration.

Would typical 'academic activities' be useful for spiritual formation? According to Kanarek and Lehman (2013:18), assignments may also be used to help students integrate their faith lives with their learning. Classroom discussions alone cannot help students to integrate their knowledge – written assignments can help to make the connection between knowledge and application. The assignment must challenge the student to apply the knowledge to a contemporary issue and voice their own opinion. In this way, students can be helped to see the connection between academic study and spiritual formation. In a study done by Astin, Astin and Lindholm (2011:10), it was found that study abroad, interdisciplinary studies, and service learning had a big impact on students' spiritual growth. Employing these different ways of learning also for spiritual formation purposes can lead to an enriching experience for the theology student. Although these activities can be very useful in spiritual formation, these aspects mentioned in the study are not always possible within a theology curriculum.

Faculty members can play a significant role in students' lives through mentoring, amongst other things. The mentor/mentee relationship can play a significant role in the formation of the theology student (cf. Wood 2008:297). Mentoring 'postures' which may be helpful in spiritual formation include welcoming, sitting, listening, and reflecting on what the student has to share (Yaghjian 2013:221). Experiencing a sense of welcoming in the contact between the student and the mentor encourages the student to be open to discussion of his/her spiritual journey. In listening thoroughly and refracting the student's experience through the knowledge and experience of the mentor, spiritual formation can take place.

However, are faculty members adequately equipped for the spiritual formation of students or for mentoring them for the sake of spiritual formation? Criteria for appointing academic staff are primarily based on their academic credentials. Academic staff may see academic formation as their main responsibility, even though this neglects the fact that students are being prepared for a spiritual career. Furthermore, not all academic staff are involved in ministry and might lack experience in spiritual formation. The format of the relationship between the student and the lecturer can be problematic as to how much the student will be prepared to share for the sake of faith formation on the one hand, and the academic assessment by the lecturer on the other. Higher education has certain requirements that need to be met, and spiritual formation is not one of them. Within institutions assessment of work performance of lecturers mainly focuses on research and teaching responsibilities. Especially in public universities, this institutional focus does not encourage lecturers to spend time on the spiritual formation of students.

If spiritual formation is to form part of theological education, the question remains whether it should be measured and how? "Around the world, academic accrediting bodies are requiring educational institutions to demonstrate the achievement of expressed competencies" (Brynjolfson 2010:198). How can this be done for spiritual formation? Assessment of spirituality has been the topic of various studies (Hall and Edwards 2002; Emmons 2000; Naidoo 2011). Emmons (2000:3) proposes that spirituality be studied within an intelligence framework. He identifies five components of spiritual intelligence (2000:3): a) The capacity for transcendence; b) the ability to enter into heightened spiritual state of consciousness; c) the ability to invest everyday activities, events and relationships with a sense of the sacred; d) the ability to utilise spiritual resources to solve problems in living; and e) the capacity to engage in virtuous behaviour. Using an intelligence framework opens new ways of seeing and measuring spiritual formation. This can unfortunately also give rise to problematic issues, like equalling intelligence, to spirituality.

The Spiritual Assessment Inventory (SAI) of Hall and Edwards (2002) was developed as they sensed a need for an instrument that integrates a clinically-relevant theoretical framework, a design for clinical application, as well as a sound psychometric foundation. They propose a theistic model and measure for assessing spiritual development. This tool measures a more 'spiritual dimension' (awareness) as well as a more 'psychological dimension' (relational maturity). It can be used as a clinical tool to assess spiritual development, as well as help identify an individual's strengths and weaknesses (Hall and Edwards 2002:353). Being more 'theologically informed', this measuring instrument can be useful in measuring spiritual formation. Naidoo (2011:130) suggests six dimensions of spiritual formation: Intentional commitment towards spiritual formation; services offered by the institution; formal and informal learning; community life; staff involvement in spiritual formation, and spiritual activities on campus. These dimensions can be utilised in a measuring instrument to assess spiritual formation at different institutions. It can also help develop more integrated educational and nurturing environments for student spirituality in theological education (Naidoo 2011:141). When taking different dimensions of spiritual formation into consideration, a broader picture can be drawn of the spiritual formation practices of an institution.

What would the purpose of measuring spiritual formation be? Measuring could be used by the student as a method of self-improvement, to ascertain whether certain goals were achieved, or maybe to evaluate the readiness of the student for ministry. In the last case, the assessment of spiritual formation influences the outcome of the student's studies. Can the student be awarded a degree but not be accepted for ministry on account of the spiritual formation assessment? This will have implications for new students enrolling into programmes. Students will have to be informed, from the beginning, that a degree in theology alone will not guarantee work in the ministry, but that their spiritual formation will be a significant part of their assessment.

Communal realities

From the different definitions of spiritual formation it is clear that experiencing the sense of community is also one of the important aspects of spiritual formation. Vassiliades, Kasseluri and Kalaitzidis (2010:608) even go so far as to say that "… theological education should always refer to communion as an ultimate constitutive element of being." The relational dimension is of utmost importance. Experiencing community on a vertical (with God) as well as a horizontal level (people) is shown by various studies to play an important role in spiritual formation (Hess 2008; Lowe 2010; Naidoo 2011). Interactions with faculty on an intellectual and social level had a positive impact on spiritual formation, according to Lowe (2010:7). The communal aspect of spiritual formation can be seen in community experienced between students and faculty. This immediately raises the question of whether there is enough possibility for students to experience this community with faculty. The opportunity for contact can be influenced by the model used for theological education, e.g. where distance learning is utilised. Studies done on the influence of distance education in theological training, indicated that spiritual formation can take place; however, a combination of face-to-face training and online training could have more benefits in this regard (Naidoo 2012a; Lowe 2010). In the African context with its growing need for ministers, distance education can help fulfil that need (Nguru 2004:245). However, special attention will have to be given to students' spiritual formation.

Another aspect regarding the communal facet of spiritual formation, is a sense of community experienced amongst fellow students. Gaikward (2010:270) refers to a team spirituality that must be cultivated amongst theology students. It can enrich their relationships and let them experience the grace and joy of being part of the body of Christ. This 'team spirituality' can prepare them for collaborating with fellow-ministers when they are in a congregational setting. A Training in Ministry (TiM) project was launched in a collaboration between some seminaries and congregations from different denominations in the United States. The aim of this project was to help prepare theology students with the transition from university/seminary to a congregational setting. It was found that the deep engagement between peers in this programme established a deeply formative experience (Wood 2008:298). Where students come from diverse cultural backgrounds and different denominations in a public university setting, experiencing this community might be more difficult. This is also true of theological training through distance education. Physical as well as cultural and other boundaries may pose a challenge for the communal aspect of spiritual formation. Formal and informal learning of spirituality should take place in the context of shared lives (Naidoo 2011:125). This should happen both inside and outside the classroom. With the academic pressure of finishing a certain amount of work, this 'sharing of lives' becomes problematic. Perhaps not enough attention is given to informal learning as an opportunity for spiritual formation.

Other aspects that also refer to community in spiritual formation, were used by Naidoo (2011:144-145) in her research to assess spiritual formation in institutions. These include: A nurtured sense of community; chapel and worship services for students and staff; recreational/fun activities available for the community, and the ability of the whole community to pray and work together. These community activities not only include 'spiritual aspects', but also non-spiritual social aspects like recreational activities that can foster communion. The social aspect of spiritual formation can also be traced to the Biblical metaphor of the Church as the body of Christ, growing together in faith. Theological institutions should ask themselves: Are enough methods used to foster communion amongst our theology students? A fellowship of faith is "… born out of the matrix of community" (Marty 2008:314). The community aspect of spiritual formation should thus never be underplayed.

The influence of spiritual formation on the pastor in the congregation

A particular sort of spiritual maturity is asked of church leadership – a spiritual maturity that internalised the religious tradition, a theological grasp of the human condition before God, and also some personal qualities where one's spiritual life plays an important role (Naidoo 2010:190). All these form part of the ministerial identity to be formed in the theology student during and after his/her studies. An important role of the minister is to shape a rich communal life in the congregation (Marty 2008:312). For this role, a theology student must be prepared through knowledge, skills and spiritual formation. Forming theological students to become this kind of minister, is a daunting task. Spiritual formation, together with theological study and ministerial practice, play important roles in the developing of ministerial identity (Cahalan 2008:96). What kind of ministerial identity will the student be formed into with a specific kind of spiritual formation (Naidoo 2010:225; 2012b:165)? Where spiritual formation mainly takes place on an intellectual level, the ministerial identity will be more that of a 'scholar pastor'. However, spiritual formation taking place mainly through religious experiences might result in an identity of the 'mystic pastor', whereas focusing on experiencing spiritual formation through practical deeds of faith can give rise to an 'activist pastor' identity.

Theological education should be a dialogue between academy and people of faith, and contribute to the self-understanding of faith communities (Ackerman 2013:6). Where a minister's theological education does not contribute to the self-understanding of faith communities, something went amiss. This can easily happen when a future minister is just prepared academically for ministering in faith communities. A minister trained in only the academic aspects of theology will be challenged to minister to people in a holistic way – addressing their spiritual needs, not only their cognitive need for knowledge. His/her ministerial identity must be formed holistically in order to minister to all aspects of congregation members' needs.

Theological studies inform students' knowledge, shape their skills and also their spiritual life. Stepping into ministry, the pastor brings these aspects with him/her into the congregation. The knowledge and skills gained will influence their sermons, pastoral care, managing of the congregation, and all other aspects of their ministry. However, the spiritual formation that took place during their theological studies will also shape their ministry in more ways than one.

Resources secured through interpersonal attachments refer to social capital, while the degree of mastery of and attachment to a particular religious culture, refers to religious capital (Finke and Dougherty 2002:106). Theology students build relationships with one another, congregations where they participate, institutions where they do practical work (e.g. old age homes, etc.), faculty, as well as relationships with people outside their study circle. In this way they gain experience and acquire social capital that can be useful in their later life. Through constant connection with churches in one way or another, students' attachment to their religious culture is strengthened. Theological knowledge of the religious scripts helps students to 'master' their religious culture. While studying theology, the theology student thus accumulates social and religious capital that he/she takes to the congregation which he/she serves as pastor. Spiritual formation in the sense of 'attachment to religion' forms part of the religious capital that students accumulate. Theological education has a responsibility to build the social and religious capital of the student in preparation for ministry. Where this capital is only scantly built, if, for instance, insufficient attention is given to spiritual formation, an insufficiently equipped pastor is sent into ministry. The pastor will not be able to effectively address the spiritual needs of the members of the congregation due to 'insufficient religious capital'. However, Finke and Dougherty (2002:108) found that the religious capital of the pastor is often distinctly different from that of the congregation. Knowledge and experience gained at the theological institution shape the pastor in ways that might differ from that of the congregation. A church tradition will, therefore, do well to assure that the spiritual formation of their students that is received at a seminary or public university, is in tune with the general spirituality of their tradition.

The growing awareness of the professional misconduct of some clergy (Naidoo 2010:190) has made spiritual formation an even bigger priority for churches. This spiritual formation should take place during theological studies, but also while in ministry, to prevent misconduct amongst clergy. As stated earlier, spiritual formation does not only happen during theological education, but also takes place before and after theological studies. Unfortunately, due to changes like unstable families and less participation by youth in the church, it can lead to the situation where many theology students might not be as well versed as one would expect in their church tradition before they start their theological studies (Naidoo 2010: 190).

Churches have a responsibility to make sure that their future ministers not only receive spiritual formation during theological training, but that they also give ongoing attention to their own spiritual formation. Theological training should equip ministers to sustain their own spirituality. Spiritual formation is a lifelong process to which the minister must attend. Sustained spiritual disciplines in the lifelong journey of spiritual formation should be encouraged for the minister to be a good steward of his/her spiritual formation (Hess 2008:23). The responsibility of the church towards the minister's spiritual formation starts before their theological studies, then continuing as a lifelong responsibility – a responsibility with consequences for the whole church. Examples of this responsibility taken seriously are centres like Communitas, Excelsus and Shepherd, offering courses in the continued development and enrichment of pastors, including their spiritual formation (cf. communitas.co.za; excelsus.org.za; theology.ufs.ac.za).

Conclusion

Spiritual formation forms an important part of theological education. Spirituality is integral to theological construction (Pobee 2010:339), although spiritual formation is not without contention. Addressing the conceptual, institutional, operational and communal issues mentioned above may resolve the queries regarding the spiritual formation of theology students. Conceptually, spiritual formation should be filled with the same meaning for all involved at the same institution. Spiritual formation is not just something for churches to decide, but should be addressed on an institutional level. The 'how-to' (operational issue) of spiritual formation needs to be planned carefully in line with how it was conceptualised. Lastly, emphasising the communal aspect of spiritual formation, interpersonal intimacies between the individual, God, other human beings and oneself, can be developed in order to shape the spirit of the minister-to-be into a person who is well-equipped and ready for the challenges of ministry (Hess 2008:21).

Bibliography

Ackerman, D., 2013. Foreword. In: I.A. Phiri and D. Werner (eds.). *Handbook of Theological Education in Africa. Regnum Studies in Global Christianity*. Oxford: Regnum Books International. xxv.

Astin, A.W., Astin, H.S. and Lindholm, J.A., 2011. *Cultivating the Spirit: How College can enhance students' inner lives*. San Francisco: Jossey-Bass.

Brynjolfson, R.W., 2010. Missionary training and spirituality: Spiritual formation in theological education. In: D. Werner, D. Esterline, N. Kang and J. Raja (eds.). *Handbook of Theological education in world Christianity*. Oxford: Regnum Books International. 196-202.

Cahalan, K.A., 2008. Introducing ministry and fostering integration: Teaching the bookends of the Master of Divinity program. In: D.C. Bass and C. Dykstra (eds.). *For Life Abundant. Practical theology, theological education and Christian ministry*. Grand Rapids, Michigan: William B. Eerdmans Publishing Company. 91-116.

Communitas, 2014. *Communitas*. [Online] Available from: www.communitas.org.za [Accessed: 2 December 2014].

Elias, J.L., 1983. *Psychology and religious education*. Malabar: Krieger Publishing Co.

Emmons, R.A., 2000. Is Spirituality an Intelligence? Motivation, Cognition, and the Psychology of Ultimate Concern. *The International Journal for the Psychology of Religion*. 10(1). 3-26. DOI: 10.1207/S15327582IJPR1001_2

Excelsus, 2014. *Excelsus*. [Online] Available from: www.excelsus.co.za [Accessed: 2 December 2014].

Finke, R. and Dougherty, K.D., 2002. The effects of professional training: The social and religious capital acquired in seminaries. *Journal for the Scientific Study of Religion*. 41(1). 103-120.

Gaikward, R., 2010. Curriculum development in theological education: The case of senate of Serampore colleges in South Asia. In: D. Werner, D. Esterline, N. Kang and J. Raja (eds.). *Handbook of Theological Education in World Christianity*. Oxford: Regnum Books International, Oxford. 263-270.

Githuku, S., 2004. Challenges of theological education in the twenty-first century. In: G. LeMarquand and J.D. Galgalo (eds.). *Theological education in contemporary Africa*. Eldoret, Kenya: Zapf Chancery. 227-236

Glennon, F. et al., 2011. Formation in the Classroom. *Teaching Theology and Religion*. 14(4). 357-381.

Hall, T.W. and Edwards, K.J., 2002. The spiritual assessment inventory: A theistic model and measure for assessing spiritual development. *Journal for the Scientific Study of Religion*. 41(2). 341-357.

Hauwerwas, S., 2007. *The state of the university. Academic knowledges and the knowledge of God.* Malden (MA), Oxford (UK), Victoria (Australia): Blackwell Publishing.

Hess, L.M., 2008. Formation in the Worlds of Theological Education: Moving from 'What' to 'How'. *Teaching Theology and Religion.* 11(1). 14-23.

Kanarek, J. and Lehman, M., 2013. Assigning integration: A framework for intellectual, personal and professional development in seminary courses. *Teaching Theology and Religion* 16(1). 18-32.

Keely, B.A., 2003. Spiritual Formation for Ordained Ministry: An Ecumenical Approach. *Teaching Theology and Religion.* 6(4). 202-207.

Laytham, B., 2010. Let Us Pray: Classroom Worship in Theological Education. *Teaching Theology and Religion.* 13(2). 110-124.

Lowe, M., 2010. A summary of the findings of the study: Assessing the impact of online courses on the spiritual formation for adult students. *Christian Perspectives in Education.* 4(1). 1-18.

Martin, T.W., 2008. Faith in the Classroom: The Perspective of a Pastor Called to College Teaching. *Teaching Theology and Religion.* 11(4). 213-221.

Marty, P.W., 2008. Shaping communities: Pastoral leadership and congregational formation. In: D.C. Bass and C. Dykstra (eds.). *For Life Abundant. Practical theology, theological education and Christian ministry.* Grand Rapids, Michigan: William B. Eerdmans Publishing Company. 306-328.

Mokitimi, S., 2014. *Seth Mokitimi Methodist Seminary.* [Online] Available from: http://www.methodist.org.za/work/education/smms [Accessed: 4 December 2014].

Naidoo, M., 2008. The call for spiritual formation in Protestant theological institutions in South Africa. *Acta Theologica.* 11. 128-146.

Naidoo, M., 2010. Spiritual formation in theological education. In: D. Werner et al. (eds.). *Handbook of Theological Education in World Christianity.* Oxford: Regnum Books International. 185-195.

Naidoo, M., 2011. An Empirical Study on Spiritual Formation at Protestant Theological Training Institutions in South Africa. *Religion and Theology.* 18. 118-146.

Naidoo, M., 2012a. Ministerial formation of theological students through distance education. *HTS Teologiese Studies/ Theological Studies.* 68(2). Art. #1225, 8 pages. [Online] Available from: http:// dx.doi.org./10.4102/hts. v68i2.1225 [Accessed: 2 December 2014].

Naidoo, M. (ed.), 2012b. *Between the real and the idea: Ministerial formation in South African churches.* Pretoria: UNISA Press.

Nguru, G., 2004. Residential and distance approaches to theological education. In: G. LeMarquand and J.D. Galgalo (eds.). *Theological education in contemporary Africa.* Eldoret, Kenya: Zapf Chancery. 237-247.

Palka, J., 2004. Defining a theological education community. In: *International Review of Research in Open and Distance learning.* 5(3). [Online] Available from: http://www.irrodl.org/index.php/irrodl/article/view/197/279 [Accessed: 30 June 2014].

Pobee, J.S., 2010. 'Stretch forth they wings and fly': Theological education in the African context. In: D. Werner, D. Esterline, N. Kang and J. Raja (eds.). *Handbook of Theological Education in World Christianity.* Oxford: Regnum Books International. 337-345.

Scharen, C., 2008. Learning ministry over time: Embodying practical wisdom. In: D.C. Bass and C. Dykstra (eds.). *For Life Abundant. Practical theology, theological education and Christian ministry.* Grand Rapids, Michigan: William B. Eerdmans Publishing Company. 265-289.

Shepherd, 2014. *Shepherd.* [Online] Available from: theology.ufs.ac.za [Accessed: 2 December 2014].

Stellenbosch University, 2014. *Seminarium.* [Online] Available from: http://www.sun.ac.za/afrikaans/faculty/theology/_layouts/15/WopiFrame.aspx?sourcedoc=/afrikaans/

faculty/theology/Documents/Kerklike+Vennote/NGK+en+VGK+Seminarium/Seminarium+Afr+WEB.pdfandaction=default [Accessed: 3 December 2014].

Tolmie, D.F. and Venter, R. (eds.), 2012. *Transforming theological knowledge: Essays on theology and the university after apartheid*. Bloemfontein: SUN MeDIA.

Uniting Reformed Church of Southern Africa (URCSA), 1997. Policy document on theological training. Acta General Synod. URCSA.

University of the Free State, 2014. *Faculty of Theology*. [Online] Available from: http://theology.ufs.ac.za/ [Accessed: 3 December 2014].

Vassiliades, P., Kasseluri, E. and Kalaitzidis, P., 2010. Theological education in the orthodox world. In: D. Werner, D. Esterline, N. Kang and J. Raja (eds.). *Handbook of Theological Education in World Christianity*. Oxford: Regnum Books International. 603-610.

Venter, R. (ed.), 2011. Faith and religion at a public university. *Acta Theologica*. 14. 1-2.

Walvoord, B., 2008. *Teaching and learning in College introductory religion courses*. Malden, Mass: Blackwell Publishing.

Warford, M. (ed.), 2007. *Practical Wisdom: On Theological Teaching and Learning*. New York: Peter Lang. Quoted in Naidoo, M. 2011. An empirical study on spiritual formation at Protestant theological training institutions in South Africa. *Religion and Theology*. 18. 118-146. 123.

Wood, D.J., 2008. Transition into ministry: Reconceiving the boundaries between seminaries and congregations. In: D.C. Bass and C. Dykstra (eds.). *For life abundant. Practical theology, theological education and Christian ministry*. Grand Rapids, Michigan: William B. Eerdmans Publishing Company. 290-304.

Yaghjian, L.B., 2013. Hidden treasures in theological education: The writing tutor, the spiritual director, and practices of academic and spiritual mentoring. *Teaching Theology and Religion*. 16(3). 221-245.

Challenges in moral formation for ministerial training

John Klaasen

Introduction

The formative years of ministers are very important for the sustainability of effective ministry in a transforming society such as South Africa's. The South African nation is not only struggling with the disintegration of a united nation – however limited the unity may be – and with the widening gap between rich and poor, but, more importantly, also with corruption amongst leaders that is spiralling out of control. Shutte (2001:1) sums up the moral vacuum in South Africa:

> In recent time there has been much talk in South Africa of a 'moral vacuum'. Something has gone and nothing has replaced it. Our President and other public figures, religious and community leaders with various outlooks, all express concern at the absence of a moral sense. Increasing crime, callous and often gratuitous violence, corruption in public office and private financial affairs, self-centred retreat into private security, the equally self-centred 'culture of entitlement' or rampant consumerism taking the place of traditional family values – these are some of the things they mention.

The first democratically elected government under the leadership of the late President Nelson Mandela, reacted with the establishment of the Moral Regeneration Movement. "The origins of the Moral Regeneration Movement (MRM) date back to a meeting in June 1997 between former President Nelson Mandela and key faith-based organisation leaders, the then Deputy Minister of Education, Father Smangaliso Mkhatshwa, and the SABC, to discuss spiritual transformation. At that meeting, former President Mandela spoke about the role of religion in nation-building and social transformation, and the need for religious institutions to work with the state to overcome the 'spiritual malaise' underpinning the crime problem."[13] Since its official launch, the MRM has had various national and regional events to address the scourge that was threatening the moral fibre of the South African nation. The results of this movement is difficult to measure, as corruption is still rife, violence is escalating, the gap between the rich and the poor is at its worst since the birth of democracy, and abuse of power is common practice.

Division, materialism and greed are not limited to government officials or corporates, but is also prevalent amongst church ministers. Child abuse, financial scandals, substance abuse, abuse of power, and extra marital affairs are some of the serious moral issues that

---

[13] Moral Regeneration Movement. *The history of the Moral Regeneration Movement*. Viewed on 31 August 2014, from http:www.mrm.org.za/index.php?option-com_contentand view=articleandid=1219@itemid=592

have confronted the Church in post-apartheid South Africa. The landscape of ministry has shifted drastically since the dawn of democracy. Communities are disintegrating, societal structures are changing, traditional societal roles are shifting, and social problems are increasing in both types and levels. For the most part, these problems have become the concern of the Church and, to a large extent, that of those in Christian ministry. The church community is part of society and is exposed to the same moral challenges as other communities.

Moral formation is important if the South African society wants to overcome the increasing moral failures of leaders and the broader members of society. Christian ministers are not exempted from the moral decay in society. To a large extent they are regarded as part of the custodians of the moral fibre of society. For many the restoration of society and the moral vacuum that is evident in the South African society since the dawn of democracy, is even further complicated by the lack of moral leadership by church ministers. The lack of moral formation of ministers makes the moral task of ministers more difficult.

The problematic issue addressed in this chapter is whether church ministers are receiving the necessary moral formation to do effective ministry, and whether these programmes are adequate. To put the question differently, one may ask whether the theological training at universities and colleges provides the kind of moral leaders that are associated with Christian ministry. To answer these questions, I will firstly give a brief overview of what moral formation is and engage with the two dominant approaches of moral education. These two approaches give rise to contestations that are both within the conceptualisation of moral formation, and the institutions of training and formation of ministers. The contestations refer to the use of abstract reason as a meta-narrative in the teaching of moral formation, as well as the practice thereof. The individual (as autonomous rational being) and the self (as social being) are another contestation that I will address. The third contestation is about the absence of community within the curricula, and the distance of the theological institution from the Church as moral community. The final contested issue is the lack of ethical leaders that can serve as mentors for ministers.

Understanding moral formation in a society characterised by a moral vacuum, moral plurality, and a society undergoing transformation, has its challenges, to say the least. I will highlight important issues rather than prescriptions, since moral formation of ministers at universities and seminaries is a complex process. In addition to the complexity of the nature of moral formation, is the South African nation with its manifold diversities and pluralities.

Since 1994, the curricula for the training and formation of ministers changed from the narrow Christian approach of theology to the broader religious approach. Archbishop Ndungane, the former archbishop of the Anglican Church of Southern Africa, challenged the curriculum for Anglican ministers and caused reform within the curriculum of The College of Transfiguration (1998:113):

The way in which we develop theological formation must not only give attention to the multiplicity of expressions of our Christian faith, but also to the importance of *ubuntu* and the dominance of African traditional religion in the region, and the growth of eastern faiths such as Islam and Buddhism. We also cannot ignore the presence of other faiths such as Judaism and Hinduism.

Another example is found in the formation and training of ministers at the University of the Western Cape. The change at this University is partly because the Faculty of Theology has been incorporated into the Faculty of Arts or the Departments of Humanities. At the University of the Western Cape, the once vibrant Faculty of Theology amalgamated with Biblical and Religious Studies to form a Faculty of Religion and Theology in 1995. In 2000, this Faculty underwent another transformation due to drastic decline in student numbers in the whole university, and became a department within The Faculty of Arts. This, in turn, resulted in a change in the approach towards the teaching of ethics, since the overwhelming majority of students are from other departments and other faculties. At Stellenbosch University, where training and formation for ministers is still within the Faculty of Theology, the shift has been less drastic. This shift in training and formation intensifies the tensions between the approaches of moral formation of ministers within a context such as South Africa where moral degeneration amongst secular and religious leaders and the broader society is worsening. Instead of trying to present a comprehensive approach towards moral formation, which is beyond the scope of this chapter, I hope that the ideas rather than solutions will contribute to a more effective approach towards moral formation and training of ministers.

Moral formation: The use of reason and individual freedom

Moral formation can be explained by two complementary terms, namely ethics and morality. These are so closely related that they are sometimes used interchangeably. Ethics is a branch of moral philosophy and is defined as "rational inquiry into how to act and how to lead one's life" (Pojman 2005:xv). Unlike social sciences and the humanities which deal with the question of how life is lived, ethics asks the more important question, namely how we ought to live our life. Whereas social sciences and the humanities are descriptive, ethics is a normative enterprise (eds. Johnson and Reath 2004:1). Notwithstanding the importance of reality with regard to how people actually live, the main aim of morality is to give direction to moral conduct and responsible decisions. Ethics has two sides, namely ethical theory and applied ethics. One side is the theoretical aspect (ethical theory) which deals with theories about the good life, what is right or wrong, and what is appropriate or inappropriate. The other side of ethics (applied ethics) deals with moral problems such as euthanasia, abortion, the death penalty, war, and affirmative action. Practice and theory goes hand in hand (Pojman 2005:xv-xvi).

How do I make the right, appropriate, or responsible decisions? What is right, appropriate or responsible must be substantiated with reasons. The Greek roots of reason date back to Plato's theory of human nature. Plato explains human nature as that which is the essence of being human. And that which is the essence of being human sets human beings aside from other living beings. Reason is the one quality that is both common to all human beings, and sets human beings aside from animals (Shutte 2001:37-38). Plato's student, Aristotle, built on this theory and came up with the idea that ethics is the theory of how to live or develop our full humanity. The implication that we can draw from Aristotle's theory, is that if reason is the core of what it means to be human, then living in accordance with reason would be the most satisfying and fulfilled life (Shutte 2001:39).

Reason, as a system of morality, has reached its climax in the fifteenth century with the philosopher Rene Descartes. Descartes' famous argument, *dubito ergo cogito, cogito ergo sum* (I doubt, therefore I think; I think, therefore I am), became the catalyst for what it means to be human (Shutte 2001:45). Another modern attempt to argue for the normativity of reason for moral formation, is Immanuel Kant's 'Copernican revolution'. Kant argued that knowledge is not something that was caused from outside of the human being, but was part of the human being. Since every human being has the capacity to reason and since reason is the source for a fulfilled life, rational decisions and actions are judged to be good (Shutte 2001:46).

Good decisions and right actions are supported by logical and persuasive reasons. If an action cannot be rationally supported it is accepted as wrong or inappropriate. The consequence of rational action can be applied universally or beyond the boundaries of the person. What is rationally supported is right for you as much as it is right for me. "People who engage in oral inquiry and discussion of ethical questions do say what they believe. But they are expressing the beliefs that they think are best supported by reasoned argument, and believe that the reasons that persuade them to accept these conclusions should be rational for others as well" (eds. Johnson and Reath 2004:2).

When we apply this theory to religion it raises the question about the role of Christianity in the process of determining what is right or wrong. We could argue that when we apply reason to Christianity we conclude that, since reason is part of the nature of human beings and every human being has the potential to free itself through natural means, God and Christianity is not essential for the freedom of the person. This means that the individual does not develop through a predetermined pattern of behaviour, that of the supernatural, but rather through the ability to perform abstract reason.

The Enlightenment, as a project of modernity, has elevated rationality to a position of superiority. Van Huyssteen (1999:2) observes that, "We are indeed the children of modernity, and the often stellar performances of the sciences in our time have again managed to elevate this mode of human knowledge to a status so special and superior that it just had to emerge as the paradigmatic example of what human rationality should be about."

Coupled with reason is the centrality of the individual. The distinctiveness of the individual was a clear breakaway from the Medieval period characterised by tradition, the authority of institutions, and a sacral worldview (Shutte 2001:43). The Modern period made the individual the centre of everything and in control of everything. "Society was now seen as made up of atom-like individuals, and politics was the study of the forces necessary to form them into a harmonious whole" (Shutte 2001:44).

Individualism refers to the "moral emotions, motives, attitudes, virtues, or decisions of the individual function as the springboard for reflections on moral education" (Van der Ven 1998:21). This can mean three things. Firstly, the individual takes its own perspective and experience as the starting point for moral reflection. Secondly, the individual can be observed without attachments to any outside authority, which is typically the approach by Kant. A third and probably combined view has to do with the individual's spiritual or material needs (Van der Ven 1998:22).

This breakaway from the Medieval period to the Modern period spilled over into the Church. The authority of the pope and the Church was questioned by reformers such as Luther and Calvin. Luther rejected the notion that Christians are bound by external works or authority for their salvation. The individual does not have to pray through the priest or find absolution in the authority of the priest. The individual has direct access to God. Wogaman (1993:111) makes this analogy to illustrate Luther's ethics:

> Luther might agree with an analogy drawn from educational experience. We do not become educated by virtue of receiving good grades; we receive good grades as an effect of becoming educated. Education itself – which occurs within us – is primary; evaluation by our teachers is secondary. While bad grades may goad us into greater effort, what really counts is our love of truth and our faith in the possibility of knowledge.

Transmission as mode of moral education in universities and seminaries

Van der Ven (1998:182) describes seven modes of moral education. The first kind of moral education is in the form of discipline. This is usually in the case of a child who internalises habits through reciprocal and open communication with parents. The second approach, socialisation, like discipline, is also a form of informal education. Socialisation is the internalisation of values and norms of a community. A third approach is called the 'cognitive development' which refers to education as development, "… in which development is seen as passing through a sequence of three levels, each consisting of two stages, beginning with the concrete and specific principles and moving to more abstract and inclusive ones" (Van der Ven 1998:182). The fourth approach, the clarification approach, emphasises the process of how people come to value what they experience and to act on those values (Van der Ven 1998:182). The fifth approach is about emotions as a vehicle to come to what is good and right. Van der Ven's (1998:379) own approach, the sixth one, is called 'education for character'. Van der Ven's approach is defined as based on the three-way interrelatedness of passions, goods, and reasons, as we learn from the ancients, especially Plato and Aristotle. Then this interrelatedness must be interpreted from the perspective of interactionism between person and situation. This interactionism, being linguistic in nature, has to be understood in terms of its narrative structure.

The seventh approach of Van der Ven (1998:379) is transmission which applies to educational institutions like colleges and universities. Here the teacher transmits the values, which students might know, to the students on two levels. The first level of transmission is on the level of the curricula which is prescribed, and forms part of the official teaching material. In the university, school and seminary curricula, the notions of morality, individualism and reason have been the norm. Where ethics is taught as a major or elective to students of theology, rational theory forms part of most approaches to morality. Transmission is the process whereby unconscious rules, laws and moral assumptions – that form the basis of moral formation – are taught by the teacher and intentionally received by the student. This intentional learning makes it possible for the student to use the basis of moral formation in different situations and contexts (Van der Ven 1998:126).

This educational approach to moral formation usually consists of a set of propositions and conclusions that is widely accepted as the norm. The content is found in uncontested documents such as doctrines, canons and texts which interpret the primary sources. These can include accepted commentaries that have reached authoritative status by the particular community or group (Van der Ven 1998:129). The content is also given authority through organs such as synods, councils or religious leaders (Van der Ven 1998:130). The goals of transmission are threefold: cognitive, affective and volitive. Cognitive goals on the level of developing knowledge are the memorising of the values, rules and laws that have been transmitted. Cognitive goals involve four qualities, namely comprehending, applying, analysing and syncretising. Affective goals include motivation and attitude development. The volitive aim is to bring the student to such a point where the will is used to uphold the value propositions in both the personal and social life (Van der Ven 1998:131-132).

The second level of transmission as a mode of moral education, is rationality. In addition to the above forms of rationality described, there is also the kind of rationality that uses the values in different moral traditions to determine which become substantive (Van der Ven 1998:136). In this instance the different traditions are compared in order to determine which of the values can be taken as normative. This form of reasoning raises the questions, by what criteria do we select the traditions, which traditions, and why? Another form of rationality that can be added to the above forms refers to procedural rationality. The determining factor here is to decide what procedural principle the tradition is linked with. The question is, to what extent does tradition acknowledge the autonomy of a specific kind of rationality? The difficulty with this approach is to decide which rationality to use in the process (Van der Ven 1998:137).

While transmission is widely used in tertiary education as a form of moral formation, there are – due to moral plurality – some serious questions with regard to the appropriateness of this form. The various Christian traditions also contribute to the difficulties that arise from transmission as a mode of moral formation.

Contestations in moral formation of ministers

The first contestation links directly to the question, which reason should be taken as normative? The formation of ministers at universities must take the superiority given to reason, as a meta-narrative approach in the transmission of values, seriously. In the context of South Africa with its social challenges and moral problems, the moral formation of ministers must take cognisance of the limitation of the rational approach in ethics. In this country's context, morality is more complex than the mere application of substantive, procedural or abstract reason as a meta-narrative approach. How one comes to moral decisions, moral judgments, and ethical decisions cannot be adequately determined without taking the history of South Africa seriously. Separate development and race classification resulted in the loss of human dignity and basic human rights. Historical facts, events, persons and periods are important for moral decision-making, judgments and moral formation. These phenomena impact on the present and how the future is shaped. The experiences of colonialism in a pre-apartheid South Africa as well as the apartheid era itself contributed to the current worldview of plurality of truths, practices and morality in a post-apartheid South Africa.

Reason is not only scientific, though this has become the norm amongst those who use reason for moral formation. Another type of reason, namely practical reason, is a more appropriate use of reason for moral formation of ministers in a society characterised with moral plurality. Practical reason is the critical engagement with or reflection on experience. Reason becomes only one of the factors for determining what is right and wrong, appropriate and inappropriate, good and bad. "This prudential process makes syllogistic reasoning open, dynamic, and flexible. It does not prevent prima facie ideas, intuitions, and emotions, which clearly condition concrete problems in concrete situations, from coming into play" (Van der Ven 1998:150). For example, in the South African context one needs to consider the level of poverty when assessing whether or not stealing and violence is a means to an end. If someone steals to feed their family, or reacts with violence as a result of a violent socialisation, one should consider the role given to the circumstances of the specific person with regard to the stealing or the violence.

Practical reason does not reject principles for moral formation. However, principles on its own are insufficient for moral formation of ministers who regard tradition(s) as an important tool for their formation. By principles I mean a set of rules or laws that predetermine how one gets to what is right or wrong or good or bad. It can usually be used in different contexts. When such principles are used as a means of moral formation, it borders on indoctrination and prescription. Practical reason, on the other hand, engages with the experience of each situation or community or tradition as an authentic partner in moral formation. Differences are tolerated and taken into account, and through open dialogue, peaceful co-existence of moral plurality is possible (Klaasen 2012:115).

Unlike abstract reasoning that is deterministic and isolated from traditions and concrete experience, practical reason takes into account the plurality of religious traditions, experiences, and beliefs of the ministers. The prospective minister does not come to the university as an empty vessel, but with a wealth of knowledge (informal) and experiences that impact on their own moral formation as well as on those in their pastoral care. While tradition, experience and beliefs do not determine moral formation, they engage with principles, laws and moral propositions in a critical way in the formation of ministers.

Ministers must acknowledge the situation in which they find themselves. By 'situation' I refer to their emotional state. The upbringing of ministers, their past and their narrative all play a significant role in their leadership. Erickson's (1980) stages of moral formation show that one's earlier years determine the kind of relationships with others which, in turn, influence the virtues that one upholds. Instead of holding on to abstract rational theories about rules or utility, non-rationalism is as important for the leader to be morally sound and virtuous in its execution of leadership. Moral leaders make an effort to discover the self and accept who they are. Moral leaders do not seek affirmation through coercion or domination, but serve with integrity and sometimes unpopularity.

The second contestation relates to ministers being caught up between what it means to be an individual and what it means to be part of a community. According to Alasdair MacIntyre, the compartmentalisation of the self is one of the most devastating effects of abstract reasoning. MacIntyre (1981:204) claims that any attempt to view human life as a whole, has social and philosophical difficulties:

> The former is the tendency to think atomistically about human action and to analyse complex actions and transactions in terms of simple components… Equally the unity of a human life becomes invisible to us when a sharp separation is made either between the individual and the roles that he or she plays.

Communitarian ethicists are amongst those who were influenced by classical figures such as Aristotle (1962) and Aquinas (1928), as well as more contemporary scholars such as Richard Niebuhr (1941) and James Gustafson (1975). Alasdair MacIntyre (1981) and Stanley Hauerwas (1983) are two of the contemporary ethicists who affirm the critique of contemporary philosophical ethics and the alternative that the community is important with regard to both methodological and social ethical questions. This approach points out the weaknesses of individualism and argues that the community is central for moral formation. The individual does not live isolated from other persons, and moral formation takes place in an interdependent relationship with others. Instead of the autonomous individual of modern ethics, the community becomes the harbinger of morality.

Moral formation of ministers happens within a community, and the formation and training process must take the community serious for effective ministry. Ministers are not just social beings; they are part of a specific community with a specific history, and are, furthermore, characterised by definite virtues that differentiate the community from other communities. When they adopt a distorted view of who they are, for example as merely individuals connected for certain purposes, they fail to respond to the need of the other and ultimately fall into sin. When the minister trusts the other to challenge him/her, character is formed. In other words, the other becomes the initiator of character.

One of the most significant resurgence in the theological landscape, has been the focus on the Trinity. There is a renewed interest in the reciprocal relationship of God as the Father, Son and Holy Spirit. This focus has also spilled over to critical engagement about what it means to be human. Does being human mean to be a person with a mechanical nature, or does it refer to being made in the image and likeness of God? The former refers to the modern, independent individual, while the latter refers to personhood in a relationship. To be in a relationship means to be inter-dependent. Moral leadership means to be faithful to the Christian moral code to love your neighbour as yourself. At the heart of personhood is self-sacrifice, grace, respect for the other, and humility.

The third contestation with regard to moral formation of ministers at tertiary institutions, is the lack of involvement of the Church as part of the formation process. This conflict has come about partly because of the theoretical orientation of moral formation at universities, which resulted in the distance between the Church (as moral community) and the tertiary institution, as well as the shift in moral formation within the Church's ministerial formation processes. With regard to the latter, this is as a result of a move away from a comprehensive formation process, as found in residential training to non-residential training and distance learning.

For centuries, training was exclusively centred on the model of the Middle Ages, where priests lived in community for the whole duration of their training and obeyed a monastic spirituality characterised by work, pray and service. Training was not without tensions, caused by the formalisation of orders. Although persons were trained in community, their local community did not have the authority to affirm or confirm their calling. Formal 'orders' began to emerge with the closer relations of the Church with the Roman Empire (Gill 1990), and in the Medieval period, this formalisation took its most rigid character. Schillebeeckx (1990:82) argues that the "Third Lateran Council of 1179 and the Fourth of 1215 were the occasions of fundamental change, whereby men were ordained without being put forward for ordination by a particular community." This was a diversion from the early Patristic view of the minister, when the community could lay claim to ordination.

This process of ordination, characterised by medieval legalism and feudalism, had serious ramifications for ordained ministers. Ordained ministry became a status symbol instead of service to the community. The minister was separated from the laity with absolute authority. Ministers were able to misuse their position in society without meaningful accountability. The misuse of authority resulted in immoral acts that could hardly be challenged by the laity who have, by then, become subordinate to the ordained person. Such notions of priesthood led to the questioning of the calling and vocation of those set aside for ministry and contributed to the Reformation (Gill 1990:83).

With challenges such as escalating costs, the growing number of married candidates for ministry, non-stipendiary ministries, and curriculum changes at universities, traditional training became less practical. While the community, through the parish council or church board, has a role in the initial discernment process, the authority to ordain resides with the bishop, board or council. For example, in the Anglican Church in Southern Africa, the worshipping community is part of the initial stage of discernment. The candidate first approaches the local priest, who after some informal discernment discusses the intentions of the candidate with the parish council. The parish council writes to the bishop, recommending the candidate to be considered for the official discernment process. Although the parish council "does not decide on the progress of the candidate, their support can help the broader church with the discernment of a call on the person" (Klaasen 2012:56). Until the candidate is ordained, the worshipping community does not have any authority in the rest of the discernment process. At ordination, the worshipping community merely witnesses the authority of the bishop.

The lack of community is not only in the discernment process, but also in post ordination. Because of the medieval paradigm of ordination that is prevalent in many processes of ordination, clericalisation is still a major problem for effective ministry. The canon law of many denominations is used as the justification for the legalistic formulations of relationships between clergy and laity, as well as bishops and clergy. These relationships are expressed in hierarchical forms and place the ordained in a class above the laity. This separation is contrary to the early Church's acceptance of the equality of all the baptised and that all the members of the community are ministers by virtue of their baptism. It is perhaps not community per say that is lacking, but the self-appointed position which the clergy occupies in relation to the rest of the members. The lack of community in the training and formation of ministers subsequently results in dissociation and irresponsible moral decisions and actions.

The status that is associated with ministry can become a gateway for abuse of power, whereby the minister has complete control over the ministry that God initiated and which the community affirmed. This leads to corruption, all kinds of abuse, and negative autocracy. Ministers become an authority unto themselves when they take on a position isolated from the community who affirms their calling from the very early stages of their discernment process. Good moral leadership is reflected in the model of leadership that is exercised by the leader. The shepherd-sheep model is usually associated with the leader taking on a superior role and the ecclesia a submissive one. This usually results in clericalism. On the other hand, ministers – who view their calling as part of the body, yet distinctive in nature – take on a Body of Christ approach. Within the Body of Christ, the minister exercises particular gifts within the context of the gifts and skills of the church community. From a moral perspective the minister treats the congregation as equals and fellow ministers within the mission of God.

Suggested ideas for effective moral formation of ministers

The curricula of universities and theological colleges should aim to balance abstract reason and practical reason, in addition to the individual and the communal within moral communities. About this, Gill (1989:64) says:

> Pointing out the importance of moral communities in fashioning and sustaining values in our society, need not become an excuse for irrationality. It is rather a claim that individual, isolated rationality is quite simply, in it, an insufficient resource for a profound morality. Moral communities without the critique of rationality can become tyrannical, arbitrary and perhaps even demonic. But atomised rationality without moral communities seems incapable (despite many attempts) of fashioning and sustaining goodness beyond self-interest.

The eighteenth century emphasis of the centrality of the individual for moral formation has taken on a universal significance. Freedom is perceived as the extent to which the person is independent from outside forces such as tradition and institutions. The individual is atomistic and is the source of his/her own freedom. On the other hand, the individual is part of a community and cannot be isolated from others in the community. The self cannot be understood apart from its social roles and attachments.

Ministers ought to guard against the status attached to ministry that was evident in the Medieval period. It is this notion of ministry that has allowed ministers to act legalistic 'canonised' (Gill 1990:82). This interpretation of the authority of ministers contributes to the abuse against the vulnerable members of the community and the structures and procedures of the institution.

The university curricula should also take cognisance of the role of the family and society in the formation of ministers. Moral formation is not restricted to rules or principles, but the influence of the family through socialisation, which is another way of transmitting values and forming character. Coupled with socialisation – by entities such as the family – is the important role of the media, especially social media, in not only contributing to moral formation, but also in transmitting values. However, it has both positive and negative aspects when it comes to transmitting values, and while social media is beneficial for easy access of information, it still carries with it some dangers. The media should be used as a critical tool of moral formation.

Conclusion

Ministers are confronted with the challenges evident of the Medieval period as well as modernity. Feudalism and legalism can lead to dissociation from the community. It can also lead to ministry being a status rather than being a service to the church community and society – or being a calling by God and not by any earthly structure or authority (council or bishop). The community, through its communitarian nature, forms the minister into a morally responsible human being who has a common humanity with other selves within the community as well as with those beyond.

Universities and theological colleges must make the community of learning an important role player in the academic curricula of those being formed for ministry. Curricula will be enhanced when consideration is given for the correlation between various modes of moral formation. Therefore, moral plurality and different traditions should form part of the content of such curricula.

An example of moral leadership is found in one of the most humble Christian leaders in contemporary South Africa, Archbishop Emeritus Desmond Tutu. Lombard (2014:15) writes of him as:

> His leadership was transformative, it was definitely a form of servant leadership, it was inclusive and affirming of his co-workers, but it also had a much disciplined side to it, including prayer and meditation and real dedication to the task. He trusted people to do their own thing, he could delegate various tasks, but importantly decided to write his own sermons, speeches and letters, and he spent much time writing to South African leaders (the 'enemy'), whom he approached on the basis of their own faith commitment, bringing in the moral dimension of politics and whatever the issue was … Tutu's leadership rested on a vision and understanding of God's dream for humanity, and thus rested not on managerial gimmicks, but on deep spiritual roots, including his belief in the power of the resurrection (coming from the Community of the Resurrection), but also fed by his strong belief in what Khoza calls African Humanism or *ubuntu*.

Bibliography

Aristotle, 1962. Ostwald, M. *Nicomachean ethics*. 1099a, trans. Indianapolis: Bobbs-Merrill.
Aquinas, T., 1928. *Summa Contra Gentiles*. New York: Benziger.
Erikson, E.H., 1980. *Identity and the Life Cycle*. New York: W.W. Norton.
Gill, R., 1989. *Competing convictions*. London: SCM Press.
Gill, R., 1990. Theology and ordained ministry. In: D.B. Forrester (ed.). *Theology and practice*. London: Epworth Press. 81-92.
Gustafson, J., 1975. *Can ethics be Christian?* Chicago: University of Chicago Press.
Hauerwas, S., 1983. *The peaceable kingdom*. London: University of Notre Dame Press.
Johnson, O.A. and Reath, A. (eds.), 2004. *Ethics: Sections from classical and contemporary writers*. Belmont: Wadsworth.

Klaasen, J., 2012. Ministerial formation in the Anglican Church of Southern Africa. In M. Naidoo (ed.). *Between the real and ideal: Ministerial formation in South African Churches.* Pretoria: Unisa Press. 48-62.

Klaasen, J., 2012. Open ended-narrative and moral formation. *Acta Theologica.* 32(2). 103-124.

Lombard, C., 2014. *Desmond Tutu's style of ethical leadership.* Paper delivered at the launch of the Desmond Tutu Centre for Spirituality and Society at the University of the Western Cape, 2 December 2014.

MacIntyre, A., 1981. *After Virtue: A study in moral theory.* London: Gerald Duckworth and Company.

Moral Regeneration Movement, [n.d.]. *The history of the Moral Regeneration Movement.* [Online] Available from: http:www.mrm.org.za/index.php?option-com_contentand view=articleandid=1219@itemid=592 [Accessed: 31 August 2014].

Ndungane, N., 1998. Theological education in the last fifty years. In: J. Suggit and M. Goedhals (eds.). *Change and Challenge: Essays commemorating the 150th anniversary of the arrival of Robert Gray as first Bishop of Cape Town (20 February 1848).* Marshalltown: CPSA. 107-115.

Niebuhr, R.H., 1941. *The responsible self.* London: Macmillan.

Pojman, L.P., 2005. *How should we live? An introduction to ethics.* Belmont: Wadsworth.

Schillebeeckx, E., 1990. *Church: The Human Story of God.* New York: Crossroad.

Shutte, A., 2001. *Ubuntu; An ethic for a new South Africa.* Pietermaritzburg: Cluster Publications.

Van Huyssteen, J.W., 1999. *The shaping of rationality: toward interdisciplinary in theology and science.* Grand Rapids, Michigan: William B. Eerdmans Publishing Company.

Van der Ven, J.A., 1998. *Formation of the moral self.* Grand Rapids, Michigan: William B. Eerdmans Publishing Company.

Wogaman, J.P., 1993. *Christian ethics: A historical introduction.* Kentucky: John Knox Press.

Relations between Church and training institution: A symbiotic association?

H. Mvume Dandala

Introduction

The type of relationship which exists between the Church and theological institutions as training centres for ministers, will in one way or the other portray the quality of ministerial leadership that results both in the kind of congregations that emerge as well as the service that the Church renders to its communities. This, therefore, raises an important question on the kind of relationship that needs to exist between the Church and the theological training institutions which train ministers as leaders for the Church. In no way will the theological training of ministers have relevance and meaning to the ever-changing South African context unless church denominations and training institutions are in a collaborative relationship on the nature of ministerial formation and critical thinking required to equip their ministers. The training institutions cannot theologically train ministers without an awareness of what the expectations of their denomination are and how the Church itself identifies with the changing needs of the communities it serves.

It is envisioned that through collaborative engagement, denominations and their theological institutions are of one mind as to what service the Church should render – both to their communities of faith and their social context. Just as the thinking of the Church impacts on or shapes the thinking of a theological institution, so should the thinking of a theological institution impact the thinking of the Church. It is certainly difficult for theological institutions to train leaders who can be innovative in ministry when what is being modelled by the denomination and its decisions are not open to change. Thus, theological institutions can easily be accused of producing misfits. It is in this way that ministerial formation becomes an integral part of theological and pastoral training. The relationship that exists between the denominations and their theological training institutions should, therefore, be a symbiotic one – held together within the tensions of what ministerial formation for their particular denominations must look like on the one hand, and the necessity of critical inquiry on the other. This partnership often creates tensions and contestations – be it by the church denomination that makes recommendations to the theological training institution, requiring conformity, or the theological training institution with its own priorities. This chapter, therefore, outlines the unique relationship between the Church and its respective theological training institutions, using the Pietermaritzburg Cluster of Theological Institutions as an example. This chapter explores the tensions that develop, highlighting attempts towards new partnerships and how these relationships impact on ministerial training.

The unique relationship between Church and seminary

Most theological training institutions in Africa have adopted an ecclesial trend where their origins can be traced back to a particular denomination. This trend, in most cases, has not only informed but also greatly influenced the character and nature of these institutions. This pattern of relationship is not only unique for African church-seminary relations, but seems to be a method also accepted in the West where most theological schools were established as ministerial training centres. Emphasising this kind of relationship in the United States context, Weber (2008) shows how theological institutions were founded by denominations, reflecting the particular emphasis of such denominations. According to him, this kind of relationship between theological institutions and their establishing communities is, in the context of education, exceptional only to theological schools (Weber 2008:65):

> Most theological schools continue in some pattern of relationship. There is no parallel in other forms of graduate professional education. Law schools were not founded by courts or legislatures or law firms. Medical schools were seldom founded by hospitals ... Theological schools have a one-of-a-kind relationship with communities that established them.

Although times have changed, the traditional relationship between Church and seminary still holds strong. Some churches have continued their theological training in public institutions, while others have opted to establish or continue with their private institutions. In both instances the intention is unwaveringly that of "the training of their professional leaders, people who will both profess the faith in fresh ways and function as professionals, i.e. display the skills and competencies appropriate to their calling" (Stortz 2011:374). What is obvious, according to Stortz (2011), is that the constantly changing social landscape demands newer approaches to such training if the faith has to continue to make sense. Stortz (2011:374) further argues that the Church has to understand that "church leaders of the 21st century need training in a number of additional disciplines as well." This has to be inextricably linked to how a denomination understands the new challenges imposed by new contexts. In this case, both private and public institutions have something to offer towards training for ordination purposes. However, the critical factor becomes that of the relationship between the denomination and the theological institutions concerned.

As early as the 1960s, Louisell and Jackson (1962:751) noted that universities originated within the fold of the established Church in the Middle Ages as extensions of the medieval church schools. What remains evident from this observation is that while these institutions were not intended for ministerial training by their nature, they brought theology as a discipline into the arena of intellectual discourse, resulting in inevitable individual critical theological inquiry. With this in mind, Phiri and Nadar (2011:81) have argued that "faith and religion can and must be exposed to academic scrutiny, and the best place for such scrutiny is the public university." This evidently means that a religious faculty of theology in a public university should be viewed as having minimal creedal and character formation intentions for its students when compared to a seminary or a Bible school. In this sense the intention of a university is, therefore, to cultivate critical scholarship and make sure that students learn without a particular creedal or behavioural formational requirement being 'forced' upon them. This may or may not always coincide with what a particular denomination is looking for in the formation of its clergy. When a church seeks to impose this on a university, it compromises the primary purpose of a university. In such cases, the relationship between church denominations and the religious faculties of theology in public universities become strained and, in most cases, remains on a feeble edge.

In South Africa, for example, during the Apartheid era, some universities promoted specific doctrinal and character formational positions informed by their political weight and persuasion, thus compromising the academic independence of those universities. Therefore, it is not unfounded to suggest that church denominations often intend to have a direct doctrinal influence on their theological training institutions. This trend was evident in faculties of theology in public universities. For example, up to the year 2000, the Dutch Reformed Church (DRC) in South Africa in a certain way regarded theological training at the universities of Stellenbosch, Pretoria and Bloemfontein as their 'own', focusing on the training needs of the DRC.[14] The teaching staff at these institutions had to be members of the DRC and were appointed by the DRC in collaboration with the university. With the recent drive towards transformation in higher education, all theological faculties had to become ecumenical faculties in order to give theological students a broader exposure to different church traditions. In the case of these 'reformed' universities, a 'curatorium' (ministerial formation focus) pays special attention to reformed students by offering 'church-owned' modules which are operated separately from the university programmes at the cost of the DRC. Hence, the ability of theological institutions to freely exercise critical thinking and inquiry within the denominational confinement, demonstrates – to some extent – the nature of the relations which exist between the Church and theological institutions.

Weber (2008:85) questions how theological institutions understand their task, inquiring whether they exist to produce theological scholars or to provide the Church with ministers for ordination. It thus becomes of vital importance to consistently ascertain the relationship of the Church with its theological institution – especially when it comes to theological education and ministerial formation. McCarthy (2004:176) notes that what leads to a deepening connection between the Church and a theological institution, is when theological schools begin to correct the 'missing connection' between the faith of the Church and the critical inquiry component in the mission of training institutions. It is within this described tension between faith formation and critical inquiry about that faith,

---

[14] Information provided in conversations with Dr Flip du Toit on 11 December 2014, who is the Director of the Centre for Ministerial Development of the Dutch Reformed Church at the University of Pretoria, South Africa.

that the Pietermaritzburg Cluster becomes an example of a 'network' model for offering an ecumenical approach towards ministerial formation and theological education.

The Pietermaritzburg Cluster Model

The Pietermaritzburg Cluster of Theological Institutions (hereafter simply referred to as 'the Cluster') was founded in March 1990.[15] The Cluster was originally founded by an association of three partner institutions, namely the Saint Joseph's Theological Institute and the then School of Theology of the University of Natal (now forming part of the School of Religion, Philosophy and Classics of the University of KwaZulu-Natal) together with the Federal Theological Seminary of Southern Africa. Since 1994, the Cluster has had additional institutions seeking membership, which has included the Evangelical Seminary of Southern Africa (ESSA), the Lutheran Theological Institute (LTI), and the Seth Mokitimi Methodist Seminary (SMMS) as the current members of this association.[16] As stipulated in the declaration of intent, it is clear that the Cluster has a public commitment to the ideas upon which it was first founded. Central to this commitment, is the fact that the member partner institutions shall support and strengthen one another in their common task of educating and equipping people for Christian ministry in the Church of South Africa.

The Cluster, therefore, stands as a reminder of the centrality of ecumenism in the mission of the Church. In its Declaration of intent, the Cluster Constitution states that "the changed and changing needs of the Church and society in Southern Africa require the constant renewal of the models and methods of theological education, and a careful analysis of social, economic and political structures in the light of the Gospel."[17] With this awareness, the strongest asset for the Cluster is the capacity it has to bring different denominational traditions together for common theological reflection and ministerial formation with the richness of critical inquiry in an ecumenical setting. In this case, the institutions in partnership not only enjoys ecumenical support from member denominations involved in the Cluster, but also the involvement with those churches of partner institutions.

The Cluster also has a commitment to seek and develop models and methods of preparing people for an incarnational ministry which meets both the needs of the Church and the society in which the Church exercises its prophetic, pastoral and serving roles. The Cluster creates a space for the sharing of resources in the form of opportunities for team-teaching amongst lecturing staff, sharing of library resources, possibilities of joint publishing ventures, and research opportunities. Central to ministerial formation needs are the quarterly Cluster

---

[15] http://www.sjti.ac.za/strat_alliance_cluster.htm
[16] Each participating institution in the Cluster is autonomous and has its own credo, its own denominational and ecumenical links, its own ethos and style. The Cluster seeks to enhance the richness and the diversity which each institution brings to it - http://www.sjti.ac.za/strat_alliance_cluster.htm.
[17] http://www.sjti.ac.za/strat_alliance_cluster.htm - the Cluster Constitution approved by the Cluster Council on 23September 1994.

worships from the various traditions represented within the Cluster institution partners. The most unique feature of the Cluster is that while six of the partners are institutions set up by denominations, the seventh, viz. the school of Religion, Philosophy and Classics, forms part of a public university. The Cluster has the potential to expose its students to various forms of critical inquiry. This immediately affords the Cluster an opportunity to explore the extent to which its member institutions could have access to the other disciplines that are needed for critical inquiry, as well as a more expanded approach to ministering. The institutions within the Cluster have an opportunity to reflect together on suitable theological and pastoral responses to social, political and economic challenges of their context, thus laying the foundation for a common approach to dealing with the challenges typically facing South African Christianity. They also have an opportunity to engage with different spiritual traditions as they participate in devotional gatherings of the different denominational member institutions. Formation, to the Cluster, thus means an encounter in the lecture room, in the chapel and in the community, as well as social life within the Cluster. Students are exposed to and formed in a diverse ecumenical context which is envisioned to aid them serve more effectively in an ever-changing pluralistic, post-apartheid South African context.

In the context of nation-building in South Africa, it may, therefore, be argued that there seems to exist an overriding challenge to the churches to offer a ministry that responds to the need for social healing from the effects of apartheid. This requires an approach to ministry that focuses on building healthy relations between people and groups, as well as enlarging the capacity to constantly critique the evolving socio-political context. The latter can be better achieved within an ecumenical approach to theological training and ministerial formation. This then calls for strong relations between theological institutions and church denominations. The doctrine of apartheid essentially maintained that one's identity could only be affirmed within the context of separateness and not within a context of diversity (Motlhabi 1984). The Church, together with its theological institutions, should consistently challenge the aftermath of such a history – both in its faith expression and in its ecumenical lifestyle. In the current situation this makes a strong case for caution where the separateness of denominations is concerned. Since the demise of another ecumenical initiative, such as the Federal Theological Seminary (Denis and Duncan 2011), traditions are moving back more and more into a denominationally-based ministerial formation focus in their theological training. It is in this context that the Cluster remains a noteworthy model for theological education as denominations and theological institutions develop viable relationships, focusing both on critical inquiry and ministerial formation within an ecumenical space.

Potential tensions between Church and theological institutions

The relationship between the theological institutions and denominations may be best upheld when there is greater clarity on issues such as the right and power of the denomination to intervene and cut short a programme of a theological training institution if the theological institution defines itself out of the denomination's formational agenda. The demise of the Federal Theological Seminary points to this need (Gibbs 2014:82-83). When the terms of reference are not clearly defined, the chances of destructive conflicts are enhanced. The common understanding is often merely that the theological training institutions prepare leaders for the Church, without much clarity given on the extent beyond which the seminary may go in its theological innovation and leadership. The mission of the seminary in Alexandria, for instance, as it prepared leaders for the Church, seems to have sought to produce leaders who would delineate specific space for the Church within the context of competing philosophies (Malaty 1995:9). Finkenwalde, on the other hand, sought to produce leaders whose depth of faith was of such a nature that they would stand up to the Church and the State whenever faith was compromised – even by the Church itself (Zimmermann and Smith 1973:107). The Federal Theological Seminary sought to form ministers who would not succumb to the dictates of apartheid.

The major concern that should be pertinent for both Church and seminary relations, regards the denomination's readiness to commit resources to the theological institutions and its formational cause. Some key issues which require consideration in this regard include teaching faculty, finances, and sharing of other available resources such as properties. Churches usually equip the denominational seminary with qualified teaching faculty. On the other hand, as His Holiness Aram 1 (2000:150) observes, in spite of the multiplicity of our traditions, "there can be no churches (in the plural) except as manifestations of the one true Church." Overall, as much as denominational institutions are of teaching staff from within the tradition, they should still remain open to other traditions so as to ensure that a theological institution remains a faithful custodian of the truth with regard to the ecumenical unity of the Church.

An area of strained relations often leads to the question, who must appoint the theological institution faculty? Should the theological institution be allowed space to make its own appointments, or should these appointments be the responsibility of the denominational church? One is inclined to call for independence for a theological institution to build a staff component that will be faithful to the mandate the Church has given with its mission in mind. However, in this regard, space should be allowed for the engagement in robust but mutual conversations with the denominational church.

The same principle which applies to staffing the theological institution should apply to the financial relationship between a theological institution and the denominational church. While the denomination is the primary investor in the theological institution, it is also aware that the theological institution is governed by principles of truth seeking, critical thinking, and unwavering adherence to such truth. Financial, property and staff appointment policies should, therefore, be of such a nature that a theological institution is never put in a situation where its faithfulness to its calling is undermined or compromised by resource dependence. This point of financial dependence on denominational churches creates tremendous tension in terms of vision and mission, and eventually impacts on the quality of ministers being trained.

Theological institutions as catalysts for creative ecclesiology

If theological institutions are going to be effective in driving a process of formation that must indeed be wholly transformative of the Church, they cannot but see the need to address the training of the lay leaders of the Church as equally central to their task. Otherwise this becomes a prescription for serious tensions between the ordained and the laity. Kritzinger (2010) takes the process of ministerial training beyond a focus merely on those being prepared for ordination. Kritzinger (2010:211) argues, "By ministerial formation I mean the holistic formation of church members for ministry." In the light of this observation, His Holiness Aram 1 (2000:150) notes that, "Churches everywhere are called to witness to the Gospel," and for that reason, "Christian formation of laity remains a continuing priority for the churches." Sound relations between the denominational church and a theological institution rest on the level to which the laity understands the mission and purpose of the theological institution and their commitment to the same. Those who are being formed for the ministry need to be nurtured into a spirit of the inseparability of the laity and the clergy. In its practical sense this means that the theological institutions cannot be adequately prepared for the ministry of the Church outside daily encounters with the experiences of its people.

A conscious effort to develop the meaning and application of Christian beliefs for a particular context is an important route to follow in the process of formation. The question of Christian values and how they relate to contemporary socio-political and economic experiences is part of the struggle that must characterise the process of formation in theological training institutions. This struggle in itself is not new, as theologians like Karl Barth and many in the tradition of the Confessing Church demonstrate (see Villa-Vicencio 1988). There is always a possibility of conflict in the relations between the Church and the theological training institution as a place of testing established theological positions. The theological training institution must, therefore, constantly weigh denominational positions against the stringent requirements of the scriptures, while, at the same time, passing these on to the future church leaders without necessarily requiring conformity. In this case, the theological training institutions should be understood as the essential intellectual interlocutors of the Church. They drive theological and ecclesiastical discussions, as well as help formulate lasting Christian values and doctrines of the Church.

Historically, theologians have often been leaders in driving such discussions, including the likes of Martin Luther (1517), John Wesley (1738), and many others in their times. Such great teachers have throughout the history of the Church helped to refine its thoughts in the light of challenges encountered within the context of the growth of society and the Church itself. However, this has not always been a readily welcomed intervention by the Church, which has shown different levels of tolerance – from outright rejection and isolation, to reasonable tolerance – in requiring conformity to what the Church referred to as 'orthodoxy'. In our own South African context it took courageous theological thinkers, like the Rev. Beyers Naudé, to challenge the Dutch Reformed Church to abandon its divisive ecclesiology (De Gruchy 1979:81). Younger theological institutional teachers like Desmond Tutu and Simon Gqubule at the Federal Theological Seminary, Manas Buthelezi at the Maphumulo Lutheran Seminary, Basil Moore of the University Christian Movement, and Allan Boesak at the University of the Western Cape, not only pursued this thinking, but brought it within the domain of the theological institutions. It is in such a context that De Gruchy (1986:154) asserts that "the supporting churches felt uneasy" about such developments. The question that arises is whether or not a theological seminary can offer a safe space for critical inquiry within tensions of conformity and formation. The challenge is to ensure that the relationship between church and theological institutions withstands such legitimate tensions.

The effectiveness of a theological institution has to do with the strength of its theological innovation, its capacity to understand the challenges of the moment, and its ability to integrate these into its processes of formation rooted in the experiences of its people. Thus, the theological institution becomes a place where men and women process their faith for an effective ministry of the Church in its society. If the theological institutions are the places where the ministry of its future leaders are formed and developed, formation cannot be done outside the need for building bridges between the thinking of a theological institution and the denominational churches as to where they stand on major theological and/or socio-political issues at any given time. Two alumni of the Federal Theological Seminary, the Rev. Stanley Sabelo Ntwasa in his time – both as organising secretary of the University Christian Movement (UCM) and student at the St Peter's Anglican College in 1971 – and the Rev. Stanley Mmutlanyane Mogoba, are examples where the positions of a theological institution and that of the churches diverged. Mogoba, as an 'unstationable' probationer minister of the Methodist Church of Southern Africa, was 'shunted' to the seminary by the Methodist Church of Southern Africa because the Church could not find a station for him where the security police would leave the Church in peace (Molomo 1998:33). Some of the leaders of the Methodist Church were questioning the value of accepting a candidate for ordination whose presence within the fraternity of the ordained would attract the unwanted attention of the state security apparatus. The seminary, on the other hand, recognised his potential as a minister of the Church, and after intense dialogue with the denomination opened its doors to him. Ntwasa found the strength for his ministry with the UCM from the bold support he was offered by the St Peter's Anglican College under the Rev. Aelred Stubbs, when some of the ordained clergy who were supporters of the radical black theology, like the Rev. Basil Moore, were being eschewed by their denominations (Molomo 1998).

A matter raised by Denis and Duncan is apt and gives way for further reflection. With regard to the Federal Theological Seminary, Denis and Duncan (2011:4) posit the question: "Were the constituent churches genuinely committed to ecumenism when they established the

Federal Theological Seminary in 1963?" This question could be seen to probe the extent to which a denominational church gives thought to the kind of formation it has in mind and which it desires the theological institution to promote. This question with regard to the Federal Theological Seminary, may be viewed as being prompted by hindsight, thus calling for a process that should interrogate the earlier discussions of the constituent churches when they took the decision to establish the Federal Theological Seminary. It leaves one curious to know whether the formational intentions of the denominational churches were properly discussed, agreed and documented. In that case, one would want to know whether they included plans for an eventuality of a breakdown of relationships between the churches and the seminary.

John Mbiti (2013), in a similar vein, makes a telling observation in the evolution of the indigenisation of the Church in Africa. In his foreword to the *Handbook on Theological Education in Africa,* Mbiti retells how a few of them, as teachers of theology in Africa, were pioneers in interrogating African life and culture in the 1950s and early 1960s "… to stammer about 'Theologia Africana,' when the Church which had been in Africa for more than a hundred years, had not even begun to seek to feel the authentic African pulse" (see Mbiti 2013:xv). It has taken a titanic power struggle for theological institutions to be seen as more than a means of spiritual domestication by the churches. Theological institutions are not, and should never be allowed to be, mere vehicles of processed and packaged views of the denominations for uncritical spiritual consumption by the theological institutions. This would be a violation of the primary calling of theological institutions as cradles of formation. Having said this, the process of theological training and formation should be a continual one. It is essential that denominations develop systems whereby their students are exposed to the priority emphases of their churches before they come to the training institution. This enables them to reflect meaningfully on their theological formation and ministerial priorities. It becomes equally important for the denominations and the training institution to formulate processes by which ongoing formation is maintained, even after theological school or seminary.

The fact that theological institutions are also places of theological innovation and catalysts for creative ecclesiology, is precisely the area where the vulnerability of the Church often shows. On the whole, denominations tend to be comfortable with defined and tested theological and social positions, and uncomfortable with new theological innovations. Denis and Duncan (2011) observe that the products of the Federal Theological Seminary changed the tone of the witness of the Church after 1976 through greater robustness in their opposition to racial and ethnic segregation. For instance, with the Methodists it was at a conference held in Pietermaritzburg in 1976 after the Soweto massacre, during which black Methodist ministers under the leadership of an alumnus of the Federal Theological Seminary, the Rev. Ernest Nkatazo Baartman, refused to allow the conference to proceed with its original agenda, forcing it to address the crisis at hand. The tension between nominal and radical commitment to fighting apartheid had come to a head. It expressed itself as a collision between a sedately anti-apartheid church and a radical young clergy formed in a seminary. As things stood, Baartman was prepared to weigh the demands of scriptures in a radical manner against the demands of the existing status quo (Molomo 1998). Currently, issues that call for reflection, like HIV and AIDS as well as those of same sex relations, have taken central focus in the discussion about the ministry of the Church. Such issues have to be engaged with honestly, especially considering theological reflections and tempered emotions that are given to disciplined and rigorous intellectual inquiry and prayer. Theological training institutions have to lead this discussion even when the sponsoring churches have not yet engaged them. It thus becomes important to build a rapport between the denominations and theological training institutions, as it will allow commonly agreed values and goals to be central to relationships between them.

The impact on ministerial training

Andrew Walls (2013:4) uses the Catechetical School of Alexandria that "offered a 'rich mixture' of intellectual and religious activity" as an example of a good working model of the process of formation. He asserts that the process of formation at the Catechetical School of Alexandria was so formative that it became the basis of the Church's theological system, ensuring the "'continual development of Christian thinking and Christian understanding' in the context of many other philosophies and religions" (Dandala 2013:68). In this case, this process "sought to 'build the faculty of discrimination' in the students", where the students were equipped with the ability to discern that which is of value from that which is not (Dandala 2013:68). This established clarity about the Church's own self-understanding, as well as the understanding of its mission. The self-understanding of the Church, in turn, must inform the self-understanding of the seminary as an agent of the same mission as that of the Church. In this case the propagation of a Christian faith in the context of other contending ideologies becomes the primary mission informant for both Church and seminary. The task of the seminary, therefore, becomes that of equipping the seminarians to service a mission response that the Church has embraced, while at the same time helping the Church itself to improve and refine its own mission thinking.

In addition, ministry internships and church placements should also become central to cementing Church and theological institution partnerships. Internship for practical ministry and exposure ceases simply being a place where the skills for ministry are honed. Rather, it becomes a nurturing exercise for a healthy relationship between the minister and the Church, as well as the theological institution. It affirms and recognises the legitimate role that both the Church and the training institution play in this mutual work of forming ministers. In this case, practical training and internship both become important aspects in helping the Church as well as theological institution decide on which competencies they would like ministers to develop. In this way, they both become helpful collaborators in ministerial formation.

Just as the local Church has to keep its arms open and understands itself as an equal player in this process of formation for ministry, the seminary also has to fulfil its own obligations toward the formation of lay leadership. This is not a call for the seminary to stretch itself beyond its mandate. Rather, it is to recognise that the work of ministerial formation reaches far beyond what happens within the walls and confines of the seminary to a live encounter with the Church, and this work is incomplete without such an encounter. This cannot be achieved when relations between the Church and the seminary are not satisfactory. Thus it is essential that Church and seminary consciously nurture collaborative spirit and practise to intensify mutual theological and ministerial formation.

Conclusion

Healthy relations between Church and seminary form a critical basis and foundation for the seminary to fulfil its obligation to produce well-formed ministers of the Gospel, firmly rooted in their tradition, fully cognisant of the unity of the Church, and passionate about the mission and ministry of the Church. These have to flow from what seminarians have learned in class, experienced in chapel as well as in the field. They have to be undergirded with a strong and well-developed capacity for spiritual formation and intellectual inquiry. Both the Church and the seminary have to affirm the legitimacy of this approach. The integrated nature of this human development targets the intellect (forming the mind), the spiritual (forming the heart), and the practical (forming the moral character and skill). It leads to theological competence that marks the ordinands as capable practitioners and leaders of Church and society. The efforts of the Church and those of the seminary as training partners should, therefore, produce a process that balances "the integration of the cognitive, practical and professional apprenticeships in educating clergy" (Naidoo 2010:352). The goal must be to initiate change for a lifetime of ministry that seeks transformation of society. In order to achieve this, a symbiotic relationship between the Church and the seminary as ministerial training partners needs to be firmly established.

The trust relationship between the Church and seminary has to be worked on regularly in order for their relations to provide an acceptable environment in which formation can blossom. When these two bodies are on the same side, united in their common call and with their relations matured enough to accommodate diversity, their work together can only thrive.

Bibliography

Aram, I., 2000. *In Search of Ecumenical Vision*. Lebanon: Armenian Catholicosate.
Dandala, M., 2013. Purpose and Method in Theological Training and Clergy Formation in Africa: A Perspective. In: The College of Transfiguration (ed.). *From Root to Branch: Colloquium on Theological Education*. Held on 7-9 August in Grahamstown. Grahamstown: The College of the Transfiguration. 68-74.
De Gruchy, J.W., 1979. *The Church Struggle in South Africa*. Cape Town: David Philip.
De Gruchy, J.W., 1986. *Cry Justice!: Prayers, Meditations and Readings from South Africa*. London: Collins.
Denis, P. and Duncan, G., 2011. *The Native School that caused all the Trouble: A History of the Federal Theological Seminary of South Africa*. Pietermaritzburg: Cluster Publications.

Gibbs, T., 2014. *Mandela's Kinsmen: Nationalist Elites and Apartheid's First Bantustan.* Johannesburg: Jacana Media.

Kritzinger, J.N.J., 2010. Ministerial Formation praxis in the United Reformed Church in Southern Africa: In Search of Inclusion and Authenticity. *Missionalia.* 38(2). 211-234.

Louisell, D.W. and Jackson, J. H., 1962. Religion, Theology, and Public Higher Education. *California Law Review.* 50(5). December. 751-799.

Malaty, T.Y., 1995. *Lectures in Patrology: The School of Alexandria.* Jersey City: St Mark's Coptic Orthodox Church.

Mbiti, J., 2013. Forward. In: I. Phiri and D. Werner (eds.). *Handbook of Theological Education in Africa.* Pietermaritzburg: Cluster Publications. xv-xvii.

McCarthy, J., 2004. Deepening Connections between the Church and the Theological Schools: Implications for theological Education. *The Journal of Adult Theological Education.* 1(2). 175-183.

Molomo, L. R., 1998. *Rev. M S Mogoba.* Cape Town: Revelation Desk Top Publishing.

Motlhabi, M., 1984. *The Theory and Practice of Black Resistance to Apartheid: A Social-Ethical Analysis.* Johannesburg: Skotaville Publishers.

Naidoo, M., 2010. Ministerial training: The need for pedagogies of formation and of contextualisation in theological education. *Missionalia.* 38(3). 347-368.

Phiri, A.I. and Nadar S., 2011. 'The Personal is Political': Faith and Religion in a Public University. *Acta Theologica.* 14. 81-94.

Pietermaritzburg Cluster of Theological Institutions, 1994. *The Constitution.* Pietermaritzburg: Cluster Publication.

Stortz, M.E., 2011. Re-Imaging Theological Education for the Twenty-First Century: 'What Has Theological Ed to Do with Higher Ed?' *Dialog: A Journal of Theology.* 50(4). 373-379.

Villa-Vicencio, C. (ed.), 1988. *On Reading Karl Barth in South Africa.* Grand Rapids, Michigan: William B. Eerdmans Publishing Company.

Walls, A., 2013. Theological Education from its Earliest Jewish and African Christian Beginnings – Some Currents in the Wider History of Christianity. In: I.A. Phiri and D. Werner (eds.). *Handbook of Theological Education in Africa.* Pietermaritzburg: Cluster Publications. 3-12.

Weber, T.P., 2008. The Seminary and the Churches: Looking for New Relationships. *Thelogical Education.* 44(3). 65-91.

Zimmermann, W., 1973. Finkenwalde. In: W. Zimmermann and R. Smith (eds.). *I Knew Dietrich Bonhoeffer.* London: Collins Clear. 107-112.

PART 3

NEW DEVELOPMENTS

ENTREPRENEURIAL LEADERSHIP TRAINING AND THEOLOGICAL EDUCATION

CHRIS L. DE WET

Introduction

With the rise of the information age and the expansion of social media platforms, our society has experienced vast changes within very short temporal intervals. This wave of rapid sociocultural and economic change has serious implications for the Christian Church and theological education. One of the major consequences of these global shifts for the Church relates to an aspect at the very core of Christian identity – the pastor. Perceptions of who and what a pastor should and should not be, are more diversified than ever, which has important implications, in turn, for theological education. One model that has developed to immense popularity, is that of the pastor being an entrepreneurial leader. This chapter investigates the concept of the entrepreneurial pastor (and what I will call 'entrepreneurial pastoralism'[18]) and its implications for ministerial training, which has been a highly contested matter for some time. As we will see, entrepreneurial pastoralism draws heavily on secular business models that place an emphasis on visionary leadership. Many seminaries, universities and churches have a difficult time warming up to this emphasis, noting that it lacks theological integrity in its approach – and in our context of poverty, this blatant show of materialism is inappropriate. However, in the midst of the general discomfort there appears to be a growing recognition amongst mainline denominations that they need to pay more attention, theologically, to the issue of leadership. Hence the need for a discussion of this nature.

This chapter will unpack factors that may have contributed to the formation of entrepreneurial pastoralism, mainly focusing on churches from the Pentecostal-Charismatic tradition. It also explores the implications of entrepreneurial pastoralism for theological education in South Africa, noting some challenges and caveats as well as opportunities for training ministers. However, before proceeding with this agenda, it is necessary to briefly qualify the notions of the entrepreneurial pastor and entrepreneurial pastoralism. To a certain extent, the appellations seem self-explanatory – the entrepreneurial pastor is a church leader who leads and manages a church, fundamentally incorporating principles of business leadership and managerialism along with traditional pastoral principles. While this may be an oversimplification, for the sake of argument I will juxtapose entrepreneurial pastoralism with 'traditional' pastoralism, i.e. those manifestations of pastoralism not incorporating and centralising a business or corporate philosophy in their theological

---

[18] The concept of pastoralism (and pastoral power) is analysed by Foucault (2009:135-254), who views it as an early form of government in the West. Pastoralism denotes a form of governmentality where social systems are governed by a (mostly Christian) shepherd-flock model.

praxis. Of course, we may argue that many churches and pastors are already entrepreneurial to a certain extent, since most Pentecostal-Charismatic churches have to be economically viable in order to exist. Thus, to make a distinction between this general occurrence of business and financial management in churches, I refer to entrepreneurial pastoralism as a paradigmatic ecclesiology and poimenology that not only incorporates principles of business management, but also centralises these principles and models within the very core of its communal identity and ministerial philosophy. Entrepreneurial leadership and management are not simply meta-values within entrepreneurial pastoralism – they are, in fact, central and normative in all respects, and become a prerequisite for participating in the ministry and other operations of the Church.

The rise of the entrepreneurial pastor

It stands to reason that this new type of pastor did not develop in a vacuum – the change of pastoral identity was the result of several factors working simultaneously to influence the very nature and operation of Christian identity. One could certainly add many other factors to those I will note here, but for the sake of brevity and focus, I will only discuss those that I believe were crucial in facilitating this change. Firstly, there is the force of globalisation, especially in the Southern Hemisphere, where churches are now challenged by rapidly changing socio-political contexts that call for a more holistic approach in terms of ministry and ecclesiastical identity.[19] Although the symbolic inertia of the Christian pendulum is thoroughly directed to the South, Christianity's response to globalisation and changing social trends and needs will determine the strength and duration of the vector of Christianisation in the South. The result is that many churches have experienced unprecedented growth in both their numbers and influence, giving rise to many mega-churches developing even in middle-class suburban and impoverished areas. Globalisation, however, also translates into dramatic demographical changes. South Africa, in particular, has been subject to such changes (Chopra and Sanders 2004). In the transition from apartheid to a free democratic state, there were two fundamental alternatives in South African economic policy that was taking shape, namely the ANC's policy of "growth through the redistribution of wealth," and "a neoliberal approach with a streamlining of state functions and expenditure, privatisation and deregulation of the financial sector. It was envisaged that this would lead to growth through the attraction of foreign direct investment and redistribution would occur through the 'trickle down' of wealth" (Chopra and Sanders 2004:156). However, as Chopra and Sanders (2004:153-174) also note, these economic policies, which were adopted to make South Africa a player in the global market, had some very unforeseen and unfortunate circumstances, namely increases in poverty and inequality. Moreover, due to social pressures such as these, as well as the prominent position of religious discourse in society, there has also been an influence

---

[19] For an excellent overview and case study of the implications and effects of globalisation in South Africa, see Hart (2002).

from religion and theology on the part of business (Marty 2004:31-52). The influence is, therefore, multi-directional, and not only directed towards theology and the Church.

There is also a second factor to this entrepreneurialisation of the pastorate, which is directly related to the rise of the information and technology age, namely the rapid deindustrialisation that is taking place in urban areas. This is especially the case in South African urban areas. The result is that many suburban areas that were located slightly outside of industrial zones became highly impoverished. It was notably the case in industrial areas, for example, surrounding Cape Town (Crankshaw 2012), and also in the Ekurhuleni metropolitan area, on the East Rand of Johannesburg (Barchiesi and Kenny 2002). What does this mean for churches in those areas? Many smaller, traditional congregations suffer from these changes since their member base, and hence their financial situation, often deplete rapidly as people move away seeking work, or their member profile changes dramatically (Offutt 2010:16-19). This was a common occurrence after the fall of the apartheid regime, when traditional 'white' suburban areas became integrated (Barchiesi and Kenny 2002:35–52). Such changes come with great pressures for the leadership of the churches. It means that, on the one hand, there are some very large mega-churches developing in suburban areas, and, on the other, smaller congregations being placed under considerable ministerial and financial pressure. Furthermore, the divide between rich and poor also increases, as we have noted above. Many pastors have to take on secular occupations since churches can no longer support them in a full-time capacity, placing much strain on ecclesiastical leadership structures and personae. One may thus find the case of a large and particularly wealthy church (by comparison to smaller congregations) with a very polarised membership base – some being far less economically disadvantaged than others (Veerkamp 2008:198-204). An example of this is Alberton Lewensentrum (ALS), located in Alberton on the East Rand. A highly successful and rapidly growing church, its membership basis being predominantly white Afrikaans-speaking people, this church has grown from a very small group to a mega-church with several campuses on the East and West Rand, as well as in the Vaal Triangle. Although its strength lies in its support from white middle-class membership, it is very much involved in major social welfare and upliftment projects for surrounding disadvantaged communities. ALS is a church that is modelled on entrepreneurial pastoralism. Yet one of the many challenges that churches like ALS face, is remaining relevant to impoverished communities without appearing to be materialistic (from its growth, wealth and success) and paternalistic. Another church that also faced major changes and bifurcations in its demographic, is Rhema Church in Randburg. It moved from being an all-white church in the 1980s, to becoming predominantly black (Offutt 2010:16).

Thirdly, the tide of materialism and its responsive proliferation of managerialism and business education, also played a major role in this shift to pastoral entrepreneurialism.

More broadly speaking, this is a consequence of the intensive neoliberalism[20] that characterises some parts of South African society, and another inference of globalisation (Hart 2002:17-49, 304-310). Neoliberalism has received much (due) criticism from theological scholars, like Veerkamp (2008). Despite this, the neoliberal tide sweeping across South African ecclesiological praxes is potent (Goldberg 2009:245-376). Many churches function as corporate organisations that need to be both socially relevant and economically viable while adhering to practices of good governance and responding to a very wide and intensive social mandate of community engagement (not only based on evangelisation and soup kitchens, for instance). It is also in this sense where the idea of social entrepreneurialism comes into play. Pastoral entrepreneurialism is not only one that proliferates business strategies, but it is also firmly set on social development and outreach (Volkmann et al. 2012:69-72). It has forced both the micro- and macro-congregations to take principles of business leadership and management seriously (Kennedy 2004:81-93). Smaller assemblies need to devise other strategies for surviving financially (not only based on member contributions), while mega-churches become so large that they require to be managed like medium-sized corporations. Entrepreneurial pastoralism is, therefore, not a phenomenon limited to macro-congregations. One of the other side effects of this change in ecclesiastical structural dynamics is the professionalisation of lay ministries (Cady 1993:119-146; Frahm-Arp 2010). Especially in mega-churches, there exists a tendency to personalise and professionalise certain ministry portfolios in the church, for instance music, finance, technical issues, welfare, marketing, and counselling. Larger churches can now afford to employ people specialising in these fields and pay them salaries that are highly competitive, as is the case with ALS. Smaller assemblies tend to do the same, only using the expertise of its membership on a voluntary basis (Weideman 2008).

Finally, and in my mind this is perhaps one of the most important and significant factors, is the critical change in the cultural fabric of society. In a very influential essay published in *Philosophy Now*, Alan Kirby (2006:34-37) suggests that postmodernism is 'dead and buried', and perhaps with it, postcolonialism, as the rising number of political revolutions suggests (Dabashi 2012). It does not signify a failure in the mandate of postmodernism, but, in fact, it is reminiscent of its success. Postmodernism was defined in its very essence as a movement that challenged and resisted dominant social discourses – however, it stands to reason that in its final days, postmodernism itself became a dominant social discourse (Gutting 2013:133-148). Once postmodernism became that dominant social discourse, it slowly also consumed and negated itself – but the jury is still out on with what it is being replaced. Some have used the terms 'post-postmodernism' or 'metamodernism'. Although the candle is still burning on the name of this logical inference of postmodernism, its effects are all too clear. It signals significant changes in how we view many of the

---

[20] Neoliberalism is a type of economic liberalism that favours free trade and an open market system, advocating small and medium-sized businesses, in which privatisation occupies a central role – the private sector plays a more active part in this economy than the public sector. Profit and economic growth are its guiding principles (Chomsky 2011).

fundamentals of our reality; it is introducing new epistemologies, thereby changing the very nature, structure, and dynamic of knowledge; new spatialities – 'space' and 'place' is no longer a constant, and the defining characteristic of these new geographies is mobility. Social identity has become something that is representational, and the old existentialist desire for authenticity has somehow returned, albeit in a different garb. Architecture, art, social media, and spirituality, to name but a few, are experiencing a rebirth and reimagination in the wake of this change in cultural productivity. The development of entrepreneurial pastoralism falls within this new metamodern renaissance. Not only are church leadership structures looking different, church buildings are also starting to look different. An excellent example would be the architecture of Mosaïek, a mega-church on the West Rand of Johannesburg (Basson 2008), which does not only center on a large auditorium, but has a smaller chapel catering for people who prefer smaller, more intimate gatherings, a community centre, etc. Often the physical architecture says something about the leadership architecture of the church. Many churches make use of e-architecture in their ministry and outreach, for instance eKerk ('e-Church') (Niemandt 2007:542-557).[21]

All these changes have led to a change in the very DNA of the identity of the 'church' and the 'pastor.' We are perhaps even witness to the end of traditional pastoralism in some Christian movements, not without resistance and critique, of course, and the rise of entrepreneurial pastoralism. However, what were the main influences that made entrepreneurial pastoralism so popular in South African Pentecostal-Charismatic movements? Who contributed so dearly to the formation of this theology (or perhaps ecclesiology) of entrepreneurial pastoralism?

The development of a theology of entrepreneurial pastoralism

The tenets of entrepreneurial pastoralism are, of course, not monolithic. Moreover, due to the complex nature of entrepreneurial pastoralism, its criticisms are also varied. There are numerous theories of leadership and, in most cases, the different currents I will identify here utilise different theories. My interest is rather in those presuppositions behind the assumption of a leadership model, especially in relation to its secularity (or sacrality) and socio-cultural assumptions. Stewart (2008:301-318) provides a good overview and critique of the various leadership theories that are popular amongst churches – she especially lists charismatic, transformational, and servant leadership, although others, like systems leadership (Armour and Browning 1995) and 'authentic' leadership (Goffee and Jones 2006) are also common. These different leadership models do not function in isolation – they are in most instances combined in church organisation.

The categories delineated here are not static, but in flux – the different streams flow in and out of each other, some overlap and other show opposition, and they also

---

[21] Churches making use of e-architecture are churches that do not necessarily have physical spaces in which they meet – these communities are often semi- or fully online and operating in virtual worship spaces. For an excellent analysis, see Hutchings (2007) and several essays in Campbell (2013).

inform one another. Thus many characteristics in these different streams will be shared characteristics, which essentially make them entrepreneurial. My focus will be on both their continuities and discontinuities, and those characteristics that define a certain stream more particularly than another. The purpose of this section is to give a sketch of the development of entrepreneurial pastoralism, especially as it influenced South African Pentecostal-Charismatic movements. Typically, the influences are predominantly North American.

The first stream is what may be called 'classical entrepreneurial pastoralism'. Historically speaking, this division is characterised by the work of John Maxwell, although he did have some precursors like Robert Schuller. Maxwell especially popularised leadership training in ecclesiastical circles. Maxwell started writing in the late 1980s, although his writing gained momentum in the decades following. Some of Maxwell's books, like *The 21 Indispensible Qualities of a Leader* (1999), have sold over a million copies, and have become popular in both church and secular contexts. The popularity of Maxwell's books is related to their claim to be universally applicable in most leadership contexts. Although Maxwell himself started out as a pastor, he has become very popular in non-ecclesiastical circles. The book mentioned above has no scriptural references and very little practical examples related to church leadership. Some of his other books, however, do apply themselves to ecclesiastical contexts (Maxwell 1996). Maxwell has obviously received much critique from ecclesiastical circles, notably about the 'secular' nature of his works and models (Howe 2003). This is a problem in general for many Christian movements – to what extent is it appropriate to import secular business principles into the Church (Stewart 2008:313-317)? There have been, however, many authors after Maxwell who use his principles and apply them specifically to ecclesiastical contexts. Andy Stanley, for example, applies many of Maxwell's leadership principles in the management of an assembly. Stanley's work is a good example of the popularisation of the concepts of vision and mission in ecclesiastical concepts. Stanley's popular book entitled, *Visioneering* (2005), highlights the importance of visionary leadership for church ministry. Yet Stanley uses numerous examples from the world of business, and also writes his book for the Christian business leader and pastor. Rick Warren's *Purpose Driven Church* (1995) also falls within the category of using credible business principles in church ministry.

We then have the charismatic stream that is especially influenced by currents of so-called prosperity theology and televangelism. Leadership and financial management are also very important features in this stream, although it will look very different than classical entrepreneurial pastoralism. Whereas the former manifestation tended to also reach out into secular contexts, this stream aims to fix itself firmly within conservative Pentecostal-Charismatic identity. Authors in this group include T.D. Jakes (2014), Benny Hinn, etc. There is a very characteristic theology present in this stream – one that tends to be more biblicistic and fundamentalist than classical entrepreneurial pastoralism. In the South African context, the works of Joyce Meyer have become increasingly popular. Although Meyer also comes from this grouping, she has managed to craft her own, very distinct identity that has become very appealing to South African Christians, especially women. The title of one of her more popular books on leadership shows a clear departure from the secular-sensitive writing of classical entrepreneurial pastoralism – *A Leader in the Making: Essentials to Being a Leader after God's Own Heart* (2008). Similarly, the works of Joel Osteen (2013) have also become very popular. Both Meyer and Osteen, and others in this stream, have also not been without criticism, especially from conservative American evangelical movements (LeMay 2012). In South Africa, this group has especially shaped Rhema Church's philosophy of ministry.

Finally, there is a very popular group of authors who have formulated a postmodern and neo-orthodox entrepreneurial pastoralism – this is an approach that is less secular-oriented than classical entrepreneurial pastoralism, yet also less confrontational and fundamentalistic than the currents inspired by prosperity theology. The model of leadership and ministry that this group promulgates has been described as 'seeker-sensitive' and 'missional', with an emphasis also on public theology (Dreyer 2006:1311-1335). It should be noted that many of the authors mentioned above, like Stanley, Warren and Osteen, could also fit in very comfortably into this category. However, the authors that especially stand out in this regard are Bill Hybels, Leonard Sweet and Brian McLaren. These three authors have been very influential also in South African contexts, all of them having visited at one time or another one of the South African mega-churches – their philosophy has been very influential in the identity formation of the Mosaïek church. Hybels was especially influential in the emerging period of this group (Stewart 2008:301-302). He is senior pastor of Willow Creek Community Church in Illinois which also hosts an annual leadership summit that is widely attended. The principle of missional Christianity features extensively in Hybels' work, in which the mission and outreach field is brought closer to home and universalised to include all Christians, not only pastors, evangelists and missionaries (Hybels and Mittelberg 2008). Hybels' later work on leadership do, however, show similar traits to that of Maxwell (Hybels 2009). Leonard Sweet's work became popular in its call for the Church to become more receptive to the societal and cultural changes and challenges that it faces (Sweet 1999), with similar but perhaps more conservative work also being done by George Barna (2011). Brian McLaren (2004), on the other hand, is a very prominent voice in the so-called Emergent Church, a branch of neo-orthodoxy in which the leadership style has a very strong focus on inclusivity, missionality and participational spirituality.

These categories are somewhat superficial in that many of them overlap one another broadly and extensively. The purpose here was to note emphases, discontinuities and dissonances within the varied voices of entrepreneurial pastoralism. Several South African Pentecostal-Charismatic movements adopt some voices from all of these currents, while others are more dominantly influenced by one or two of the groups. The problem we face, specifically for theological education, is two-fold. Firstly, as is evident from the discussion above, most of the prominent literature on the subject has developed from grass-roots level of church activity, with many of the books being classified as popular rather than academic reading. There is, therefore, a great need for a critical stance and approach when it comes to these groups of literature. Secondly, we also see that there is not one ideal model of the entrepreneurial pastor, but rather a kaleidoscope of models and epitomes that differ from context to context, and church to church. It is not a one-size-fits-all scheme. The important question that remains for this chapter is how entrepreneurial pastoralism impacts on the training of pastors, and what the response could be from institutions involved in theological training.

Entrepreneurial pastoralism and theological education

Although many churches, especially the more traditional (and perhaps smaller) Pentecostal-Charismatic churches, exhibit some resistance to entrepreneurial pastoralism and business leadership models (Frahm-Arp 2010:170-179), the reality is that theological education can no longer ignore the importance and prevalence of business leadership training and entrepreneurial pastoralism. Johnston (2008) has shown the important role Pentecostalism plays in social and economic development in South Africa, and, therefore, an extensive and critical approach to entrepreneurial leadership amongst the clergy is of utmost relevance (see also several essays in Attanasi and Yong [2012]). There are some challenges faced by theological education in this regard, but there are also many opportunities that will assist in the transformation and evolution of theological education to be relevant for metamodern thinking and the demands of post-apartheid South African society.

In the first instance, and this may be one of the greatest challenges, we have the issue of sources and literature relating to entrepreneurial pastoralism. As we have seen above, many of the best-selling sources that inform and shape attitudes towards leadership in assemblies, are of a popular nature. The challenge then for theological education is to approach the popular sources for leadership formation in a critical and investigative way. It implies that theological education on pastoral leadership should be research-intensive; the body of critical analyses of leadership theories, models, styles, and also effects and consequences, need to be expanded. There is a great need for studies like those of Stewart (2008) and Frahm-Arp (2010), to mention but two, that critically analyse and investigate entrepreneurial leadership in ecclesiastical contexts. This is especially crucial in Pentecostal-Charismatic contexts where there often tends to be an ideology of anti-intellectualism (Elinson 1965:404-410). Such critical examinations are especially important in that they will exhibit both the strengths and weaknesses of certain entrepreneurial leadership dynamics. For instance, Frahm-Arp (2010:171-178) has shown that in many South African contexts, entrepreneurial-pastoral leadership dynamics tend to be highly patriarchal and androcentric, and also shows how such challenges may be managed and overcome by female church leaders. The dissemination of the research is also an issue – along with dissemination in the usual academic venues like monographs and journals, there also needs to be a popularisation of this research, and a highly public dissemination, as the source of most of the literature is the public and popular domain. Since the source is popular, the response should also include a popular audience. Specialists in theological leadership training, as any academic, should strive to be public intellectuals. Moreover, due to the popular nature of engagement in this field, strict measures of quality control need to be in place (Houston 2013:875-880). Yet, as a corollary to the research-intensive impetus, there also needs to be a balance of practical experience and exposure for potential leaders and ministers (since leadership training is a dynamic and ongoing formative process), which implies that institutions of theological education need to have close and ongoing relationships with the various stakeholders – whether it be churches (as in most cases) or even NGOs, etc. Thus, a fine balance should be struck between teaching potential ministers *about* leadership and teaching them *in* leadership; that is, how to become better leaders.

Another challenge that theological education faces is the influence of neoliberalism on entrepreneurial pastoralism (Veerkamp 2008:198-209). In this regard, South Africa does perhaps have an advantage with its strong public and liberation theological legacies (Dreyer 2006:1311-1335). There needs to be a close cooperation between liberation theology and entrepreneurial leadership training for pastors, so as to avoid a type of commodification of 'spiritual capital' or delivery of 'spiritual services'. It is also in this regard that social entrepreneurialism can be incorporated, so as to remind prospective leaders of the social mandate that the Church has, as well as create a sensitivity and passion to uplift, empower, and transform impoverished and disadvantaged communities. The danger of entrepreneurialism is that it can become answerable to a form of Christian consumerism and materialism, and also poses the risk of making churches and Christian organisations profit-driven rather than transformation-driven. Stewart (2008:312-317) is, therefore, correct in highlighting the advantages of transformative leadership models for ecclesiastical contexts.

Furthermore, education in entrepreneurial-pastoral leadership in South Africa should be contextualised. This is especially the point illustrated by Hendriks (2013:818-831), who calls for a new missional hermeneutic (one notices the influence of post-modernist entrepreneurial pastoralism, especially McLaren, on the work of Hendriks). It means that there is a need for responsive training, and training that remains very close to the community of the Church (Hendriks 2013:828-829). Entrepreneurial-pastoral leadership may fail disastrously if not contextualised, especially due to its suspicious nature in some contexts.

The phenomenon of using professional people in traditional 'lay' ministries also poses certain challenges. The pastor of the assembly no longer needs to know and do everything that requires attention in an assembly. Pastors cannot be experts in everything, although this is expected and even required at times. The implication is that many lay 'workers' and 'leaders' in churches have little or no theological education at all; their training lies in other fields that may benefit an assembly. It is in this respect that theological education should not only focus on those prospective pastors and leaders doing a theological qualification, but also give attention to training programmes within churches for lay professionals working in the church. The church that centralises its ministry philosophy on entrepreneurial pastoralism should be training-intensive institutions (Frahm-Arp 2010:66-70). Institutions of theological education need to evaluate and review their involvement also in continuous theological education – not only of pastors in the ministry, but also in training programmes for lay professionals. Once again, a close relationship with stakeholders is essential. Post-graduate and extra-graduate theological training programmes (like short-learning programmes) and qualifications need to receive more attention, as well as initiatives for coaching, mentoring, and other means of support (De Gruchy and Holeness 2013:852-857). It also calls for an interdisciplinary initiative in theological education, which needs to provide opportunities for students studying non-theological qualifications to receive some basic training in theology. Unfortunately, the opposition to electives outside the area of specialisation and selection of subjects for non-degree purposes (due to subsidy limitations) as well as the contested position of the field of theology in many South African universities, make this somewhat difficult.

Finally, a more practical consideration needs to be taken, namely the position and weight of entrepreneurial-pastoral leadership training in the theological curriculum. As a case in point here, I would like to refer to research done by Maré (2003) and Putter (2006) regarding the experience and expectations of pastors training for ministry in the Apostolic Faith Mission (AFM), one of South Africa's largest Pentecostal churches (see also Putter [2010:1-9]). The training was done by the Auckland Park Theological Seminary (ATS), the AFM's most influential (and currently, controversial) theological training institute. Interestingly enough, all the interviewees indicated that their theological training equipped them quite well for biblical exegesis and systematic theological issues, but all felt that they did not receive ample preparation for the practical aspects of ministry, especially related to leadership and management (i.e. entrepreneurial-pastoral preparation) (Maré 2003:111-113). Maré's suggestion to address these challenges is to lengthen the time spent to qualify for a degree and ordination from a three- to four-year course to a seven-year course (Putter 2010:3). He is, however, against having one theological discipline (like Practical Theology) being given preference at the cost of others (like Biblical Studies or Greek and Hebrew). He is also in favour of closer cooperation between churches and theological training institutes, and continuing theological training (Putter 2010:3-4). Putter (2006), on the other hand, focused more closely on which type of leadership models enjoyed preference amongst AFM pastors and members – a type of hybrid between servant and transformational leadership, especially role-modelling, seemed to have had preference (Putter 2006:81-110). There was also a great need (and preference) for pastors with post-graduate Masters and Doctoral degrees (Putter 2010:7-9).

These two studies, done within a Pentecostal context, provide some very important insights for the challenge of entrepreneurial pastoralism to the curriculum of theological education. In the first instance, it would be unwise to simply introduce another subject, like leadership, to the curriculum, or expand Practical Theology at the cost of other theological disciplines. The approach should be more integrative and holistic – instead of adding a subject on leadership and management, leadership should rather function as a recurring motif in all the theological disciplines. So, for instance, in New Testament and Early Christian Studies, the topic of leadership and church management in the early Church could be incorporated as a study unit. In this way, the positive aspects of theological training (which pastors noted), namely biblical and systematic theological training, are not compromised. In fact, introducing a topic like leadership in their sub-curricula increases pastors' relevance to their context. It also curbs the danger of producing a skills-based graduate with little critical theoretical and cognitive grounding. Maré's suggestion of extending the length of time to receive a theological qualification that allows for ordination, should also be taken seriously. And in this instance, theological training institutions and churches need to consult in order to determine the best course of action. Finally, as stated above, more attention should be given to practical training as well as continuing theological education.

Conclusion

The purpose of this chapter was to present the phenomenon of entrepreneurial pastoralism and the pastor-as-entrepreneur framework, with special attention given to its implications for theological education (focusing specifically on South African Pentecostal-Charismatic traditions and movements). It became clear that entrepreneurial pastoralism resulted from numerous economic, political, social and cultural shifts, especially within a post-apartheid South African society. Although it remains a highly contested issue, the changes in pastoral leadership may challenge theological training institutions to start thinking outside their established paradigms. Whereas these institutions need to fulfil their task as a critical voice in theological education, they also need to take up a creative and innovative stance in training ministers who will be active in this challenging yet exciting context.

Bibliography

Armour, M.C. and Browning, D., 1995. *Systems-Sensitive Leadership: Empowering Diversity Without Polarizing the Church.* Joplin: College Press.

Attanasi, K. and Yong, A. (eds.), 2012. *Pentecostalism and Prosperity: The Socio-Economics of the Global Charismatic Movement.* New York: Palgrave Macmillan.

Barchiesi, F. and Kenny, B., 2002. From Workshop to Wasteland: De-industrialization and Fragmentation of the Black Working Class on the East Rand (South Africa), 1990-1999. *International Review of Social History.* 47(S10). 35-63.

Barna, G., 2011. *The Power of Vision: Discover and Apply God's Vision for Your Life and Ministry.* Regal: Regal.

Basson, K.L., 2008. 'n Kwalitatiewe Ondersoek na die Leierskapstyle van Mosaïek Gemeente: 'n Gevallestudie. Unpublished M.A. Thesis. Johannesburg: University of Johannesburg. [Online] Available from: http://ujdigispace.uj.ac.za/handle/10210/403 [Accessed: 20 May 2014].

Cady, L.E., 1993. *Religion, Theology, and American Public Life.* Albany: SUNY Press.

Campbell, H.A. (ed.), 2013. *Digital Religion: Understanding Religious Practice in New Media Worlds.* Abingdon: Routledge.

Chomsky, N., 2011. *Profit Over People: Neoliberalism and Global Order.* New York: Seven Stories Press.

Chopra, M. and Sanders, D., 2004. From Apartheid to Globalisation: Health and Social Change in South Africa. *Hygiea Internationalis: An Interdisciplinary Journal for the History of Public Health.* 4(1). 153-174.

Crankshaw, O., 2012. Deindustrialization and Racial Inequality in Cape Town. *Urban Affairs Review*. [Online] Available from: http://uar.sagepub.com/content/early/2012/08/26/1078087412451427 [Accessed: 20 May 2014].

Dabashi, H., 2012. *The Arab Spring: The End of Postcolonialism*. London: Zed Books.

De Gruchy, J. and Holeness, L., 2013. Mentoring Younger Scholars in Theological Education in Africa. In: I.A. Phiri and D. Werner (eds.). *Handbook of Theological Education in Africa*. Oxford: Regnum Books International. 852-857.

Dreyer, Y., 2006. Postmoderne Kerk-Wees in die Lig van Publieke Teologie: Eenheid en Verskeidenheid. *HTS Theological Studies*. 62(4). 1311-1335.

Elinson, H., 1965. The Implications of Pentecostal Religion for Intellectualism, Politics, and Race Relations. *The American Journal of Sociology*. 70(4). 403-415.

Foucault, M., 2009. *Security, Territory, Population: Lectures at the Collège de France 1977-1978*. M. Senellart et al. (eds.). New York: Palgrave Macmillan.

Frahm-Arp, M., 2010. *Professional Women in South African Pentecostal Charismatic Churches*. Leiden: Brill.

Goffee, R. and Jones, G., 2006. *Why Should Anyone Be Led by You?: What It Takes To Be An Authentic Leader*. Harvard: Harvard Business Review Press.

Goldberg, D.T., 2009. *The Threat of Race: Reflections on Racial Neoliberalism*. Malden: Blackwell.

Gutting, G., 2013. *Thinking the Impossible: French Philosophy Since 1960*. Oxford: Oxford University Press.

Hart, G.P., 2002. *Disabling Globalization: Places of Power in Post-Apartheid South Africa*. Berkeley: University of California Press.

Hendriks, H.J., 2013. Contextualizing Theological Education in Africa by Doing Theology in a Missional Hermeneutic. In: I.A. Phiri and D. Werner (eds.). *Handbook of Theological Education in Africa*. Oxford: Regnum Books International. 818-831.

Houston, B., 2013. What is 'Quality' in Theological Education? In: I.A. Phiri and D. Werner (eds.). *Handbook of Theological Education in Africa*. Oxford: Regnum Books International. 875-880.

Howe, R.G., 2003. Some Concerns about John C. Maxwell. *Midwest Christian Outreach Journal*.

Hutchings, T., 2007. Creating Church Online: A Case-Study Approach to Religious Experience. *Studies in World Christianity*. 13(3). 243-260.

Hybels, B., 2009. *Courageous Leadership*. Grand Rapids, Michigan: Zondervan.

Hybels, B. and Mittelberg, M., 2008. *Becoming a Contagious Christian*. Grand Rapids, Michigan: Zondervan.

Jakes, T.D., 2014. *Instinct: The Power to Unleash Your Inborn Drive*. New York: Faith Words.

Johnston, S., 2008. *Under the Radar: Pentecostalism in South Africa and Its Potential Social and Economic Role*. Johannesburg: Centre for Development and Enterprise.

Kennedy, R.G., 2004. Spirituality and the Christian Manager. In: O.F. Williams and M.E. Marty (eds.). *Business, Religion, Spirituality: A New Synthesis*. Notre Dame: University of Notre Dame Press. 81-93.

Kirby, A., 2006. The Death of Postmodernism and Beyond. *Philosophy Now*. 58. 34-37.

LeMay, M.D., 2012. *The Suicide of American Christianity: Drinking the 'Cool'-Aid of Secular Humanism*. Bloomington: West Bow Press.

Maré, L.P., 2003. AGS-Pastore se Belewenis van Hulle Teologiese Opleiding. Unpublished M.A. Thesis. Johannesburg: Randse Afrikaanse Universiteit.

Marty, M.E., 2004. Non-Religion, Religion, and Spirituality: Competing for Business. In: O.F. Williams and M.E. Marty (eds.). *Business, Religion, Spirituality: A New Synthesis*. Notre Dame: University of Notre Dame Press. 31-52.

Maxwell, J.C., 1996. *Partners in Prayer*. Nashville: Thomas Nelson.

Maxwell, J.C., 1999. *The 21 Indispensable Qualities of a Leader: Becoming the Person Others Will Want to Follow*. Nashville: Thomas Nelson.

McLaren, B.D., 2004. *A Generous Orthodoxy*. Grand Rapids, Michigan: Zondervan.

Meyer, J., 2008. *A Leader in the Making: Essentials to Being a Leader after God's Own Heart*. Nashville: Faith Words.

Niemandt, C.J.P., 2007. Ontluikende Kerke – 'n Nuwe Missionêre Beweging: Deel 1 – Ontluikende Kerke as Prototipes van 'n Nuwe Missionêre Kerk. *Verbum et Ecclesia*. 28(2). 542-557.

Offutt, S., 2010. The Transnational Location of Two Leading Evangelical Churches in the Global South. *Pneuma*. 32. 390-411.

Osteen, J., 2013. *Break Out! 5 Keys to Go Beyond Your Barriers and Live an Extraordinary Life*. Nashville: Faith Words.

Putter, A.P.J., 2006. Die Voortgesette Akademiese Ontwikkeling van die AGS-Pastoor. Unpublished DLitt et Phil Dissertation. Johannesburg: University of Johannesburg.

Putter, A.P.J., 2010. Teologiese Opleiding in die AGS-Kerk: Verkennende en Ontwikkelende Beskouings vir die Nuwe Millennium. *HTS Theological Studies*. 66(1). 1-9.

Stanley, A., 2005. *Visioneering: God's Blueprint for Developing and Maintaining Vision*. Sisters: Multnomah Books.

Stewart, A.C., 2008. The Workplace of the Organised Church: Theories of Leadership and the Christian Leader. *Culture and Religion*. 9(3). 301-318.

Sweet, L.I., 1999. *Soultsunami: Sink or Swim in New Millennium Culture*. Grand Rapids, Michigan: Zondervan.

Veerkamp, T., 2008. Neoliberalism and Reclaiming a Theology of Economy. *International Review of Mission*. 97(386-387). 198-209.

Volkmann, C.K., Tokarski, K.O. and Ernst, K. (eds.), 2012. *Social Entrepreneurship and Social Business: An Introduction and Discussion with Case Studies*. Springer: Wiesbaden.

Warren, R., 1995. *The Purpose Driven Church: Growth Without Compromising Your Message and Mission*. Grand Rapids, Michigan: Zondervan.

Weideman, H.J., 2008. Die Rol van Leraars in die Ontwikkeling van Leiers vir Bedieninge in die Gemeente. Unpublished M.A. Thesis. Johannesburg: University of Johannesburg. [Online] Available from: http://ujdigispace.uj.ac.za/handle/10210/231 [Accessed: 20 May 2014].

Educational technologies: Exploring the ambiguous effect on the training of ministers

Anita Cloete

Introduction

The advent of technology in theological education, and specifically the training of ministers, has surely stirred much discussion on why we educate and how we educate, as well as the theological nature of theological education. Although previous research suggests that there is no significant difference (Russel 1999) between online or face-to-face education, research on the topic continued as there is still the drive to explore and demonstrate the benefits or dangers thereof in education (Condon 2014:23). As Kelsey (2002:2) rightly notes, unexamined practices are not worth engaging in and, therefore, technology in higher education calls for critical assessment. Van der Laan (2012:242) notes that although we are surrounded and dependent on technology, the effects on us remain poorly understood. Therefore, this chapter will highlight the contested nature of technology as medium by identifying and discussing a few ambiguous effects that the use of technology has on theological education.

The most important frameworks that guide the current discussions on technology and training of ministers, seems to be focusing on pedagogical issues and the theological nature of training of ministers (Delamarter 2004; Delamarter 2005; Delamarter 2005; Hess 2002; Ascough 2002; Kelsey 2002). However, a broader understanding of the effect of technology and how it is intertwined with human existence could provide a helpful framework for this ongoing discussion and its impact on the training for ministers. Therefore, this chapter firstly situates the use of technology in theological training in a broader understanding of technology as part of living in a digital age (with specific reference to the South African context). This discussion will highlight the fact that technology is much more than merely a tool that could be used – it also represents a culture whereby humans are co-creators of different digital spaces for connection, community formation, meaning making, identity formation, and learning. A summary of the use of technology in the training of minsters, as well as responses thereto, is offered. In the last section, the ambiguous effect of technology will be demonstrated by discussing how the medium could simultaneously offer opportunities and challenges to the training of ministers. This discussion will focus on the cost associated with the use of educational technology, the digital divide, disembodiment, and the role and status of knowledge in a technological age.

Training of ministers in a digital culture

The world in which we are living today is characterised by the pervasive presence of technology through which we communicate, work, play and learn. "… we now rely on and use technology in every sphere of life: from agriculture, energy, medicines, telecommunication and transport, to business, education, finance, politics and psychology" (Van der Laan 2012: 242). Technology, however, is more than a tool. It also presents a way of living. Social shaping as a theoretical perspective on media, postulates that technology is created by humans as part of a social context, but also affects being human and the context we are living in (Wessels 2010: 31). Therefore, technology says as much about us as it says about the societies we live in (Baym 2010:23). Several years ago, Murphy (1986) argues, technology did not have autonomy and logic of its own, apart from that given by human agency, as technology is created and sustained by humans. Although technology creates the illusion that it operates without the human agency, it is not possible (Murphy 1986:140), as human action should be understood in order to be at the centre of technology (Murphy 1986:144). However, the mediatisation theory proposed by Hjarvard (2011:123) differs, and postulates that technology does in fact have a logic of its own to which institutions have to adhere to. This means that technology is no longer just in service of institutions, but that institutions need technology to communicate effectively in the present day. Technology, therefore, nowadays mediates communication between people, as is also the case with educational technologies. This implies that new worlds are created as digital platforms, and become the primary locations of communication and symbolic connections (Soukup, Buckley and Robinson 2001:370). Medrano (2004:147-148) is of the opinion that digital technologies represent a culture, a way of living, in which the internet plays an integral part. According to Wicker and Santaso (2013), the use of technology is so important these days, they even argue that it should be considered as a human right. Kerr (2005:1006), however, is of the opinion that the enthusiasm for using technology for education is not because there is conclusive evidence which improves student learning, but because internet communication technology (ICT) is a generator of contemporary culture (2005:1007). Against this background, the use of technology in education seems inevitable, although not without the need for an examination of what it really means for being human and, in this case, for theological education.

The path travelled with technology and training of ministers

The use of technology in or for training of ministers could be ascribed to several factors. These include advanced technology – the demands of an increasingly mobile and diverse population and dissatisfaction with traditional models, seem to be some of the most important factors contributing to the need thereof (Naidoo 2012:1). In South Africa, education is one of the rights that is enshrined within the Constitution. Therefore, the demand for access to basic and further education also rises. One of the ways of providing access to education (especially at tertiary level) is online distance learning, whereby learning is mediated through technology. Print-based correspondence courses marked the earlier stages of distance education, but with the ongoing development of telecommunications, distance education has several new opportunities (Ascough 2002:17). The University of South Africa (Unisa), the only fully distance-university in South Africa, positions itself as an institution that embraces and harnesses the potential of information and communication technologies (ICT) in Africa in providing students with an inherently online teaching and learning experience. The teaching and learning process is further strengthened and enhanced by support facilities and services like counsellors and volunteer peer helpers (Chetty 2014:54). An example of a smaller private institution that specifically provides theological training through distance, is the South African Theological Seminary (SATS). Different online platforms are created through a central hub called MyStats, where study material is obtained and communication with a course facilitator and other students are possible.[22] One of the main supporting elements of theological training at SATS is the prominence of partnerships with the various churches where students are located. This means that learning is embedded in a specific local context that assists and compliments the online learning experience.

The use of technology as the basic medium to guide the learning process, is always in direct relation to other developments. Declining enrolment at residential institutions, specifically for theological studies, makes online distance education a favourable option to attract new students (Ascough 2002:20). The growth of open distance learning (ODL) in Africa resulted in distance education becoming the policy option in Africa, with significant enrolments in South Africa, especially at the University of South Africa (Unisa), being the largest provider of distance education in South Africa (Naidoo 2012:1). Ascough's (2002:18-19) explanation of online distance education – by pointing out the characteristics thereof – is helpful. The characteristics of online distance education could be summarised as follows:

- It has the sponsorship of a reputable educational organisation.
- Teachers and learners are separated from one another.
- It requires special technical skills.
- The nature of the medium changes the social dynamic of the learning environment, class, race and gender issues.

The presence of technology in training of ministers currently has basically two forms, namely distance education and the use of technology in combination with face-to-face teaching, referred to as the 'hybrid model'. The hybrid approach is pointed out by some as being the most effective, as it has the best of both worlds – the online as well as the traditional classroom situation (Naidoo 2012:5; Delamarter 2005:52; Delamarter 2004:138).

Based on the results gathered from interviews with theological educators from 45 different seminaries in North America, Delamarter (2005) gives a good overview of the path travelled with technology and theological education. Initially, staff members used personal computers merely to send emails and gain information for research and teaching. However, within the short span of a decade, it became almost unthinkable not to use the World Wide Web for obtaining information. And since information literacy became

---

[22] *The South African Theological Seminary* – www.sats.ed

a necessity to function effectively and efficiently as a citizen living and operating in the information era, faculty members had no choice but to develop certain technical and computer skills (Delamarter 2005:52). From there the use of technology became part of face-to-face instruction. "Perhaps the most significant development in technology for theological education, was the use of web-based tools for asynchronous teaching and learning" (Delamarter 2005:52). The road ahead points to an increasing need for the use of technology, since the potential students enrolling know only a world filled with technology and will, therefore, expect technology to be a part of how they are trained (Delamarter 2005:53-55). This could lead to criticism of lecture-based pedagogies and could lead to where technology is no longer viewed as a helpful tool for the educator, but rather as a necessary and responsible aid for the sake of the student (Delamarter 2005:53). This implies that educators who stick to the classroom-based approach will be held accountable for explaining why they do not make use of or neglect the powerful tools provided by technology (Delamarter 2005:53).

Reponses to the use of educational technologies

Delamarter's (2004) typology of the use of technology in theological training provides a helpful description on the responses of especially theological educators to the use of technology. Delamarter (2004:136) differentiates between three types of reactions: Stage one, where technology is used to teach together with electronic library management; stage two, in which educators try to replicate what they do in class to some online mediated form; stage three, which includes responses on individual and institutional level. Educators in this stage claim to have made some useful pedagogical findings and have started to transform the classroom with a more sophisticated use of technology (Delamarter 2004:138). On an institutional level, new pedagogical discoveries have been reported in a way that would enhance the training of ministers (Delamarter 2004:138). It seems important for theological faculties and seminaries to have some idea of how educators view the use of technology, and how the relationship is between technology and the institutional expectations with regard to the use thereof. It also seems important to get feedback on how students experience the use of technology, or lack thereof, within the educational process. It will be irresponsible to assume that all students want and find the use of technology helpful in their learning process.

The developments with regard to technology and theological education, however, were not without some rather divergent responses – especially on the part of educators, resulting in adherents and opponents of the new approach towards education. It should be noted that responses originate mostly against the backdrop of the existing, classical classroom-based approach to education, which means that the new approach is valued or questioned on that grounds. Delamarter (2004:135) notes that the classical paradigm entails theological training which includes full immersion of at least three years of training in a residential programme with face-to-face, lecture-based pedagogies, supported by library research and writing. For decades this has been viewed as the best pedagogical paradigm for reaching the goal of training ministers. Although the use of technology is evaluated in the light of the classical, face-to-face, classroom-based pedagogy, it does not mean that the classical paradigm necessarily accomplishes everything that is now questioned in the new paradigm (Delamarter 2004:137).

The concerns and preferences of educators with regard to technology and training of ministers, could be understood within at least two broad frameworks, namely pedagogical and theological (Delamarter 2005; Naidoo 2012; Ascough 2002). Delamarter (2005:131) has done empirical work in seminaries in North America in order to find out what the concerns of theological educators are by establishing their attitudes towards the use of technology for teaching and learning in theological education. These concerns were sorted under practical and personal, pedagogical, educational, philosophical and theological (Delamarter 2005:131-143). The different concerns listed under the different frameworks were interrelated, as could be expected.

The ambiguous effect of technology on theological education

According to Ascough (2002:17), the nature of the medium needs to be understood before it could be conceptualised and designed in the educational environment. Although technology could provide us with creative and endless opportunities for quality education, it could also lead to poor pedagogical practices if the medium is not understood.

1. The digital divide and cost associated with the use of educational technologies

It seems that one of the most valuable contributions of online education is the creation of greater access, especially for marginalised groups. Although there seems to be a misconception that all countries have access to technology. Roos and Jordaan (2006:2) indicate that internet access in South Africa has increased, but at a diminishing rate. South Africa still has a long way to go when it comes to making the internet widely available and affordable. This is directly linked to the digital divide that refers to the divide between those who have access to technology and technological skills, and those who do not. The narrow and broader definitions of the digital divide are noteworthy as the former refers to the lack of access to computers between racial groups, while the latter includes sufficient training and relevant content on the web that will enable users to use the internet effectively (Roos and Jordaan 2006:4). The digital divide further implies that people who have the financial means already have access to technology and skills to use it, while the majority have no access and are, therefore, marginalised and unable to participate in an information-based economy. In an empirical study done by Chetty (2014) on the integration of ICT at the College of Human Sciences at Unisa, similar findings emerged as in the study done by Delamarter (2005) with regard to the opportunities and challenges that the use of ICT poses to learning and teaching. Inadequate infrastructure like server capacity, down times, and interruption of connectivity, is singled out as the most challenging factors in the process of integrating ICT in teaching and learning practices. Almost half of the respondents in the study (59 out of 130) pointed out that ICT in teaching and learning disadvantages students who are already in a disadvantaged position, since most of these students have limited access to the internet as well as limited skills to participate in the ODL process. Closely linked to this challenge is the cost factor which is implied in sustaining and upgrading infrastructure and continuous training of staff and students (Chetty 2014:58).

The digital divide thus entails much more than access or skills, but includes stable infrastructure across different sectors. It is, therefore, closely linked to the cost factor of using the internet. Naidoo (2012:1) and Ascough (2002:20) confirm that in order to be able to use technology to its full potential, certain infrastructure, the socio-economic viability of the end user, and staff development are needed. Although the internet may become less expensive, the infrastructure and software of different programs need to be upgraded continuously at a huge cost. And although older technology may also become less expensive and more accessible, newer versions are pricy and not accessible for the majority in a country like South Africa with its high levels of unemployment. Thus, while technology could give greater access to education, it could also exclude, for instance, students living in rural areas. A person who does not have access to technology, usually also lacks technological skills, which means even if they have access to education through distance, they will not be able to participate due to the lack of technological skills. Barraket and Scott (2001:209) provide a helpful explanation of information literacy, namely an awareness of the kinds of information available, possible sources of this information, the means of retrieving the information, and an understanding of information required in relation to existing knowledge. Information literacy, therefore, does not simply refer to the ability to use a computer or surf the net, but entails a variety of interrelated skills. Training to obtain these skills implies additional cost as the lack thereof could compromise the educational process. Ascough (2002:20) adds an important factor, namely that the use of technology in education could be time consuming, as educators have to manage two platforms – the classroom as well as the online platform. As universities become more competitive and expect staff to be involved in community interaction, as well as to teach and deliver higher quality research outputs, the use of technology in teaching could place an extra workload and pressure on academics.

Barraket and Scott (2001:204) identify the digital divide as a key concern, "which has the potential to create disadvantages that mirror traditional inequalities." Students with particular disabilities are also vulnerable to the economic cost involved for modified hardware and adaptive software (Barraket and Scott 2001:207). The increased cost associated with the use of technology could lead to unreasonable price increases of education fees, which could compromise the right of access to education. Education is viewed as one of the weapons to eradicate poverty, but if the cost of technology compromises that, we surely have to scrutinise the effect of educational technologies. The costs associated with the use of technology pose a significant challenge to the training of ministers, as many theological training institutions are faith-based with limited budgets and, therefore, cannot engage fully in technological infrastructure development. Hence, in a country like South

Africa with the highest division between rich and poor, anything like the digital divide that increases inequality, should be examined and critiqued beforehand.

2. Disembodiment as part of educational technologies

Education that is mediated by technology is characterised by bodily absence. This virtual reality is believed to provide an increased possibility of irresponsible conduct of students, like developing fake online personae (Delamarter 2005:135). At the same time it is argued that it could lead to deeper learning as students have more time to reflect, whereas in a traditional classroom an immediate response is needed (Delamarter 2004:137). Furthermore, students who seldom participate in class, could participate online, which could lead to greater student participation. The underlying question that seems of importance is whether the virtual reality and face-to-face reality are the same, and whether the same outcomes could be accomplished in both? In other words, is the virtual reality real and authentic? The physical togetherness created by residential face-to-face pedagogy has been viewed as community in a theological sense, where educators carried out their work under the guidance of the Holy Spirit (Delamarter 2004: 136) and where students could be transformed (Delamarter, Alanis, Haitch, Hofmann, Jones and Strawn 2007:64). Isolated individuals in virtual reality made possible by technology, is seen as non-conducive for what is key to theological education, namely spiritual formation (Naidoo 2012:3). Questions like how people could be formed outside the learning community, and when they are absent and isolated, arise (Delamarter 2004:137). These questions suggest that community is not possible in the virtual reality created by educational technologies. Disembodiment, therefore, seems to pose a great pedagogical and theological challenge to the training of ministers. Campbell (2013:59), however, claims that online communities still entail the basic act of social exchange, although these communities are often viewed as inauthentic and unreal (Campbell 2013:63).

Condon (2014:24) raises her concern with online education by asking if this engagement through technology really creates a sense of presence. She argues that, especially for the nursing profession, it is important for students to learn the art of being and knowing how to be present with patients. Could it be that theology students could unlearn the art of being present with people, which is such a vital component of being a religious leader? Kelsey (2002:3) is of the opinion that the training of ministers brings with it a particular type of critique which is centred on the theological nature of theological training. According to him, the theological nature is in line with the purpose of theological training. He plots his theological critique around theological anthropology with specific reference to the fact that it is humans who undergo theological training (Kelsey 2002:6). Kelsey (2002:7) further points to the incarnation according to which "Christ came amongst us as one of us, joyfully created, sustains and affirms us as human beings." The bearing of this on theological training is that students and educators should not be viewed as spiritual souls contained in a body, but rather as complex personal bodies with an extraordinary range of powers. This personal body and the corporate body of the Church are further understood as an extension of the body of Christ. In short, the body matters a great deal, especially in the Christian tradition. In the technological culture of the day, Kelsey (2002:8) claims "… there is a strongly spiritualising and dualistic picture of being human." Therefore, his central question is whether theological students are seen as personal machines or personal bodies? His well-articulated critique is thus directed towards disembodiment in educational technologies. Bulu (2012) describes several types of presence in the virtual space, namely place-presence, co-presence, and social presence. Kiran (2012:78), however, contends that technological presence is not the same as physical presence, but with the presence of technology there are both actuality and potentiality. However, these different kinds of presence could be seen as artificial and, therefore, not be viewed as similar to physical presence. If spiritual formation is one of the core elements of ministerial formation, we have to make time to reflect theologically on the reduction of the body in educational technologies. Is bodily absence really conducive for spiritual formation, which we believe to be intergenerational and primarily takes place in community? (Cloete 2012) The individual nature of educational technologies could be viewed as being in direct opposition to the communal nature of Christian spiritual formation. Dykstra (2005:95) argues that the life of faith is communal before it is individual. This means that we need each other for spiritual formation. Grenz (2002:95) confirms that the understanding of spiritual formation as communal project is endemic to all Christian traditions. Westerhoff (1976:53) even suggests that different generations are needed as part of the community for spiritual formation. The educational process in theological training should thus contribute to community formation that fosters spiritual formation. Naidoo (2012:2) contends that, for many years, theological institutions were concerned about the end product by asking the question what sort of person the Church needs, and tried to align programmes accordingly. In other words, what is aimed for or is expected of theological training, and what are the best pedagogical methods to deliver that? It could be argued that being is as important as knowing and doing in the training of ministers. Nel and Cook (2010:3) emphasise that the adequacy of the person in theological training is even becoming more important, since the person of the pastor or ministerial identity plays an increasingly more important role in ministry today.

However, disembodiment as part of educational technology, according to Esselman (2004:160), leads to the depersonalisation of the learning process, because it is mainly self-directed through instructional technologies. Esselman (2004:160) also points to the commodification of knowledge in a technological culture and refers to the two competing understandings of the role of higher education today, namely the 'gown approach' and the 'merit badge approach'. The first approach aims towards transforming the whole person into a productive and responsible citizen, while the latter stresses the acquisition of particular skills that will make the candidate more suitable for the labour market. It is argued that the 'gown approach', where the person is being regarded as valuable, is eroded in a technological age which is primarily market-driven and, therefore, directs the educational goals and processes to deliver candidates that will fit the market. Information is viewed as a commodity and educational processes are packaged and presented as such, too. Therefore, the homepage of a faculty of theology often does not look much different from that of any other educational programmes and services (Esselman 2004:160). Naidoo (2012:2) also alludes to the tension that already exists between the educational goals of public universities and that of theological training, which could become even more complex in a technological era. Communication is central to education and, as is discussed early on in educational technologies, communication is mediated by technology. The fact that the body is absent in this kind of communication is problematic in many ways, as our bodies "… are inherently involved in our efforts to communicate ourselves as persons" (Kelsey 2002:9). Put differently, we need our bodies in order to communicate meaningfully and, therefore, the presence of both the educator and the student is of utmost importance in education. The key question that needs attention here is whether or not spiritual formation, as an integral part of ministerial formation, is being served by educational technologies. More empirical research is needed in order to give insight into this area.

3. Knowledge in a technological culture

It is important to take note of the role and status of knowledge in a technological culture. Mary Hess (2013:13) describes the way of learning in a digital age as "a new culture of learning." In a world where there is a large body of stable knowledge, teaching about the world might be functional and adequate, but in a digital age, knowing is changing all the time and deeply embedded in personal agency and experience. Therefore, learning through engagement is necessary (Hess 2013:14). In a context where there is a large body of established knowledge, an inquiring mind is of essence in order to establish what we do not know. This implies a new way of educating and learning at the same time. Shifting to new paradigms could cause uneasiness and take some time to be implemented and appreciated. If educators in theological institutions have been trained in an age of stable knowledge and teaching-based education, the new learning culture could seem too different and even impossible for them to facilitate.

Despite the fact that the information age is marked by a vast amount of available information, knowledge is regarded as more important than information, specifically for education. Sajjadi (2008:185) points out two developments with regard to knowledge in a technological culture: Knowledge is reduced to information which led to the delegitimatisation of knowledge, and quantitative information becomes the authoritative scientific analysis. Both the quantification of knowledge and the minimised responsibility on the side of the knower is problematic for religious education. Religious education requires a qualitative epistemology characterised by understanding, reasoning and critical rationality (Sajjadi 2008:186). Theological training is not only about transferring information, but also requires critical engagement with what is known, is needed in order to transform the knower, and create a responsibility towards what is known. Theological students are trained to be spiritual leaders and, therefore, spiritual formation and religious discipline will be paramount as part of the educational process. Hess (2013:16) thus warns that the unlimited access to information does not mean unlimited access to wisdom. Wisdom is closely linked with spiritual formation which refers to an integration of everything that is part of our being.

The fluid nature of information in a digital culture is also viewed as both threat and opportunity to theological education, since it means there is no central canon or core of information that all must master to be considered educated (Kerr 2005:1011). Sajjadi (2008:188) explains hypertextual learning as "a nonlinear method of reading and interpreting information that is principally achieved in digital form." The hypertext took the monopoly of knowledge from elites and created a democratic space where knowledge is made available to all. At the same time it led to the death of the author, as the reader becomes an active co-author or, sometimes, even the primary author of the text. Kerr (2005:1012) describes the fact that information could be altered and updated in radical and subtle ways, as mutability. Although the mutability of information gives agency to students to not only be consumers of information but also producers thereof, it means, on the other hand, that there is no place for an authorised version of any given item. Religious education, however, needs a core or a canon since traditional religious education has a hierarchal component. In traditional religious education, "teachers are considered the authoritative basis of religious information and knowledge" (Sajjadi 2008:187). However, in a technological culture, the teachers and students are on the same level, which means a weakening role of the teacher to transfer or interpret knowledge (Sajjadi 2008:189). Idiosyncrasy makes it possible for individuals to tailor their individual learning experience. This means that there is no common learning experience, because in a technological culture learning could be a solo activity (Kerr 2005: 1012-1013).

Van der Laan (2012:242-244) argues that although educational technologies make use of the imaginary in order to create experience, understanding and the ability to read are limited in a digital age. Educational technologies summarise and reduce content to such an extent that it is hardly possible to have in-depth understanding thereof. The content becomes superficial because "… a technological society desires and conceives its world in terms of graphs, drawings, tables, charts and diagrams. PowerPoint turns everything into those forms" (Van der Laan 2012:245). Language has to conform to the fundamental principle of technology, namely efficiency (Van der Laan 2012:245). This also has a direct bearing on critical thinking, since intellectual processes of reasoning is related to the word which is reduced in a technological culture. The overarching aim of especially tertiary education, is to assist students to be able to read with comprehension, critically engage with material and enable them to present their understanding in a systematic and coherent way. In the light of Van der Laan's arguments, it seems that educational technologies could jeopardise this aim. The expectation from theological training is no different in this regard, as Nel and Cooke (2010:3) suggest theological students should be able to demonstrate the ability to reproduce knowledge in a conceptual and narrative manner. If reading is not favourable in a technological culture, it could lead to the inability to read with comprehension. This will hinder critical thinking, making it almost impossible to reach the above-mentioned aims. Due to the vast amount of information available, selection is not only possible, but is the norm, which contributes even more to the loss of mastering long, complex arguments and descriptions (Kerr 2005:1012).

One of the important questions is how teaching and learning, by using ICT, could be integrated best in order to serve the aim of training ministers. The integration of ICT in teaching and learning implies more than just a medium or tool that carries information (Hess 2002:31). It actually creates a complex process that facilitates meaning-making – not only of theory, but also of the self and the world. The creation and use of technology is, therefore, closely linked to who we are and are becoming (identity), the world that we create through communication, and the way we live our lives (ethics). These elements, namely identity formation, meaning-making and ethics, are at the heart of the training of ministers. Therefore, despite the challenges brought along with the integration of ICT, it could also be of tremendous value to theological education. Questions like how could and should theology and pedagogy interacts in cyberspace, could guide the training of ministers using ICT.

Conclusion

The expectations surrounding the training of ministers are very high, as such training is often seen as the most efficient way to influence and shape the leaders of the Church (Anderson 2011:185). Therefore, theological reflection on the training of ministers as well as the mode by/in which the training is done, are of utmost importance. The context in which training of ministers takes place today, is described as a digital culture – making the use of educational technologies inevitable. It will thus be irresponsible for any training institution not to explore and find ways to integrate ICT in teaching and learning. Overall, the change brought about by technology is unpredictable and complex, and at best described as incomprehensible. Hence, it demands adaptability in real time, here and now (Allenby and Sarewitz 2011:162).

Bibliography

Allenby, B.R. and Sarewitz, D., 2011. *The Techno Human Condition*. Cambridge: MIT Press.
Anderson, P., 2011. Theological Education as Hope for a New Ecclesiology. *Currents in Theology and Mission*. 38(3). 183-192.
Ascough, R.S., 2002. Designing for Online Distance Education: Putting Pedagogy before Technology. *Teaching Theology and Religion*. 5(1). 17-29.
Barraket, J. and Scott, G., 2001. Virtual Equality? Equity and the use of Information Technology in Higher Education. *Australian Academic and Research libraries (AARL)*. 33(3). 204-212.
Baym, N.K., 2010. *Personal Connections in the Digital Age*. Malden, MA: Polity Press.
Bulu, S.T., 2012. Place-presence, social presence and co-presence in virtual worlds. *Computers and Educations*. 58. 154-161.
Campbell, H.A., 2013. Community. In Campbell, H.A. (ed.). *Digital Religion: Understanding Religious Practice in New Media Worlds*. Abingdon: Routledge.

Cloete, A., 2012. Spiritual formation as focus of Youth Ministry. *Nederduitse Gereformeerde Teologiese Tydskrif (NGTT)*. 53(3 and 4). 70-77.

Condon, B.B., 2014. The Present State of Presence in Technology. *Nursing Science Quarterly*. 26(1). 23-28.

Delamarter, S., 2004. A Typology of the Use of Technology in Theological Education. *Theology and Religion*. 7(3). 134-140.

Delamarter, S., 2005. Theological educators and their concerns about Technology. *Teaching Theology and Religion*. 8(3). 131-143.

Delamarter, S., 2005. Theological educators, Technology and the Path ahead. *Teaching Theology and Religion*. 8(1). 51-55.

Delamarter, S., Alanis, J., Haitch, R., Hoffman, M., Jones W. and Strawn, B., 2007. Technology, Pedagogy and Transformation in Theological Education: Five Case Studies. *Teaching Theology and Religion*. 10 (2). 64-79.

Dykstra, C., 2005. 2nd edition. *Growing in the life of Faith: Education and Christian Practices*. Kentucky: Westminster John Knox Press.

Esselman, T., 2004. The Pedagogy of the Online Community: Forming Church Ministers in a Digital Age. *Teaching Theology and Religion*. 7(3). 159-170.

Grenz, S.J., 2002. Christian Spirituality and the Quest for Identity: Towards a spiritual-theological understanding of life in Christ. *History and Heritage*. 37(2). 87-103.

Hess, M., 2013. A New Culture of Learning: Implications of Digital Culture for Communities of Faith. *Communications Research Trends*. 32(3). 13-20.

Hjarvard, S., 2011. The mediatisation of religion: Theorising religion, media and social change. *Culture and Religion*. 12(2). 119-135.

Kelsey, D.H., 2002. Spiritual Machines, Personal Bodies, and God: Theological Education and Theological Anthropology. *Teaching Theology and Religion*. 5(1). 2-9.

Kerr, S.T., 2005. Why we want it all to work: Towards a culturally based model for educational change. *British Journal of Educational Technology*. 36(6). 1005-1016.

Kiran, A.H., 2012. Technological presence: Actuality and potentiality in subject constitution. *Human Studies*. 35. 77-93.

Medrano, A.M., 2004. Making Religious Media: Notes from the Field. In: P. Horsfield, M.E. Hess and A.M. Medrano (eds.). *Belief in Media: Cultural Perspectives on Media and Christianity*. Burlington: Ashgate Publishing Limited.

Murphy, J.W., 1986. Humanizing the Use of Technology in Education: A Re-Examination. *International Review of Education*. 32(2). 137-148.

Naidoo, M., 2012. Ministerial formation of theological students through distance education. *HTS Theological Studies*. 68(2). 1-8.

Nel, M. and Cook, F.T., 2010. Die Keuring vir Teologiese Opleiding: Noodsaak en Toepassing. *HTS Theological Studies*. 66(2). 1-6.

Roos, L. and Jordaan, A.C., 2006. Access to information and communication: estimating the determinants of internet usage in South Africa. *Communicare*. 25 (1). 1-22.

Russel, T. L., 1999. *The Significance Difference Phenomenon*. Raleigh: North Carolina State University.

Sajjadi, S. M., 2008. Religious Education and Information Technology: Challenges and Problems. *Teaching Theology and Religion*. 11(4). 185-190.

Soukup, P.A., Buckley, F.J. and Robinson, D.C., 2001. The influence of information technologies on Theology. *Theological Studies*. 62. 366-377.

South African Theological Seminary. *About us/History* [Online] Available from: www.sats.ed [Accessed: 2 December 2014].

Van der Laan, J.M., 2012. Language and Being Human in Technology. *Bulletin for Science, Technology and Society*. 32(3). 241-252.

Wessels, B., 2010. *Understanding the Internet: A socio-cultural perspective.* New York: Palgrave MacMillan.

Westerhoff, J. H., 1976. *Will our Children have Faith?* New York: The Seabury Press.

Wicker, A. and Santaso, S.M., 2013. Access to the Internet is Human Right: Connecting Internet access with freedom of expression and creativity. *Communications of the ACM.* 56(6). 43-46.

DIVERSIFICATION IN TRAINING MODELS: A KEY TO OVERCOME CHALLENGES IN MINISTRY TRAINING

JOHANNES P. VAN DER WALT

Introduction

With the radical changes in world Christianity, any discussion on ministry training needs to consider the changing landscape of theological education. In South Africa, this would involve a reflection on the need to diversify models of training so that all people of God can access training and the missional vision of theological education can be reached. There is a very large need for ministry training[23] of pastors in less formal church settings, who, in the past, did not have access to formal training. There is also a growing need for formal training of 'lay members' of churches. The formalisation of training for these target groups should be taken seriously as part of future processes aimed at reshaping ministry leadership development in the country. The need to reshape training is relevant to informal churches. However, it is also valid for formal churches (such as the Dutch Reformed, Anglican and Lutheran churches), as they will have to fall back more and more on the utilisation of lay leaders within ministry who did not receive any formal training in the past. Diversification should play a key role in the process to rethink and redesign ministry training in order for it to meet the needs of these groups.

The concept of diversification of ministry training could be construed in different ways. One possibility would be to conceive of it in terms of diverse thematic emphases that would be relevant in diverse contexts. For example in Southern Africa, where the legacies of colonialism and apartheid are still freshly remembered and acutely experienced, a focus on themes such as justice and peace, race and human dignity, class and poverty, reconciliation, and social cohesion would be deeply relevant (Botman 2013:xx); or a focus on "raising self-awareness and self-discovery ... that would, at the same time, focus on the foundations of the faith" (Mofokeng 2012:149). In African contexts where the legacies of former, and even some recent and current, religious and ethnic practices are viewed as influential in communities, such as "evil foundations" and "strongholds" precipitated by "ritual killings, bloody inter-tribal wars, sacrifice of new-born babies, twins and virgins to the gods of the land ..." (Olukoya 2001:9), themes such as inter-faith relationships, spiritual mapping, deliverance from evil powers or witchcraft, and the breaking of strongholds, may be deemed essential. Another possibility of viewing diversification may be to deal with

---

[23] The term 'ministry training', as it is used in this chapter, is meant to imply a close link with and embeddedness in theological education. The term is also used instead of the more common 'ministerial training'. The concept 'ministerial training' emphasises 'who' is being trained, namely the 'minister' - normally interpreted as the 'professional clergyman or –woman'. The concept 'ministry training' relates to 'what' the training is aimed at, namely 'preparation for ministry'. This is a wider concept than 'ministerial training' and should be interpreted as including any person who is being prepared for any kind of church or faith-related ministry.

it in terms of teaching and training that focus on diverse categories of ministry and the need for specialist ministries. An example of this would be a focus on child ministry (such as presented by Petra Institute for Children's Ministry);[24] or a focus on sound Biblical interpretation and exegesis (e.g. the Veritas College);[25] or a specialist leadership focus (e.g. the Dael Institute of Leadership based in Lagos, Nigeria).[26] There could be several more angles towards approaching the concept of diversification.

This chapter, however, will deal with diversification from a different angle, namely that of the contested nature of our current models of ministry training. Existing challenges related to formal ministry training opportunities for pastors and other ministry leaders in the informal church environment, will be unpacked. It will be shown that few formal training opportunities are available to the disproportionately large group of leaders of informal churches. Most training initiatives currently available to this group are informal in nature in the sense that they are not formally recognised by the official qualification authority of the country. This leads to a series of consequential problems for the relevant group. It will be argued that two levels of diversification will assist in overcoming the challenges, namely diversification in the overarching framework that regulates training in the country, as well as diversification within ministry training itself. Reference will be made to new training policies recently introduced by the Government, and to a new initiative which aims at utilising opportunities in the new policies to bring about the relevant diversifications – and by doing so, contribute to the solution of the problems as identified. The discussion will commence with a theological motivation for training of all of God's people involved in ministry, with an emphasis on those who were marginalised by the formal training system in the past.

Theological motivations for training

A missional understanding of the Church is fundamental for a proper understanding of theological education and ministry training. Training of leadership for ministry is an obvious task of the Church, embedded in God's mission. Ministry training has to be understood within "the movement of the Trinitarian history of God's dealings with the world" (Moltmann 1977:65). During the 20th century, especially since the paper read by Karl Barth at the Brandenburg Missionary Conference in 1932, theologians began to understand mission as an activity of the triune God himself (Bosch 1991:389). This grew into a conviction that the Church does not have mission "as one of its activities", but rather that its existence is embedded in God's mission. Jürgen Moltmann states (1977:64):

> In the movement of the trinitarian history of God's dealings with the world, the Church finds and discovers itself ... It finds itself on the path traced by this history of God's dealings with the world, and it discovers itself as one element in the

---

[24] Petra Institute – www.petra.co.za
[25] Veritas College International – www.veritas.org.za
[26] See ng.linkedin.com/pub/basil-ibeh

movements of the divine sending ... It is not the Church that has a mission of salvation to fulfil to the world; it is the mission of the Son and the Spirit through the Father that includes the Church, creating a church as it goes on its way.

It is not the Church that brings the Spirit and the grace of God to the people. The Church is the witness and the instrument used by God in his act of reaching out to the world. And if this is the case, says Moltmann, the Church needs to understands itself "as one element in the power of the Spirit and has no need to maintain its special power and its special charges with absolute and self-destructive claim" (Moltmann 1977:65).

Ministry training should be understood within this wider perspective of the Trinitarian *missio Dei*. It is not 'owned' by the training institutions as if it is 'our work'. Instead, teaching and training is part of God's work to be done by members of the universal Church as the body of Christ. As Christ was sent by the Father, He sends his members, in the power of the Spirit (Jn 20:21-22) to do as He instructs. He sends them to serve, to bear witness of his death and resurrection (Lk 24:45-48; Ac 1:8), to make the peoples into his disciples, to teach (Mt 28:19-20) so that there could be life, and that in abundance (Jn 10:10).

Understanding ministry training as embedded in the *missio Dei* means that ministry training initiatives should be conceived of and designed around what Ross Kinsler calls 'a mission paradigm' – that is, around the core questions, "What was Jesus's understanding of God's mission?" and following from that, "What does it mean to follow Jesus in today's world?" (Kinsler 2009:13). Based on this fundamental point of departure, Kinsler comes to the conclusion that ministry training practices should reflect Jesus's emphasis. Jesus gave priority to "action on behalf of the hungry, the thirsty, the stranger, the naked, the sick, and the prisoner. His ministry on behalf of the 'little ones' ... was at the same time a denunciation of the powerful and the rich and the structures of oppression and marginalisation" (Kinsler 2009:15). Against this background, Kinsler makes two comments that have a bearing on content and organisation of ministry training. Regarding content of training he states: "To follow Jesus in our time ... we need to consider whether our programmes of theological education are equipping local church leaders to defend and support the weak ..." (Kinsler 2009:19). Regarding organisation and focus of training he states: "Priority should be given to the theological formation of local leaders, especially those who have traditionally been marginalised" (Kinsler 2009:15). This ties in with Bosch's understanding of the new missional identity of the Church, and also that of ministry training initiatives – see, for example, the need for the local Church to be heard; the need to change the rather paternalistic idea of the "church for others" into a "church-with-others" (Bosch 1991:378); or the concept of "teachability" of those who find themselves in the stronger position (Bosch 1991:456); or that of "self-theologising" (Bosch 1991:451-452), which is easily forgotten today.

Providing this theological mandate does not imply that the importance of solid theological education is questioned. Important to note, however, is that the training of leaders for church ministry may never be structured as an elitist undertaking that disregards the needs and the contributions of the 'little ones' in the kingdom of God.

Training needs for Christian ministry

Formal, established churches such as the Catholic, Dutch Reformed, Anglican, Presbyterian, Baptist, Methodist churches and the like, have relatively strong structures for the training of their leaders. These churches all have a history of thorough theological education and ministry training for their pastors, most of that on tertiary level and at registered and formally accredited universities (Naidoo 2012:15-114; Landmann 2013:241-244). The position, however, with regard to training of leaders in the less formal or informal churches, is different.

Over the last century there was a significant change in the religious and denominational profile of South Africa, with a disproportionate growth in churches initiated by black Africans. The following statistics tell the story. The total number of Christians in South Africa in 1911 was approximately five million, of which about 50% were black and 25% were classified as white, while the rest were classified as coloured or Asian. By 1996, these proportions have changed dramatically. According to the national census of that year, the total number of Christians were more than 30 million, of which 78% (slightly more than 23 million) were black Africans. The proportion of Christians in other race groups has obviously decreased accordingly (Hendriks and Malherbe 2002:18,25). Amongst black Christians, nearly 11 million (42%) were reported being members of African Initiated Churches (AICs) in 1996 (Hendriks and Malherbe 2002:18). Five years later, the 2001 national census found a further growth in the AIC membership. A total of 14 254 031 persons were reported belonging to AICs, with another 3 422 749 persons reported as being members of Pentecostal or Charismatic churches (Department of Government Communication and Information Systems 2011:12).[27] Together these two groups of less formal churches made out nearly half of the Christians in the country (49.5% to be exact).

The important point to focus on is the estimated growth in the number of leaders in the informal church environment, and the training needs implied by this. Siaki's study from 2002 provided information on the average number of church members per pastor in several of the formal churches (Siaki 2002:38). Based on this, a rough estimate can be made of the number of pastors in these formal churches. The result of this calculation is shown in Table 1, where the estimated number of members per pastor is related to the number of members per church tradition as reported from the 2001 census. Siaki (2002) unfortunately did not report information on the average number of members per pastor

---

[27] It may be assumed that a certain proportion of this last number can also be deemed as 'initiated in Africa', especially churches from the so-called third wave Pentecostal tradition which position themselves as responsive to typical African needs, but are critical of certain trends amongst AICs that are interpreted as syncretistic. (Information from the orally presented course entitled Advanced Level of Studies in the Pastors/Ministers Training Institute in Africa, presented by Prophet Laurette Mkati, Sandton, February 2013, also from a discussion with Barr Emeka Nwankpa, leader of the Pastors and Ministers Prayer Network in Africa, Lagos, Nigeria, 2011.)

in the AICs. To make a preliminary estimate of this statistic, information obtained by the Centre for Contextual Ministry (CCM) at the University of Pretoria in a small sample of nineteen AICs in the Rustenburg area, is used as a substitute. The number of members per pastor in this sample varied from 20 to 300, with an average of 83 and a median of 60. Due to a lack of better information this average of 83 is used to make a rough estimate of the number of pastors in AICs. The result of this calculation is also shown in Table 1.

Table 1: Estimated number of pastors per denomination/church group

Church tradition/group	Number of members*	Members per pastor	Estimated number of pastors	Number expressed as percentage of AICs
Roman Catholic	3 181 336	2 897**	1 098	0.6%
Anglican	1 722 076	1 126**	1 529	0.9%
Methodist	3 305 404	1 373**	2 407	1.4%
Reformed churches	3 232 193	843**	3 834	2.2%
Pentecostal/Charismatic	3 422 749	246**	13 914	8.1%
African independent churches	14 254 031	83***	171 735	100%

Although these numbers and proportions may not be completely accurate, Table 1 shows that the number of pastors in the AIC and to a certain extent in the Pentecostal/Charismatic tradition, is totally disproportionate to the number of pastors in formal churches. This relates to the phenomenal growth over the last century of Christianity in the global south.[28] A century ago, about two-thirds of the world's Christians lived in Europe, where most Christians were to be found for more than a millennium. This has changed dramatically. At present, only about 26% of all Christians lives in Europe, with approximately 37% in the Americas. About one-quarter of Christians lives in sub-Saharan Africa (24%), and the rest (about 13%) in Asia and the Pacific (Pew Research Centre 2011).

A very large proportion of leaders of the informal church environment who need training, do not hold the necessary prior qualifications that afford them access to registered or accredited ministry training. Many leaders in informal churches do not have the literacy skills and academic proficiency that are needed to successfully enter or enrol in formally accredited courses. Theological education on tertiary level is currently only accessible to a relatively small 'academic elite' – certainly not to the masses of leaders with lower levels of prior learning who need training. Another reality is that most leaders who are in need of training are in full-time ministry, or are in part-time ministry while employed elsewhere to earn a living. They cannot attend courses that would take them out of their ministries or other places of work for extended periods of time.

---

[28] This term is to a large extent becoming synonymous with the concept of 'non-Western Christian' (Charles 2009:15).

Training challenges related to non-formal education

There is a surprisingly high number of non-formal (i.e. not formally registered or accredited) ministry training institutions that provide training to this group. In a recent report compiled by the Centre for Contextual Ministry (CCM), approximately 80 training institutions that are active in this field were listed (Van der Walt 2014:21-26). Some of these institutions are entities within universities, for example CCM at the University of Pretoria, Shepherd at the University of the Free State, Ekklesia at Stellenbosch University, and the short course programmes of Unisa and North West University. Most are, however, private initiatives that were developed by visionary individuals who had the training of untrained pastors at heart. This varies from private tertiary institutions offering bridging courses to leaders of this group of churches, to Bible colleges using material by institutions such as the Nehemiah Bible Institute, small institutions that developed own training material, etc.

Several problems related to the training of pastors and other leaders in AICs and related churches are experienced by these institutions. Research done by CCM amongst a sample of 53 ministry training institutions that provide training to leaders in the informal church environment, highlighted the following as important challenges (Van der Walt 2014:32-38):

Table 2: Problems reported by ministry training institutions

Issue	Intensity of problem			Percentage of institutions participating in study experiencing the problem
	Serious	Slight	None	
Curriculum/course design	2	26	25	53%
Developing or finding appropriate training material	2	21	30	43%
Determining and maintaining appropriate training standards	5	23	25	53%
Finding well-qualified/effective teaching staff	5	24	24	55%
Accreditation of courses in South Africa (including courses on tertiary level)	22	15	16	70%
Accreditation of courses on sub-tertiary level	44	0	9	83%
Accreditation of the training institution within South Africa	25	11	17	68%
Financial constraints/financial viability	19	27	7	87%
Lack of physical resources	8	23	22	58%
Limited geographic reach/geographic restrictions	24	7	22	58%

Table 2 suggests that formal accreditation issues and financial constraints are amongst the most serious problems experienced by ministry training institutions in South Africa. Problems with regard to accreditation are especially important in the case of institutions that focus on the training of leaders in the informal churches of whom a large proportion have to be trained on a pre-tertiary level (National Qualification Framework Level 4 and lower).

A core issue is that most ministry training institutions could not succeed in registering as a Further Education and Training (FET) College which is officially entitled to award qualifications on the pre-tertiary level. Virtually all pre-tertiary courses presented by ministry training institutions in South Africa fall outside the ambit of the National Qualification Framework (NQF) and do, therefore, not carry credits towards recognised qualifications. Discussions with the leadership of the training institutions revealed that there are several reasons why registration is so difficult. A factor often mentioned, is that the process to register courses and institutions is extremely complicated. Problems with the complexity of the process are compounded by the fact that theology and church ministry are 'strange birds' with no 'home' within the framework for the registration of FET level courses and institutions. Registration of pre-tertiary theological and ministry courses had to be done via the framework of Sectoral Education and Training Agencies (SETAs),[29] all of which are designed in terms of the needs and realities of other sectors and none for the specific realities of the religious sector.

Another critical challenge is that of financial viability, which has a limiting impact on the level of service that institutions are able to provide. Viability problems are mainly due to the fact that the vast majority of informal churches operate in less affluent to very poor communities. Many churches have difficulties to pay their pastors who, in turn, find it difficult to pay for their tuition. The tuition fees of most of the training institutions serving this target group represent only a fraction of the fees of 'financially sustainable' training in the corporate environment – and yet the experience is that most leaders from the informal churches struggle to afford even the highly subsidised fees of the courses they want to attend.

An important challenge is the absence of a common vision and strategy regarding ministry training needs. A total of 98% of the respondents in the CCM study stated that "there is no joint vision amongst the relevant training institutions regarding the desired outcomes of Christian leadership training in the country and over the continent" (Van der Walt 2014:5). Training institutions stated that most of the training institutions seem to be working in

---

[29] See for example http://mobi.careerhelp.org.za/page/mobile/learnership_information for a list of SETAs. There are 21 of these agencies, each designed to provide for the specific training needs of the sectors they represent. The SETA operations are funded from the national Skills Development Fund. There is, however, no sectoral agency which provides for the specific characteristics of religious and church-related leadership training. At the same time, the Skills Development Fund does not provide for training in the religious and church ministry environment

varying levels of isolation towards own objectives. It was reported that there was a lack of coordination and optimisation of effort towards jointly formulated objectives. It was found that many of those involved in more or less the same kind of service, were "at best blind or indifferent to the work of the others, and at worst even offensive and working in opposition to one another. The result is that much energy is wasted due to a lack of clubbing together of forces" (Van der Walt 2014:15).

Although reported on a slightly lower level, the remaining problems identified by training institutions seem to be a fairly general experience: problems with curriculum and course design, obtaining appropriate training material, determining and maintaining appropriate training standards, finding well-qualified and effective teaching staff, limited geographic reach, and a lack of physical resources. These should also be taken into account when re-thinking ministry training in the country.

Diversification of training models as a solution

Diversification of theological education and ministry training can significantly contribute to the solution of the challenges identified above. Diversification on two levels is intended – in the overarching framework that regulates education and training in the country; and in the internal world of theological education and ministry training itself.

1. Diversification of training within the overarching national framework

Many leaders in the informal church environment have years of ministry experience. However, officially approved methods and procedures to quantify and to recognise this, do not exist. Ways should be found to enable pastors and other leaders to enter the ministry training framework on any level as the need may be – from ABET level 1 (where there is only rudimentary or even no literacy skills and academic proficiency), to pastors who could successfully make a first entry on post-graduate level. Ways should also be found to allow for the recognition of prior learning in a way that will recognise relevant learning that has taken place through practical ministry involvement and to present this as part of the process to identify the appropriate access level into formal ministry training, while identifying gaps that need to be filled through bridging courses. Current deficiencies related to these issues lead to a very large proportion of informal church leaders remaining excluded from the formal training system.

A fundamental challenge that deserves attention is the 'homelessness' of pre-tertiary ministry training within the overall regulatory framework of education in South Africa. As stated in a previous section, ministry training institutions presenting pre-tertiary courses currently have to work through educational and training agencies (SETAs) that are geared towards the characteristics and realities of other sectors of the national activity structure. Theological and ministry training institutions and their courses do not fit properly into the 'moulds' of these agencies that were actually designed for other sectors. Thus, while the other sectors (e.g. agriculture, banking, construction, health and welfare, engineering, mining, public service, etc.) can successfully develop and register training institutions, unit standards, courses and qualifications within the pre-tertiary (FET) bands, this proved (for all practical purposes) not possible for ministry training since this sector had no say in the design of their regulatory 'home'.

Since there are deficiencies in the interaction between the national education regulatory environment and training provision in the religious and ministry sector – specifically on the lower (pre-tertiary) levels – there is a need for further diversification within the national regulatory framework to provide for an own 'tailor-made home' for ministry training. The good news is that an innovative opportunity for this has recently been created through the introduction of a new set of education and training policies by the Government. This was encompassed in the National Qualifications Framework Act of 2008, which *inter alia* provides for the establishment of non-statutory professional bodies for the wide variety of professions that are included in the Department of Higher Education and Training's Organising Framework for Occupations (OFO) (SAQA 2012:5).

In terms of the new policy, any 'industry' (individuals and institutions involved in a specific category of professions or vocations, referred to as a 'community of expert practitioners') may jointly form a professional body to formally represent that 'industry' in its relationship with the national qualification authorities. Significantly, the OFO includes what is referred to as 'religious professionals' and 'religious associate professionals' (Department of Higher Education and Training 2012: Codes 2636 and 3413). The fact that 'religious professionals' are included in the framework for relevant occupations, implies that religious professions are now formally recognised within the regulatory framework, and that a dispensation can now be created that will specifically deal with the unique realities of the Christian ministry training environment.[30] SAQA may now formally recognise such non-statutory professional bodies. A recognised professional body may *inter alia* define and register professional designations (recognised types of profession), determine the underlying qualifications for those designations (the qualifications an individual must obtain in order to register for a designation), be involved in the development of curricula and assessment standards, formally recognise[31] suitable education and training providers, and develop Recognition of Prior Learning (RPL) strategies and guidelines (SAQA 2012:5).

This novel development in the country's official educational and training policy constitutes an important opportunity for diversification on the regulatory level in the sense that an opening has now been created for the ministry training fraternity to establish their own, diverse track within the national regulatory framework. It is now potentially possible

---

[30] During meetings held with the SAQA Directorate for Registration and Recognition, SAQA representatives have indicated that, although the policy states that a "(p)roliferation of professional bodies within the same community of practice" will be discouraged, different religions (Christian and others) will be allowed to develop their own, unique bodies. This was *inter alia* reflected in the resolutions of the November 2013 convention of training institutions (Van der Walt 2014:10).

[31] The term 'recognise' is used instead of 'accredit' in the relevant legislation and policy documents.

to deal with regulatory issues of ministry training 'within its own house' – forming the professional body in a way that will fit the unique characteristics of this 'industry', defining its own 'house rules', etc.

Obviously, having the opportunity to establish an 'own house' is not equal to having the 'house' already built and fitted out. An intensive process and much hard work will be required before the opportunity will actually have come to fruition. A first step towards the utilisation of the new opportunities has recently been taken with the establishment of an Association of Ministry Training Practitioners (AMTP). The association was established in August 2014 by representatives of 25 theological education and ministry training institutions, who acted upon a suggestion by SAQA. They convened to discuss the challenges jointly experienced and to respond to the opportunities that exist for overcoming those challenges. One of the main objects of AMTP (apart from opening it up to all training institutions who would want to opt in to the initiative), will be to work towards registration as a professional body which will be in a position to open up the new opportunities for ministry training institutions (AMTP 2014). The emphasis will be on realising the benefits of being recognised as a formal role player within the regulatory framework for education and training for the affiliated institutions, as well as to pursue solutions to the problems that were identified in previous sections.

2. Diversification within ministry training itself

It was shown in previous sections that formally recognised ministry training is nearly exclusively available on tertiary level, where it is inaccessible to a disproportionately large component of ministry leaders in need of training. Minimal education and training services that are formally recognised or accredited within the South African regulatory framework and that constitute formal progressive learning paths towards recognised qualifications, are available to the very large body of pastors in the AICs and related churches (Mofokeng 2012:149-150). What is needed is a diversification of formal, recognised ministry training that will allow access to formally recognised training opportunities for leaders with prior qualifications, academic proficiency, and literacy skills on any level – from the lowest to the highest.

The new SAQA policy framework, together with the AMTP initiative, has the potential to bring about a diversification that will allow leaders from all levels to successfully enter and exit formal education and training on any level. The NQF Act determines that "where a professional body that is recognised … wishes to give formal recognition to an occupational qualification … it must enter into a formal agreement with SAQA's Quality Council for Trade and Occupations (QCTO), to attain authority to develop and/or quality assure such occupational qualification" (SAQA 2012:6). This means that the work of the professional body must be done in close cooperation with the QCTO, which is one of three quality councils within the SAQA and NQF environment.[32]

The role of the QCTO is to oversee training provision in the trade and occupational environment, from NQF levels 1 to 8. Recognised professional bodies may enter into agreements with the QCTO regarding the development and recognition of qualifications (including part qualifications and training modules), curriculas, courses, assessment, and the recognition of prior learning on all levels, up to NQF level 8. If correctly dealt with, this opportunity could be used to create fully diversified (flexible, modular) courses and qualifications that will allow those ministry training institutions that are affiliated with the professional body to offer courses and award occupational qualifications on all levels – from the lowest ABET and NQF levels, up to NQF level 8 – and will provide access and exit points to leaders at any level, from the lowest up to NQF level 8 (Hlekane 2014:2-10). The intention is to create such a level of diversification that learners will be able to choose a progressive learning path that will take them from where they are in terms of previous qualifications, if any, prior learning, relevant workplace experience, literacy level, and academic proficiency, and 'deliver' them on the level where they want to exit.

To do this, the professional body will have to facilitate a process to develop curricula, to implement assessment systems, and to formulate RPL policies and strategies that will allow the required level of diversification. The process will involve the QCTO, Development Quality Partners and Assessment Quality Partners designated by the QCTO, and a community of expert practitioners to work out the detail surrounding this whole process (Hlekane 2014:12). The point is that the opportunity to develop a fully diversified and flexible training dispensation for leaders in the informal church environment who need access to formal, recognised training (irrespective of their prior qualifications, literacy skills and academic proficiency), can finally be opened up.

The QCTO-related qualifications (occupational qualifications) do not only provide access on the different NQF levels. Provision is also made for what is called diverse learning contexts (vocational, occupational, academic and professional), and diverse teaching or training environments (classroom, laboratory, field, clinic, community, etc.) (SAQA 2012:4). Occupational qualifications overseen by professional bodies have to provide for teaching and learning that take place in a diverse variety of settings – there needs to be a knowledge component, a component of practical work during training, and a workplace-experience component. Qualifications and courses can, therefore, now be designed to form a perfect fit to the situation of practising ministry leaders who want to enrol for formally recognised ministry training, by being responsive to their contextual experience as well as the informal and non-formal learning environments that fit their situations best.

---

[32] The other two are the Council for Higher Education, which oversees the functioning of tertiary educational institutions that operate on NQF levels 5-10, and Umalusi, which oversees the functioning of public and private schools that operate up to NQF level 4.

These distinctions (level, context and environment) form useful parameters of differentiation and diversification that can now be used in developing an appropriate future ministry training dispensation. In terms of these distinctions, the challenge in diversifying education will be to determine the optimal combinations of course content levels, context of learning, and environment of training that will be adequately responsive to the situation and needs of church leaders who want to enter a training path – a combination that will guarantee the most effective achievement of the required teaching and learning outcomes.

Conclusion

There is a massive need for formally recognised ministry training that will fit the needs structure of pastors, in particular those of the informal churches and the growing number of 'lay' workers in informal as well as formal (historic) churches. Formal (accredited, officially recognised) training is mostly available and accessible only to the very small minority of leaders of formal churches. A creative, strategic drive is necessary to ensure that the very large need for good training of leaders in the AIC and related churches will be met with a sufficient offer of relevant and formally recognised training on appropriate levels, with an appropriate response to context and environment.

The recent establishment of the Association of Ministry Training Practitioners (AMTP) is seen as a first step towards the creation of a framework that will be able to utilise the new opportunities in the national regulatory framework that were recently created. It holds the potential for ministry training institutions to overcome the challenges that, in the past, prevented a large proportion of leaders from entering into a recognised progressive path of theological education and ministry training.

There is thus an expectation that a new training dispensation stands to be developed where the diverse needs of the large number of leaders in the informal church environment – many of whom can be described as little, marginalised ones for whom there is a special place in the heart of the Jesus we met in the Gospel – will be met with appropriately diverse and adaptable training solutions.

Bibliography

Association of Ministry Training Practitioners (AMTP), 2014. *Memorandum of incorporation.* Founding document prepared during the AMTP founding conference held on 20-23 August 2014.

Basil Ibeh. *Nigeria LinkedIn.* [Online] Available from: ng.linkedin.com/pub/basil-ibeh [Accessed: 25 August 2014].

Bosch, D., 1991. *Transforming mission: Paradigm shifts in theology of mission.* New York: Orbis Books.

Botman, R., 2013. Foreword. In: I.A. Phiri and D. Werner (eds.). *Handbook of theological education in Africa.* Oxford: Regnum Books. xx

Career Advice Services, [n.d.]. *List of SETAs and contact details.* [Online] Available from: mobi.careerhelp.org.za/page/mobile/learnership_information [Accessed: 27 August 2014].

Charles, J.P., 2009. *Global Christianity: Trends in mission and the relationship with non-Western missionaries working cross-culturally in Thailand.* MTh thesis. South African Theological Seminary.

Department of Government Communication and Information Systems (GCIS), 2011. *Pocket guide to South Africa 2011/12.* Pretoria.

Department of Higher Education and Training (DHET), 2012. *The organising framework for occupations (OFO).* Pretoria.

Hendriks, J. and Malherbe, J., 2002. General statistical picture of religion in South Africa. In: D. Kritzinger (ed.). *No quick fixes: The challenge of missions in a changing South Africa.* Pretoria: IMER. 13-30.

Hlekane, N., 2014. *Quality Council for Trades and Occupations (QCTO): Advocacy on Qualifications.* Presentation made to the AMTP establishment conference on 21 August 2014, Melk River.

Kinsler, F.R., 2009. *Diversified theological education: Equipping all God's people for God's mission.* [Online] Available from: www.oikoumene.org/.../education.../diversified-theological-education-eq [Accessed: 29 August 2014].

Landmann, C., 2013, Theological education in South Africa. In: I.A. Phiri and D. Werner (eds.). *Handbook of Theological Education in Africa.* Oxford: Regnum Books. 239-245

Mofokeng, K., 2012. African spiritual churches and theological training. In: M. Naidoo (ed.). *Between the real and the ideal: Ministerial formation in South African churches.* Pretoria: Unisa Press. 134-146.

Moltmann, J., 1977. *The church in the power of the Spirit.* Translated by M. Kohl. London: SCM.

Naidoo, M. (ed.), 2012. *Between the real and the ideal: Ministerial formation in South African churches.* Pretoria: Unisa Press.

Olukoya, D.K., 2001. *Your foundation and your destiny.* Lagos, Nigeria: Battle Cry Christian Ministries.

Petra Institute for Children's Ministry, [n.d.]. *Petra Institute for Children's Ministry.* [Online] Available from: www.petra.co.za [Accessed: 25 August 2014].

Pew Research Centre, 2011. *Global Christianity: A report on the size and distribution of the world's Christian population.* [Online] Available from: http://www.pewforum.org/2011/12/19/global-christianity-exec [Accessed: 2 September 2014].

Siaki, P., 2002. Christianity in the new South Africa: Another look at the statistics. In: D. Kritzinger (ed.). *No quick fixes: The challenge of missions in a changing South Africa.* Pretoria: IMER. 31-60.

South African Qualifications Authority (SAQA), 2012. *Policy and criteria for recognising a professional body and registering a professional designation for the purposes of the National Qualifications Framework Act, Act 67 of 2008.* Pretoria.

Van der Walt, J.P., 2014. *Phase 1 Report: Establishment of a coordination forum and professional body for service providers involved in the training of practising pastors and other community leaders.* University of Pretoria: Centre for Contextual Ministry.

Veritas College International, [n.d.]. *Veritas College International.* [Online] Available from: www.veritas.org.za [Accessed: 25 August 2014].

www.ingramcontent.com/pod-product-compliance
Lightning Source LLC
Chambersburg PA
CBHW080323170426
43193CB00017B/2885